DAMAGE NOTED

_____

DATE _____

Jan 4 9 1988

East Wind
Over Africa

ALSO BY JOHN K. COOLEY

BAAL, CHRIST, AND MOHAMMED: RELI-
GION AND REVOLUTION IN NORTH
AFRICA *(Holt, Rinehart & Winston)*

East Wind Over Africa

RED CHINA'S AFRICAN OFFENSIVE

JOHN K. COOLEY

WALKER AND COMPANY
NEW YORK

Author's Introduction

Red China has moved into Africa, and it intends to stay there. By the beginning of this decade, it had become clear that Communist China's moves to win allies, subvert adversaries and gain influence in Africa formed a significant part of its design for global recognition and power. Some newsmen began to report this move about 1960 and even earlier. But few editors and only a limited number of scholars took Chinese efforts in Africa seriously until 1963.

From then until after the postponement of the Afro-Asian or "second Bandung" Conference at Algiers in June 1965—a postponement Peking fought vainly to avert—China's diplomacy took a new and ambitious tack. It sought to muster all Asia, Africa and even Latin America against both the United States and the Soviet Union. Whereas the first Bandung Conference of 1955 had produced a bloc of "nonaligned" nations, China's objective now became an end to nonalignment, and enrollment of the "non-aligned" nations on China's side. One major reason Peking failed at Algiers in June 1965, following President ben Bella's overthrow, was China's growing tendency to lump African and Asian neutrals, like Nasser and Shastri, with the Soviets and Americans as "imperialists." The details of the considerable defeat the Chinese suffered at Algiers are set forth in Appendix A.

Much of this book results from culling published material, not least the voluminous daily file of news and propaganda in French and English that Hsinhua, the New China News Agency, sends to Africa. In Africa I taped and transcribed many Radio Peking broadcasts in English, French, Spanish and Portuguese. As I do not know Chinese, I have had to rely on translations into European languages made by others, but have sought to make transliterations of Chinese names as uniform as possible.

6990

Many people gave gracious help, especially officials of the North African governments and diplomats of sub-Saharan countries. For information on areas I could not visit myself, I have relied on documents. Many of these are official and therefore not citable here. Much material comes from personal interviews with diplomats, businessmen, missionaries and soldiers, and also fellow newsmen, African, Western and Communist. Where material is taken directly from publications or lectures, I have tried to indicate this in the text.

I am grateful to Professor L. Gray Cowan, Director of the Institute of African Studies at Columbia University, for his help and encouragement in the final stages of preparing this book for publication. His assistant, Mrs. Annette Stiefbold, graciously permitted me to profit from her own seminar paper comparing the Guinean and Chinese party systems. Other members of Professor Cowan's seminar, in which I participated during the academic year 1964–65, were also helpful.

Miss Margaret MacCartan's untiring, patient and imaginative help with research, the manuscript and her index were major contributions. Others, such as Robert Bass, Roger Jellinek, John Kirk and Arthur Cohen and Hymie Cohen, gave valuable help and criticism. The Christian Science Publishing Company—publishers of the *Christian Science Monitor*—the *Commonweal,* NBC News, The Canadian Broadcasting Corporation and others were understanding about permitting me to incorporate in this book some thoughts and data from reports I made to them earlier. Any flaws and errors are, of course, entirely my own.

John K. Cooley
New York City, 1965

Contents

Contents

"In the struggle between the socialist and capitalist camps, it was no longer the West wind that prevailed over the East wind, but the East wind that prevailed over the West wind."

—MAO TSE-TUNG, NOVEMBER 1957, TO CHINESE STUDENTS IN MOSCOW.

"When I first meet someone, I believe what he says. Now that I have experience, I listen to him and watch his acts. Though I am a Marxist, I accept this principle. You adopt it too. Don't be fooled by the Chinese. Don't be satisfied with our words. Look at our actions!"

—MARSHAL CHEN YI, TO WESTERN NEWS-MEN IN PEKING, MAY 4, 1964.

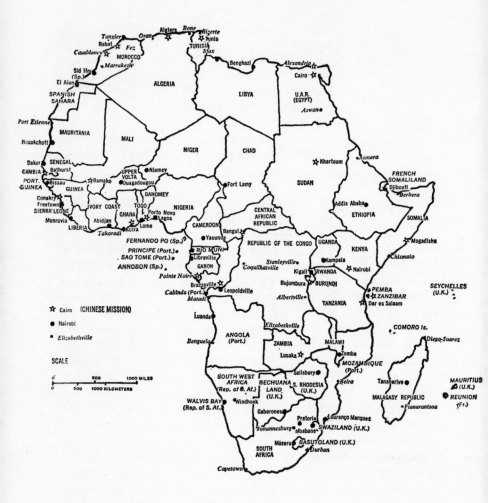

CHAPTER ONE

Red China's African Offensive

FROM CAIRO TO CAPETOWN, AND FROM THE ISLANDS OF THE INDIAN
Ocean across the mountains and bushlands to the Gulf of Guinea, a
new wind from the East is blowing across Africa.

This is a wind that says Revolution. Every day, in all the major
tongues of Africa, Radio Peking broadcasts the rigid message of the
Chinese Communists: "Only through violent revolution and armed
struggle will the colonialists, the white men, be thrown out. Only
through violence and fighting will real freedom come to Africa. Only
by fighting for it will the oppressed peoples of Africa, Asia and Latin
America defeat their worst enemy: American imperialism."

Since Peking's split with Moscow in 1960, China's 650 million
people have been told repeatedly that theirs is a nation of destiny. It
is China's destiny to prove to the world's peoples, especially those
people who, like the Chinese, are struggling to catch up with the rich
countries in the race for development, that the dogmatic Chinese
prescription of armed revolution is correct. Increasingly, the Chinese
Communist Party under Chairman Mao Tse-tung and the government
of Premier Chou En-lai have widened the scope of their action from
Asia to Africa.

The Chinese example and the Chinese experience in revolution and
self-help on the road to development are the proper models for Africans, as well as Asians, to follow says Peking. *You are our underdeveloped brothers, our black and brown-skinned brothers,* the Chinese diplomats and propagandists incessantly tell the Africans. *We*

have known oppression and adversity and you have known oppression and adversity. You can expect no real help or sympathy from the white imperialist West; least of all from the United States. You can expect no help from the Soviet Union. Its leaders are white men like the rest. Khrushchev preached that goulash is more important than revolution, and a full belly more vital than freedom. Because of his errors, Khrushchev fell from his high seat of power. We only wish you to be yourselves. But in seeking out your socialist destiny, a part of the socialist destiny of all of us, we are certain that you will discover your way to be our way.

Paradoxically, though China is desperately poor itself and grappling with a thousand economic problems, it is intensively aiding chosen governments, groups and individuals throughout Africa. By training selected Africans in guerilla warfare, as well as in simple technical skills, and by bringing African leaders and students to China, the Peking government seeks to convince Africans that only its own rigid analyses of world society and what is required to change it are acceptable. Wherever there is an unstable situation or a conflict in Africa, Peking sides, more or less discreetly, with whatever faction is most likely to reduce Western or Soviet influence and increase its own. It has worked to subvert both colonial and independent African regimes that were too "bourgeois," especially where there seemed to be a possibility of reshaping a society along the lines of the drastic Chinese agrarian revolution. Chinese planners appear to hope that armed revolution in one area will touch off a chain reaction of revolution in others: the spread of Chinese-encouraged rebellion in the Congo from one area to another was a case in point.

Peking's tactics, unlike its revolutionary dogmas, are not rigid and doctrinaire. They are supple and flexible. Each country and each situation in Africa is dealt with on its merits. Peking backs socialist strong men. But it has also supported monarchs like the Mwame Mwambutsa IV of the kingdom of Burundi because it needed Burundi as a lookout station for advice to the Congo rebels, or King Hassan II of Morocco because it needs Morocco's cobalt for nuclear weapons.

In the Congo, a handful of Chinese helped to fan fires that threatened all semblance of order, stability and legal government. These fires blazed from traditional inter-tribal hostility. The Chinese, like the Soviets, sought to use them for their own political ends. When Moise Tshombe came to power in Leopoldville in 1964, Peking played skillfully on Africans' deep-seated dislike of him. From their bridgeheads in the Congo (Brazzaville) and Tanzania, Peking's diplomats extended this influence into the neighboring countries.

In some places they suffered setbacks. Statesmen such as Dr. Hastings Banda, the Prime Minister of Malawi, denounced their conspiracies. Their boycott-breaking trade with the white-supremacy government of the Republic of South Africa was exposed, as was their own racial discrimination against African students in Peking. In Burundi, blatant Chinese interference with local political processes, culminating with the assassination of an anti-Chinese Prime Minister in January 1965, led the king to close the Chinese Embassy and to suspend diplomatic relations.

But Africa, especially Black Africa, is vulnerable to subtle personal diplomacy like that of the Chinese. Great unrest and political uncertainty have replaced the stability imposed by the departing European colonial powers. Each new African country seeks to organize its own "take-off" in national economic development, in the most efficient way it can. Each hopes that this will be an original way: African leaders generally do not wish to be beholden to any outside country or social system. At the same time, African countries must sell their raw materials to the outside industrial or industrializing powers, including the West, the Soviet Union and China, in order to survive. All these powers need Africa's strategic goods: its copper, cobalt, beryl, uranium and industrial diamonds, now controlled largely by the West. Peking has set out to do what Moscow failed to do between 1956 and 1960: to promise the Africans disinterested aid, deny their strategic commodities to the West, and capture what it needs for itself.

Among the countries where Western controls and Western political formulas are most rejected, the competition between the Chinese and the Soviets is hottest. This was true in the Congo, where in 1964 and 1965 both backed Christophe Gbenye's rebel "Congo People's Republic." Here the "militant" Arab and African nations joined in the effort. Through the neighboring Sudan and Uganda, using the air corridors southward from Cairo and Algiers, the Soviets and the Algerians, Egyptians and Ghanaians, determined not to be outdone by the Chinese, sent the guns, ammunition and military "experts" for which the late Patrice Lumumba over four years earlier had asked in vain.

In North Africa, Chinese competition obliged Nikita S. Khrushchev to promise more assistance to the United Arab Republic than his colleagues in Moscow wished to support. This was a contributing cause of his downfall in October 1964, even as Peking enhanced its prestige in African and Asian eyes by exploding its first nuclear device.

Through Egypt and Algeria, Khrushchev before his fall launched a Soviet bid for influence in North Africa that would offset the spreading Chinese influence south of the Sahara. Whereas Chinese economic aid stressed modest-self-help projects, the Soviet strategy was to offer dams, roads, hardware and solid capital goods that had the value of both prestige and long-term economic growth: the Soviet-backed Aswan High Dam in Egypt, said one Western diplomat, was being built strong and massive enough to survive any future revolutions. Not only hundreds of millions of dollars but also vast amounts of military equipment and Russian advisors were involved in the new Russian effort to counter China's revolutionary push. Khrushchev had stressed that the underdeveloped world needed more goulash and fuller stomachs much more than it needed new and immediate revolutions, despite his willingness to provide arms aid. The Chinese leaders, on every possible occasion, chided the new Soviet rulers, Brezhnev and Kosygin, for continuing this course in 1965.

In his efforts to identify Arab nationalism and "Arab socialism" with the Soviet rather than the Chinese branch of world Communism, Khrushchev had developed a Leninist thesis: the Communist bloc, together with the "third world" of developing countries, constitutes a force that will inevitably "bury" the Western world. The offensive of the Chinese Communist schismatics in Africa forced Moscow to put more urgent emphasis on this, with ever-diminishing respect for the "non-alignment" of those African states that most interest Moscow. This was the tactic Moscow tried to employ after Chou En-lai's tour of ten African countries in the winter of 1963–64, when it became clear that Peking hoped to win exclusive control of the liberation movements on the continent. Sino-Soviet rivalry focused on Algeria and Kenya, continued in the Somali Republic and Tanzania, and moved into freshly independent African countries such as Malawi (formerly Nyasaland). Peking adopted a far more militant line in support of the Arabs against Israel than did Moscow.

In their appeals to the "third world," the Chinese now began to stress the solidarity of race rather than of class. In August 1963 the Soviets issued their historical statement accusing Peking of trying to separate the African, Asian and Latin American continents from European and Communist states on the basis of the "color of skin." From this, and again mainly for African consumption, it was only a short step for the Chinese to accuse the Soviets of supporting United States "racial policies." At the same time, Chinese official statements began to disclose one of China's foremost propaganda objectives: the linking-up of the Afro-Asian struggle against American "imperialism" with that of the American Negro. A statement of Mao Tse-tung in August 1963, and many others to follow it, was made in reply to a query by Robert Williams, an American Negro fugitive from the summary justice of North Carolina. Mao's statement, distributed to Africans in Peking, called for unity "against racial discrimination by U. S. imperialism and in support of American Negroes." This has remained a major Chinese theme ever since.

The immediate purpose of Red China in Africa, to eliminate Western and particularly American influence, seems clearer than its longer-term goals. China seeks to check the rise of Soviet influence, which it professes to see forming an unholy alliance with the United States to retard the course of true revolution. But even as Sino-Soviet competition weakens the world Communist movement, it intensifies Communist activities in the "third world." Certainly Peking seeks to form its own sphere of influence, with the African continent part and parcel of this sphere. By expelling the United States entirely from Africa, Mao Tse-tung's planners could advance far toward their declared objective of isolating the United States on the world scene.

To use Toynbee's terms, Red China's African offensive is partly a response to a historical challenge. The power of the Soviets opposed and checked the dynamic expansion of a great empire in Central Asia and Mongolia, where the interests of the Czars and Chinese Emperors of other ages once collided. The United States halted it, at least temporarily, in Southeast Asia. Africa is a newer and, in some ways, more tempting arena. In Africa nothing is settled. Few final boundaries, ideologies or national loyalties are clearly drawn. To Peking's planners, Africa is the flux of a new world Afro-Asian society, the stuff of a major revolutionary outpost in a Sinocentric world.

CHAPTER TWO

The Bandung Breakthrough

A MOMENTOUS CHAPTER OF HISTORY BEGAN WITH A DISASTER OVER the South China Sea.

On April 10, 1955, the chartered Air India Constellation "Kashmir Princess" flew southward from Hong Kong toward the conference of twenty-nine African and Asian countries at Bandung, Indonesia. Leaders in Africa and Asia looked eagerly to Bandung. For the first time, the voices of 1.3 billion people, most of them non-white and comprising more than half the world's population, were being raised in an international forum.

Thus far the rest of the world had not taken much notice of the event. The chief Chinese delegate was Premier Chou En-lai. At fifty-seven he was a suave and accomplished diplomat who clearly showed his cultured origins and cosmopolitan Western education. Chou had been scheduled to fly from Peking to Bandung via the British Crown Colony of Hong Kong. At the last minute he and a Hungarian journalist had switched to another flight. Eleven other Chinese delegates and Communist journalists from Vietnam, Austria and Rumania were aboard the "Kashmir Princess" when it left Hong Kong.

Suddenly, at an altitude of 18,000 feet in the vicinity of Sarawak, the "Kashmir Princess" exploded in a blinding flash of fire. All its passengers were lost. The shock of the crash riveted world attention on the conference. People in the six African countries sending delegates—Egypt, Ethiopia, the Gold Coast (now Ghana), Liberia,

Libya and the Sudan—suddenly realized that their leaders were actors on the world stage.

Peking claimed that it had warned the Hong Kong police thirty-two hours ahead of time that a sabotage attempt would be made on the plane. The explosion, Peking said, was plotted by Chiang Kai-shek's Nationalist government with the connivance of the United States. Its purpose was to kill Chou En-lai, disrupt the Afro-Asian Conference and so prevent the voices of the world's underprivileged people from being heard at last.

Washington and Taipeh denied the charges. The later Western and Chinese Nationalist version was that the Hong Kong baggage carrier who had placed two time bombs aboard the "Kashmir Princess" had been an *agent provocateur* in the pay of the Communists. With a price of $100,000 on his head in Hong Kong, he took asylum in Formosa.

The disaster of the "Kashmir Princess" placed the Bandung meeting in the full glare of world publicity. Now it was no longer just another conference: the world has not been the same since.

This was the real beginning of Red China's rapid entry on the African scene. Though the Communist revolution had been victorious since 1949, the Peking regime in 1954 still had no diplomatic relations with any African country. The Nationalist regime in Formosa had only a few consulates in Africa—mostly set up before the Kuomintang government was established in 1927.

China's isolation from Africa up to 1954 was merely a part of her almost total isolation from the rest of the world. American foreign policy was dedicated to maintaining this isolation and, where possible, reinforcing it. Peking was to devote the decade that followed to breaking out of this isolation.

China had made its alliance with the Soviet Union the bedrock of its early foreign policy. Chairman Mao Tse-tung, Premier Chou En-lai and the other Communist leaders on the Chinese mainland had taken every possible opportunity, it seemed, to proclaim that Soviet Russia was the only model for China and the rest of the world to follow. Stalin, who had meddled mightily in Chinese politics, wanted things this way. Moscow was the capital of the "socialist camp," the "New Rome" that the orthodox had to obey.

But straws of coming change were already drifting in the wind. A few African nationalists, along with millions in India and the rest of Asia, took note of a speech that President Liu Shao-chi made in

Peking to the 1949 conference of the Moscow-led World Federation of Trade Unions (WFTU). President Liu asserted that China's revolution was the proper model for underdeveloped or "semi-colonial" countries. This was a clear challenge to Moscow's leadership, fully four years before the death of Stalin.

Another Chinese leader, Lu Ting-yi, repeated the implicit challenge to Moscow in a speech on June 25, 1951. He made it clear that Chairman Mao had officially added this momentous new dogma to the Chinese Communist code. Peking was bidding for the leadership of the Asian and African revolutions yet to come. In a historical sense, the Chinese were reasserting their ancient Confucian belief in their own superiority, a belief they had held for half a millennium. China was the source of all light, the center of the civilized world. Sinocentrism, frustrated by centuries of containment by foreigners, barbarians, was coming back into its own.

The Bandung meeting was the first opportunity for leaders of the six participating African states to meet the rulers of Communist China. Of these six, Egypt, Ethiopia, Liberia and Libya were then independent. Many unofficial nationalist emissaries from territories still under colonial control, and numerous political exiles from such territories as Tunisia, Algeria and Morocco, were also present.

Indonesian Prime Minister Ali Sastroamidjojo had taken the original initiative. At a meeting in Colombo, Ceylon, with the Prime Ministers of Burma, Ceylon, India and Pakistan, he proposed a conference of Asian United Nations members, without African participation.

India's Jawaharlal Nehru argued in favor of inviting Chou En-lai. He pointed out that all five sponsoring powers had relations with Communist China. Some of the territories and states of Africa were then added to the list. Only the Central African Federation (the British-ruled Rhodesias and Nyasaland) declined. The Union of South Africa was not invited. Its apartheid policy of racial separation was bound to come under heavy attack at the conference, and these attacks might disrupt other business.

The two mightiest world powers, the United States and the Soviet Union, were explicitly barred because they belonged neither to Africa nor to Asia. This was an argument the Chinese used again in 1965 to keep the Soviets, now their rivals for Communist hegemony, from the postponed "Second Bandung" meeting of Afro-Asian powers in Algiers.

Chou was left to lead the Communist delegations at Bandung, and all the participants in the conference seemed to feel that he had made a brilliant diplomatic debut on the Afro-Asian scene. To the "Five Principles of Peaceful Coexistence" he had already signed with Nehru in 1954, Chou proposed additions that would appeal to all African and Asian countries. At Bandung the Five Principles became Seven Principles: (1) Respect for sovereignty and territorial integrity of nations; (2) Abstention from aggression and threats; (3) Non-interference in the internal affairs of nations; (4) Racial equality and non-discrimination; (5) Equality of all nations; (6) Respect for the freedom to choose a political and economic system; (7) Mutually beneficial relations between nations. At the same time he encouraged militant anti-imperialism.

Chou's meeting with Gamal Abdel Nasser at Bandung gave China the opening and the opportunity it needed in Africa.

The young President of Egypt, still insecure in the power he had seized from King Farouk, and then from General Mohammed Naguib, must indeed have had mixed emotions as he first shook hands with the austere Chinese statesman with the wise, humorous eyes. Nasser later said that Chou had impressed him no less than had Pandit Jawaharlal Nehru. "Together," he recalled, "these two men represented more than one-third of the entire population of the world."

Russia had not yet made a strong bid for influence on the African scene. Premier Nikita Khrushchev's intentions were still obscure to Nasser. Chou and Nehru, friendly and available, represented much of the potential power of both the "non-aligned" and the Communist world. For their part, they competed furiously at Bandung to present Nasser to the rest of the Afro-Asian world as the leader of all the Arabs, and even of the world's 350 million Moslems.

Nehru needed Nasser because he was locked in a deadly conflict with Moslem Pakistan over Kashmir. India was as hostile as was Egypt to the Baghdad Pact, which the United States and Britain were hoping to make a main "bulwark against Communism" in the Near and Middle East. Logically, Egypt would have sided with its Moslem brothers in Pakistan. But it did not. In Colonel Gamal Abdel Nasser, Nehru had won a star recruit for his neutral camp.

Nasser went to Bandung determined to establish himself as leader of all the Arabs. To do this, he needed recognition as a non-aligned leader as well. For Chou he offered the advantage of being the only up-to-date African nationalist who was also chief of a sovereign African state. Chou realized how deeply the Arab defeat in the Palestine war of 1948-49 had wounded Nasser. He hoped to draw Nasser completely away from Britain and the other Western powers that backed Israel. Perhaps he hoped to use Nasser to destroy Western power positions in the Near and Middle East. Chou and Nasser embraced each other, and seemed to emerge from the conference good friends. President Nasser's government recognized Communist China on May 5, 1956. Cairo established full diplomatic relations with Peking on May 30, 1956.

Nasser was the first African leader to play the Russians off against the Chinese. In early 1956, British Prime Minister Anthony Eden had received tacit Soviet agreement to set up machinery to halt the arms race in the Middle East. But official Egyptian recognition of Communist China, and the increasing Chinese interest in African affairs, probably prompted the Russians to come through with an arms deal, via Czechoslovakia. This aroused Western wrath, especially that of the United States Secretary of State, John Foster Dulles, and in that fateful summer before the abortive Anglo-French-Israeli attack on Egypt, Dulles withdrew the offer of American financial aid for the Aswan High Dam project.

By shouldering the enormous cost of the dam, perhaps $1 billion, the most ambitious and possibly the most useful development project ever undertaken anywhere, the Soviet Union forged ahead of both the West and China. Significantly, Moscow was soon to refuse similarly favorable terms to China for its crucial Yangtze and Yellow River projects, with the result that they bogged down completely. In May 1964, Nikita Khrushchev promised a further $270 million toward the Republic's economic development. Since Red China's struggling economy simply cannot raise amounts of capital comparable to Western or even Soviet aid to Africa, Chinese material aid to Egypt (and the rest of Africa) has been small by comparison. There were small amounts in 1958 and 1963, and a promised loan of $90 million in December 1964.

Peking's military interest in the Middle East has been generally remote and largely abstract, except for concrete aid to the Algerian revolutionary army and for promises of Chinese support to Arabs against Israel. There was one important exception. When Khrushchev uttered his famous warning of Soviet rocket retaliation against the West if the Anglo-French-Israeli attack on Egypt did not cease, Peking felt obliged to add its own menace. It threatened to send 300,000 Chinese "volunteers" to Egypt. None of them ever left

China. But the threat carried some weight at the time. Perhaps this was partly because of Western ignorance of China's real intentions and capabilities.

The Chou-Nasser understanding at Bandung had another chain of consequences. Egypt and Red China signed a cultural accord on May 31, 1955. A trade agreement followed in August. It was now thoroughly clear to Africans and Asians that Peking, as well as Moscow, was perfectly willing to support bourgeois and even anti-Communist regimes—Egyptian Communists were languishing in concentration camps—if this support happened to suit its other policy objectives.

The trade agreement with Egypt was the beginning of Peking's search for markets and vital raw materials in Africa. In 1955 the total volume of mainland China's trade with Egypt had been only $9 million in Chinese exports to Egypt, and $24 million in Chinese imports from Egypt. By 1957 these figures had nearly doubled. China placed big orders for Egyptian cotton, bartered for manufactured products.

This was the starting signal for useful trade missions to Africa. The Foreign Trade Minister, Yeh Chi-chuang, and Vice-Ministers Kiang Ming and Lu Hsu-chang headed them. They went to Egypt (the United Arab Republic since the union with Syria, which lasted from 1958 to 1961), Tunisia, Morocco, Mali, Guinea, Ghana and Sudan. Nearly all of these became zones of intense Chinese diplomatic activity in the 1960s. The total of all Communist China's commerce with its African trading partners in 1957—Egypt, Algeria (then legally a part of France, but already in revolt), the Union of South Africa, and the Sudan Republic—was under $60 million. By 1965 it had increased nearly sevenfold, and had been extended to nearly all of the thirty-five African states that were by then independent.

Much had happened since the explosion of the "Kashmir Princess." From the summer of 1956 on, Red China had a base of operations on the African continent: its embassy in Cairo. This base had been established without Soviet aid and through the efforts of Chinese diplomacy alone. This was a great psychological success. The Cairo Embassy quickly became the point of departure for Chinese activities of all sorts, clandestine and overt, throughout Africa.

At Bandung the Chinese took several major steps on their long march out of isolation, and it was Africa that promised a field of action and a recognition that Chou En-lai and his compatriots were not long in taking.

CHAPTER THREE

Afro-Asian "Solidarity"

FROM ITS NEW BRIDGEHEAD IN CAIRO, CHINESE COMMUNIST DIPLO-macy looked for "people's" organizations through which it could spread the doctrines of the Chinese revolution in Africa.

The framework already existed. Moscow had created it at an "Asian Conference for the Relaxation of International Tension" in New Delhi, called by the Moscow-dominated World Council of Peace just before the Bandung meeting. It formed an "Asian Solidarity Committee," which in March 1956 held an Asian Writers' Confer-ence, also in the Indian capital.

As at Bandung, Egypt's battle against Western domination once again gave the Chinese the opportunity they sought. The Egyptian delegates basked in the glory of Nasser's moral and diplomatic vic-tory over the West at Suez. Mindful of the profound repercussions of Suez, the Asian Solidarity Committee and its Chinese members de-cided to extend its activity to Africa. It was renamed the "Afro-Asian Solidarity Committee." Its first move was to send a mission, in 1957, of Chinese, Soviet, Indian and Japanese delegates to President Nasser to ask his approval for a big "Afro-Asian Peoples' Solidarity Confer-ence" in Cairo. Nasser delegated the task of making arrangements to Anwar as-Sadat, his leading propaganda specialist. Shrewdly, Nasser laid down the absolute condition that the Committee's permanent secretariat be established in Cairo, and that Egyptians hold most of the key posts in it. This condition and Nasser's suspicious attitude toward Peking prevented complete Chinese control of the movement.

Unlike Bandung, the Cairo conference of December 1957 was nongovernmental. Its organizers were "Afro-Asian Solidarity Committees" in several countries, notably China, the Soviet Union and India. Forty-seven delegations attended. They included members of political parties, labor unions and other "mass" organizations. Some were controlled or infiltrated by Communists; while some were neutral, and some were pro-Western. The Philippines, Turkey and Pakistan boycotted the conference. They had close political and military ties with Washington (which took a dim view of the meeting), as well as treaty obligations.

After accepting an invitation "in principle," partisans of King Mohammed V's newly independent Moroccan regime decided not to come. Only delegates of a small conservative Moroccan opposition group, the Democratic Independence Party (PDI), attended. Tunisia's Neo-Destour Party took part, after receiving assurances that President Habib Bourguiba's mortal adversary, Salah ben Youssef, would not. The major political parties of French West Africa were absent, a fact that conditioned the reluctance of those Africans to take part in the movement in subsequent years.

"We are weary of power blocs," Mme. Pandit Nehru of India told the conferees. Soviet and Chinese delegates both made glowing promises that disinterested Communist aid would help Asia and Africa build "factories, dams, ports, railroads, hospitals, schools," all without political strings.

In accordance with Nasser's wishes, the conference set up an "Afro-Asian Peoples' Solidarity Council." Its seat was in Cairo, and Anwar as-Sadat was its president. There was one Indian and one Russian vice-president. The general secretary, who still held the post in early 1965, was another Egyptian, Youssef as-Sibai. Red China was among the countries permitted to nominate ten other secretaries.

Though the Egyptian role might have remained strong, in practice it has weakened. The Soviet and Chinese delegates, particularly the Chinese Yang Chuo and Chu Tzu-chi, came to dominate the work of the Council. When Moscow and Peking began to quarrel openly in 1960, the effectiveness of the Council and all its subsidiary organizations dropped off. Peking sought to move it to Jakarta, Indonesia, as President Sukarno increasingly pursued policy objectives that paralleled those of China. The Council's financial wing, the "Afro-Asian Solidarity Foundation," may at one time have been considered by the Chinese as a plausible channel for funds intended to foster African revolutions. They seem to have abandoned it in favor of direct payments to their chosen agents, as in Zanzibar and the Congo.

The main advantage that the Chinese derived was a series of new footholds and new bases for exchanges with Africa. The Chinese Afro-Asian Solidarity Committee in Peking immediately began to trade visits with Africans. This gave the Chinese an opportunity to catch up with the Soviets, who had maintained regular diplomatic, consular or commercial contacts in some African countries since the 1920s.

Peking now had a good forum to exploit the points of "solidarity" it could claim to share with Africans: being non-white and non-European, and having had the common experience of being a poverty-stricken country exploited by "foreign devils" ever since the fifteenth century, when the first Portuguese caravelles touched the coasts of Africa and the Orient.

At the Cairo conference of December 1957, three years before the Sino-Soviet split drew world attention, it was already apparent that the Soviet and Chinese Communist appeals to Africa were fundamentally divergent. The Soviets stressed their superior ability to grant economic aid, and pointed to the Aswan High Dam as a shining example. The Chinese, unable to compete in hard cash, appealed to African hearts, minds and race-consciousness. As Soviet delegates talked economic aid and credits, Chinese delegate Kuo Mo-jo spoke of the common cultural heritage of the non-whites of Asia, Africa and America. Delegate Chu Tu-nan contended that Chinese, Indians, Arabs and Negroes shared the heritage of ancient cultures that had been broken and ruined by the West's imperialism. The only answer, Chu told his audience, was tremendous effort by the non-white world to build a new universal civilization, incorporating these lost traditions with the revolutionary elements of socialism. During his tour of Africa in the winter of 1963-64, Premier Chou En-lai developed this theme. He said in Mogadishu:

In the course of creating a new human civilization the African peoples, who had once created a brilliant ancient civilization, will certainly leave far behind the Western civilization, which was based on colonial rule over the peoples of Africa, Asia and Latin America.

At the second All-African People's Conference in Tunis in January 1960, the Chinese agreed to a Soviet proposal to transform the Solidarity Council into the "Afro-Asian People's Solidarity Organization" (AAPSO). This was set up with an executive council of fourteen Asian and thirteen African states, and a rotating chairmanship. It included Communist North Korea and North Vietnam and also Outer Mongolia, a country under both Soviet and Chinese influence. The U.A.R. and the Chinese joined forces to block a Soviet suggestion that the secretariat be moved to Conakry, at a time when Guinea was enjoying Soviet favor.

The Solidarity Fund was set up at the Executive Council's meeting at Beirut in November 1960. Its headquarters was in Conakry. The chairman was Ismail Touré of Guinea. His deputies were Mehdi ben Barka, organizer and chief foreign emissary of Morocco's non-Communist Socialist party, the National Union of Popular Forces (UNFP), and Chu Tzu-chi, the Chinese member of the Cairo secretariat. There were also one U.A.R., two Indonesian and one Soviet member on the board. The chairman and his two deputies could disburse aid to armed resistance movements in case of need, provided they informed the other members afterward.

During the early 1960s a bewildering array of "Afro-Asian" organizations, for women, workers, young people, lawyers, journalists, writers and other professions and trades, blossomed within and on the edges of the world Communist movement.

Peking has systematically sought to oust the Soviets and their supporters from these organizations, though Russian influence in some, such as the World Federation of Trade Unions, has become so traditional that it is virtually institutionalized. In AAPSO itself, Sino-Soviet rivalry grew especially bitter at a meeting in February 1963.

This was the third Afro-Asian Solidarity Conference, at Moshi, Tanganyika. President Julius Nyerere's newly independent republic, and especially its multi-racial capital Dar es-Salaam, were already providing refuge for African nationalists from the Portuguese colonies, the Rhodesias and the Republic of South Africa. It was also a hub of the moderately militant Pan-African Freedom Movement of East, Central and South Africa (PAFMECSA).

The Moscow-Peking schism was beginning to split the Communist world. Africans and Asians were developing grave doubts about the omnipotence of the Soviet power system, especially since the death of Stalin. Moscow had backed down during President Kennedy's firm

handling of the Cuban missile crisis in October 1962. But Red
China's self-drawn image as the peaceful but powerful defender of
colored people everywhere was also tarnished: the invasion of India a
month earlier had shocked and puzzled Asians and Africans.

The Soviets, mindful of the decline of Communist influence in
Africa, proposed a truce in Sino-Soviet polemics. They asked the
Chinese and the other delegates at Moshi not to discuss "controver-
sial" subjects. But Liu Ning-yi, the chief Chinese delegate, ignored
the Soviet request. He persuaded the Conference not to grant official
status to the Moscow-dominated World Peace Council's seven delegates or other international front organizations known to be favorable
to the Soviet "peaceful coexistence" line. He blocked recognition of
Nazim Hikmet, a Turkish writer living in Moscow who had become a
standby Soviet mouthpiece at such meetings.

In response to Khrushchev's message, citing the Cuban crisis as an
example of how a country's national independence can be saved
without war, Liu Ning-yi pointed to the Algerian victory in the battle
for independence. This, he said, was proof that a people's will to
revolution can defeat modern weapons. Imperialist assurances, and
the idea that underdeveloped nations would profit from disarmament
agreements by receiving more economic aid, a standard Soviet argument, were equally false and dangerous, he added. The Chinese were
able to make a number of their ideas prevail in the final resolutions.
They annoyed the Russians by identifying them as "white men" who
had no right to be on the African continent.

From this time on the Soviets and their backers, especially the
Indians, fell out with the Chinese and their supporters, especially the
Indonesians, over the goals and the methods of AAPSO. Beginning at
a seminar in Algiers of the World Federation of Democratic Youth in
April 1963, the Chinese began to form their own splinter groups.
They published their theory that colonized or recently independent
lands of Asia, Africa and Latin America constitute the "focus of
world contradictions." The populations of these lands, argued the
Chinese, rather than the "international proletariat" as argued by the
Soviets, would lead in "sweeping imperialism and capitalism from the
face of the earth."

How far such arguments could lead the Chinese in their offensive
to capture the African mind was dramatically highlighted in the auditorium of the University of Algiers in March 1964.

Under the apprehensive eyes of M'hammed Yazid, the Algerian

chairman, and before the tense faces of over 100 delegates to the sixth session of the AAPSO Council, a tough, determined little Chinese woman took the floor.

She was Mme. Kuo Chien, an articulate high priestess of Chinese militancy. At this meeting she had already criticized "peaceful coexistence" and the "reactionary reasoning" of the Soviets that frontier conflicts should be settled by peaceful means. "Your expansionism and national egoism," she told the Russians, "have long since made it difficult to draw a line between you and the imperialists and colonialists, old and new. As birds of a feather flock together, it is not at all strange that you should stand on the side of the imperialists and colonialists. But you will never succeed in deceiving us, the people of Africa and Asia . . . *Morally, you are the assassins of Patrice Lumumba!"*

A deathly hush fell over the auditorium. There was a chill of foreboding in the air: this was the gravest charge that could be made in Africa about anyone.

Patrice Lumumba, the silver-tongued, mild-mannered ex-beer salesman who had risen to lead the Congo through its first frenetic months of independence, was still Africa's chief martyr. To accuse a Belgian businessman or an American banker of having been Lumumba's murderer was usual enough. Africans, Communists and liberals everywhere often made the charge. But for one "socialist" to accuse another of this crime was sacrilege.

President Ahmed ben Bella, who suggested the Algerian revolution as a model for the rest of Africa, had done all a host could do to prevent things from reaching this pass. In his opening speech, he tried to show how Algeria's "original" pathway could guide other countries seeking their salvation outside the arena of great-power conflicts. "National egoism," said Ben Bella, "is the greatest enemy of African unity and liberation." He added that Africans themselves were not doing enough about liberating the remaining colonial areas—Angola, Mozambique, Portuguese Guinea, Southern Rhodesia and French Somaliland. He implied that neither Russian nor Chinese aid could accomplish for Africa the feats that Africans themselves were too timid or divided to undertake.

After more Russo-Chinese quarreling, chairman Yazid announced that further polemics were banned on the floor. The squabble then moved into the committees. Chinese and Russians crossed swords on Israel, South Africa and the Congo. Some of the African delegates got

up and left in disgust. A Western diplomat lunched with M'hammed
Yazid and Mehdi ben Barka, then drove them back to the meeting
hall. A small and manifestly hostile crowd of Algerians had gathered
on the sidewalk to watch the delegates return for the afternoon session. As the Chinese and Russians passed, there were catcalls and
various derogatory remarks.

"Aren't you ashamed," the diplomat was moved to ask his two
companions, "of such a spectacle, of the Chinese and Russians using
your meeting to wrangle?" They had to agree they were. At an
AAPSO secretariat meeting in Cairo a few days later, Yazid told the
Soviets and Chinese that if they did not stop their fighting in AAPSO,
the African countries would quit the organizations and the Algerians
would take the lead in doing so.

The Sino-Soviet dispute was involved rather less directly at the
Conference of Non-Aligned Nations in Cairo in October 1964. Since
the previous general conference of neutrals at Belgrade in September
1961 the African and international situations had changed radically.
The independent African states had held their own summit meeting in
June 1963 at Addis Ababa, Ethiopia, and created the Organization of
African Unity (OAU). The dangers of an international nuclear con-
flict had diminished, despite dangerous tension in Southeast Asia.
Soviet-American hostility had diminished. Differences between
France and the United States in the West and between China and
Russia in the East had created an entirely new and quite fluid situa-
tion.

Economics, especially the yawning gap between "have" and "have-
not" nations, increasingly dominated the thinking of African leaders.
They believed that falling basic prices of raw materials and high tariff
barriers in Western countries lay at the root of many of their major
difficulties. The central thesis of the Cairo meeting was that the end
of political colonialism should also entail changes in the world economic order: the "haves" should increasingly share wealth and the
means of production with the "have-nots." The Cairo conference was more aggressive toward Western "neo-colonialism" than the
Belgrade conference had been. In discussions and voting on the resolutions at Cairo, only a few African states, notably Mali, Congo
(Brazzaville), Tanzania and Algeria, supported the radical revolutionary theories of the Chinese—and the Algerians had reservations.

The Chinese did their best to exclude the Russians from the second

"Bandung" conference of Afro-Asian states scheduled in Algiers in June 1965. A year earlier Khrushchev's African and Asian diplomacy, including his history-making visit to Egypt in May, and subsequent talks he had had with President Tito and other statesmen, had centered on securing an invitation for the U.S.S.R. Peking denied Moscow's right to attend, since the Soviet "was not an Asian power." Soviet rebuttals claimed the Soviet Union was the "largest Asian power." Peking, it said, planned to erect a "Great Wall of China" between the different races. But most of the fourteen-nation committee preparing the Algiers conference remained deaf to the Russian claim, even after India backed it in December 1964.

Red China's planners see all of Africa, Asia and Latin America as a vast "intermediate zone" between the United States and the divided Communist world. "Afro-Asian solidarity" means the expulsion of United States influence from this zone. Red China's exclusion from the United Nations gave Peking a chance to strengthen this concept of "solidarity," and Peking applauded Indonesia's withdrawal from the United Nations in January 1965. On January 24, Chou En-lai proposed a "new, revolutionary U.N." free of United States influence.

This idea, judging by African reactions, appealed only to China's best African friends: Mali, Tanzania and the Congo (Brazzaville). Other African statesmen, notably Dr. Kwame Nkrumah, President of Ghana, said they regretted it, and sought to persuade the Indonesians to reconsider.

The formation of a new "revolutionary" bloc of Afro-Asian nations outside the U.N., not taking part in the latter's work even if asked to, had long been in Chinese minds. "If we should enter the United Nations," said the confidential *Work Bulletin* of the Central Political Department of the People's Liberation Army on April 25, 1961, "we would not be a majority. On the surface the situation would become easier, but in reality the struggle would become more intense and we should lose our freedom of movement . . . The area of peace is growing." But never, the article went on, could there be reliance on coexistence, and "no illusion" about "imperialism," especially as long as the United States continued to oppose the "liberation" of Formosa.

Peking actively promoted the idea of a "Conference of Asian, African and Latin American Peoples," to be held sometime in 1965 or 1966. Ahmed ben Bella had proposed the inclusion of Latin

America, and Fidel Castro eagerly encouraged the idea. AAPSO delegates of Algeria, Guinea, Morocco, the U.A.R., Tanganyika and the African National Congress Party, chief opponent of white rule in the Republic of South Africa, planned to meet with the delegations from six nations of Asia (including China) and Latin America in Havana in July 1964, to seek a formula for this super-conference. Castro wished to hold it in Cuba before the second "Bandung" in Algiers. Though Peking and Moscow both welcomed the idea publicly, they were privately more than hesitant, since Castro's allegiance was uncertain.

The July meeting never took place. In the winter of 1964-65 Castro's trusted aide, Ernesto ("Che") Guevara, made an extended tour of Africa, seeking to strengthen Cuban influence in all of the "liberation" movements, especially the Chinese-backed Congo rebellion. He also continued to campaign for the new Peoples' Conference.

Soviet Communist Party secretary M. A. Suslov, in his secret report read to the Party's plenary session on February 14, 1964, and finally published May 3, 1964, sounded a warning against underestimating the Chinese. It was meant originally for the ears of Soviet-bloc party workers only, but it deserved the careful attention it got in the West. Suslov said he believed the Chinese theories of violent revolution could affect "people unversed in politics or with insufficient experience," especially countries lacking an industrial proletariat—which includes nearly every country on the African continent.

"Afro-Asian Solidarity"—one of the most formidable catchwords in the Red Chinese vocabulary—had thus come to mean, as Soviet Professor Bojdan Gafurov put it, that "China wishes to range the yellow and black-skinned people" against the world's whites. Against the Western idea of human brotherhood, betrayed so often by the West in its own racial practice, or even against the equally tarnished Soviet idea of the "solidarity" of the world's workers, this could prove to be a deadly weapon indeed.

CHAPTER FOUR

Africa's Troubled Horn

RED CHINA CHOSE THE NORTHEAST HORN OF AFRICA, JUTTING INTO the Indian Ocean just south of the strategic Gulf of Aden, for one of its earliest and most persistent efforts. This was more than a historical accident, for the Chinese had started to visit the Somali coast more than a thousand years before. Geographers still call the area "The Somalilands."

The Somali coastlands, like Ethiopia to the northwest and Kenya to the south, guard the sea and air routes between Asia and Africa. They are a crossroads for all sorts of exchanges between Arabs, Negroes and Orientals.

Foremost among the "Somalilands" is the independent Somali Republic. This came into being in July 1960 through the merger of the former British Somaliland Protectorate with the ex-Italian colony of Somalia. The merger was a first step toward restoration of the Somali nation as the ethnic entity that had existed until France, Britain and Italy carved up the Horn of Africa in the late nineteenth century. For the Somalis, and the Chinese, it is not what is inside the Somali Republic that is most important, but rather what is still outside it. The "reunification" of all the Somalis is a point on which all Somali political parties and all regimes in the Somali Republic's capital of Mogadishu have always agreed. First of all there is the French overseas territory called Côte Française des Somalis, or French Somaliland. Then there are the disputed Hodh and Ogaden pasturelands: in 1897, Britain, to win support against the Mahdist rebellion in the

Sudan, recognized these as part of Ethiopia. As a result, they are the scene of constant fighting between Ethiopians and Somalis. Farther south lies the bleak Northern Province of Kenya. About one-third of its people are Somalis, who settled there as conquerors in the 1890s, during the last great wave of Somali tribal expansion.

Blood ties and the True Faith—Islam—are tremendously strong among the Somalis. To foreigners, the vast majority seem to be like the same rude herdsmen that the first Chinese voyagers reported seeing in the ninth and tenth centuries. They are pastoral nomads, constantly moving their flocks of camels, goats and sheep over the arid wastelands in quest of water and grass. Like other tribesmen of North Africa, the Somalis love to fight. Their loyalties are tribal. Only in northern Somaliland, where the Arab and Persian traders left their mark, is there any considerable traditional political order or organization.

The two major cities are Mogadishu, in the south, and Djibouti, capital of French Somaliland, in the north. During the colonial competition of the late nineteenth century the Italians as allies of the British obtained control over the southern ports from the Sultan of Zanzibar. The British in 1920 temporarily broke the back of the Somali opposition when they bombed the capital of a tribal chieftain known as the "Mad Mullah." Mussolini's Italy, for its part, "pacified" the interior of Somalia and occupied Ethiopia beginning in 1934, in a shameful war of conquest to which Western Europe and the United States largely closed their eyes.

When the British defeated the Italian armies in East Africa in 1941, they placed the Protectorate, Somalia, the Hodh and Ogaden under a military administration. Under this administration the Somali Youth League was formed as a political club in 1943. Its most active period of organization was between 1950 and 1960, when Italy exercised United Nations trusteeship over Somalia. The League formed the first Somali government in 1956. Its moderation and modernism made it a target for the pro-Egyptian and more extremist Greater Somalia League, in which both Russians and Chinese were soon to take an interest. Pressure increased when the Hodh grazing lands were transferred in 1954 to direct Ethiopian administration. It was still growing in the summer of 1960, when the British Protectorate won its independence. Somalia followed it, and the two states united in the new Republic.

The new nation was thus born under the triple threat of frontier claims, a militant call of an especially self-conscious brand of Islam, and a growing popularity of the idea of a true ethnic and political union of all the Somalis.

Before the Sino-Soviet split it seemed that Moscow and Peking had divided Africa into spheres of influence. The emphasis of Chinese diplomatic activity placed on Guinea and Mali, and the parallel Soviet interest in Ethiopia and nearby countries, suggested that perhaps Peking was applying its main efforts to West Africa, while Moscow concentrated on East Africa. But as soon as the split became visible in 1960, the Chinese began rapidly to mount their own diplomatic offensive in the Horn.

Peking chose one of its top Arabic and Islamic experts, Chang Yueh, to be first Ambassador to the Somali Republic in June 1961. Chang had already initiated Red China's push into the Arab world when he supervised road-building operations in Yemen. In Mogadishu he hired Indian contractors to build the biggest and most ornate embassy in the Somali capital. His initial staff numbered nearly forty, nearly all of them speaking Somali and most of them speaking Arabic as well, a language that educated Somalis admire and use to some extent.

Chang Yueh rapidly sought out "interesting" political parties and coalitions, advocating the reunification of all Somalis, including those in Ethiopia. The Soviets were deeply committed to Ethiopia because of traditional Russian policy considerations and investments. They did nothing at first, while Chang Yueh's staff toured the Somali back country, distributing encouragement and cash. Pan-Somali extremist opposition leaders were feted royally in Peking and given secret numbered accounts in Swiss banks.

Moscow's early efforts seemed to have been largely through the Somali Communists. From 1945 through 1960, while former Italian Somaliland was a United Nations Trusteeship territory under Italian administration, the Italian Communist Party worked intensively among teachers and trade unions. Many Italian residents, never very friendly toward the British military administration in British Somaliland, were heavily influenced by the Italian Communists, some of whom Mussolini had exiled to Somalia. A "Somali Communist Party" existed for a few months in 1956, but was dissolved. Even in 1964 the ruling Somali Youth League, with its red flag and doctrinaire tone, showed the influence of the Italian Communist Party.

Moscow's influence was also exercised through a labor federation,

Confederazione Generale Somala di Lavori (CGSL), which was inspired in structure and purpose by the Italian trade unions. Italian
and therefore some Soviet Communist influence was also discernible
in the 1960s through a Pan-Somali Party, which sometimes called
itself the Greater Somalia League, and sometimes the Somali Democratic Union. The CGSL was strongest in the southern part of the
Republic, especially in the southern towns of Darot, Howeia and
Rakanwena. There was a rival, pro-Western Confederazione Somala
di Lavoratori.

By 1964 the Chinese Embassy was working directly with the
Somali Democratic Union and the CGSL. Western diplomats stationed in Mogadishu observed that the Chinese operated far more
discreetly than the Russians, who had tended to compromise themselves by contacting opposition politicians openly. The number of
Somali delegations visiting China rose from two in 1960, to four in
1961, to seven in 1963. In 1962 China gave Somalis 200 of a total of
400 scholarships it distributed in Africa. Moscow, meanwhile,
granted credits and gifts ranging from a new fifty-kilowatt radio
transmitter at Mogadishu to oil drilling equipment. Together Moscow
and Prague offered arms to the Somali government on attractive
terms. Britain and Italy countered this with a secret offer, which led
to the Somali acquisition of $840,000 worth of British and Italian
armored cars, mortars and light artillery. The United States shipped
surplus food and modest amounts of other aid. Like Red China, it
offered relief supplies during the country's periodic droughts.

Though French Somaliland has never been in the African spotlight,
this blisteringly hot enclave, 12,000 square miles of gritty basalt
desert, relieved by little but the steaming capital of Djibouti, was the
cradle of an early and abortive Chinese venture on the Somali coast.
A French Protectorate since 1894, its political life has been sleepy. In
September 1958, like all the rest of the French African Community
except Guinea, it voted to keep its ties with Paris. It was given local
self-government, while France controlled foreign relations and defense. In 1965, United Nations and OAU commissions on colonialism were busying themselves with the question. Ethiopia was
advancing its own claims, though not insistently.

Just as at Bandung five years earlier, Red China's new overseas
adventure began with a mysterious air disaster.

The principal nationalist movement in Djibouti in 1960 was the
national Pan-Somali Movement, led by Mohammed Harbi Farah. He
was a fifty-two-year-old native of Djibouti who had gone into exile in

1958 and set up his headquarters in Mogadishu. In April 1960, Harbi attended the Afro-Asian Solidarity Conference in Conakry and was contacted by Chinese agents there. After receiving the usual red carpet reception during a visit to Peking, Harbi made a trip to Europe in September 1960. On September 27 the Egyptian airliner on which he and two other natives of French Somaliland were flying from Geneva to Rome, bound for Mogadishu, crashed into the sea off the island of Elba. The sea washed up nothing of the plane and its thirty passengers except for some fragments of wreckage and a few life jackets.

A few days later, a colleague of Harbi's named Ali Abdullah was attacked at Mogadishu airport by another Somali who tried to prevent him from boarding a plane for Europe.

In questioning the men, Somali police learned that Harbi had received a sizable sum of money from Peking and had deposited it in a numbered Zurich bank account. Abdullah had been with Harbi in Peking and knew about the money. He had been bound for Switzerland to collect it when Ahmed Gourmane, Harbi's second in command, challenged him at the airport. Harbi, it turned out, had accused Abdullah of embezzling party funds. It was estimated that $4,200,000, or nearly one-third of the entire national income of the Somali Republic, had been deposited in the Zurich account. Part of this money had been used to pay for a shipload of arms, probably intended for Harbi's partisans in French Somaliland. These arms were to have been landed in Berbera, the new Soviet-built port, early in October 1960.

On October 1 the Saudi Arabian freighter *Rastanura,* with an Egyptian captain, an Italian engineer and a mixed Arab crew, arrived in Berbera, showing cement on its cargo manifest. At dawn on October 5 the ship slipped out of port and was gone seventeen hours. Suspicious Somali port authorities searched it after its return, but found only cement and two voluminous secret compartments, both empty. The Egyptian captain was tried anyway and sentenced for customs offenses. Eventually five large boxes of 1952-model British anti-tank grenades turned up on the beach, probably parts of stocks the British had left in Suez when they evacuated Egypt. Some 1,500 rifles and other small arms that were also thought to have been aboard were never found. Western diplomats surmised that they had made their way to the Shifta tribesmen who regularly raid the Ethiopian or French Somali frontiers.

The cement cargo had been purchased in the name of a shipping agent, one of the Somalis who died with Harbi in the plane crash. Harbi himself had been due in Berbera the day before the *Rastanura* docked. It was assumed that when he failed to arrive the captain hastily left port to dump his hot cargo.

Peking's intervention on the Somali coast, though far more discreet than its backing for guerilla warfare in the Congo, in 1964, was nonetheless highly vexing to three Western powers: France in French Somaliland; Britain in Kenya; and the United States, which, like the Soviet Union, was deeply committed in Ethiopia by this time.

The backbone of the Chinese-backed Shiftas, Somali nomad irregulars who keep up the pressure on Ethiopia, are some 50,000 Esa tribesmen in the northern area, who love to fight. In the summer of 1960 the Ethiopian army intervened in a tribal war between the Esas and the more primitive Danakils, nomads who roam the empty deserts of French Somaliland and Ethiopia, southwest of Djibouti. The Ethiopians took revenge for the killing of a few of their men by slaughtering over 100 Esas, including women and children.

The Esa riposte was an attack on the Addis Ababa-Djibouti train in August. This railroad is Ethiopia's lifeline to the coast, and is operated by a French company holding a concession from Emperor Haile Selassie. It is an important reason why Ethiopia is anxious not to see a hostile power take over in French Somaliland. The plundering Esas went on to kill the French Consul in Harar. When Ethiopian troops chased them from French Somaliland back into the Somali Republic, the Esas were met by Ahmed Gourmane, who is reported to have promised Chinese arms to stiffen their resistance. This led diplomats then in Mogadishu to believe that the anti-tank grenades aboard the *Rastanura* may have been intended for another assault on the railroad.

At various times since then the conflict has flared anew, especially on the Ethiopian border in the Hodh pasturelands during the winter of 1963-64. This time the fighting was stopped by the Organization of African Unity, the supra-national grouping of independent African states created at the Addis Ababa African Summit Conference in May 1963. A joint Somali-Ethiopian inspection team brought about a withdrawal of troops. But there seemed little hope for a permanent truce. Neither Dr. Abdirrashid Ali Shirmarke, who was then the Somali Prime Minister, nor any other Somali politician could be moderate on the frontier issue without risking political suicide. The Pan-Somali Party's sky-blue flag has a five-point star symbolizing the

Somali Republic, Ethiopia's Ogaden and Hodh, Eritrea, French Somaliland and Northern Kenya, and most Somalis look upon it as the true flag of their nation. A Somali "liberation song" broadcast by Mogadishu Radio in September 1963, and typical of many such songs, runs as follows:

> My face is burning and will not be happy
> Until I see all the five parts sharing the flag over us,
> Until I see brothers taking the oath to die together.
> I shall not be happy until our spears are wet and we do our duty;
> I shall not be happy until we go to war to unite the Somalis,
> Until the leader gives us news of his determination.

And another added:

> Although I am dismembered,
> If a MIG could fly for me,
> I would thank God.
> When it flies high in the sky,
> And I hear the noise of its engine,
> My heart will take courage,
> And the enemy will become frightened.

Radio Peking, which by 1965 had expanded its African service in all languages to nearly 100 hours a week, wholeheartedly backed such sentiments. But it did it so discreetly that Peking's broadcasts in the Somali language played even battle hymns in soft, modulated music. A listener would never suspect they were battle hymns if he did not know Somali.

At the borders the Somali nomads move along their traditional routes. Ethiopian police stop them only if they cross. A BBC correspondent reported in June 1964 that the Shiftas say "The Ethiopians are our comrades. But we shall go on fighting them until we get our land back." The Ethiopians express equal regard for the Somalis, but equal determination not to give an inch. Though limited in scope, the Somali-Ethiopian conflict provides Red China with great opportunity for stirring up African conflict. It centers on a problem common enough in Africa, that of disputed frontiers inherited from past colonial regimes. The Charter of the Organization of African Unity tacitly endorses the preservation of these frontiers. Emperor Haile Selassie used this as his main argument against the Somali claims.

Ethiopia, the oldest independent nation in Africa, with a history and traditions nearly as venerable as China's, represents a barrier to both Soviet and Chinese designs on the continent. Ethiopia is also one of the African countries that has been aided by General Chiang Kai-shek's Nationalist Chinese regime on Formosa. As I learned in Addis Ababa in 1963, the Ethiopians are aware of the militancy and exclusiveness of contemporary Somali nationalism, and of the strength of its common language and Islamic faith. But they regard Ethiopia, the oldest Christian nation in the world, as a bulwark of Christianity. Emperor Haile Selassie, who was seventy-two in 1964, has been personally behind Ethiopia's missionary drive to push Coptic Christianity northward. He also has looked to the south, to Tanganyika, whose elder statesman Julius Nyerere is a Roman Catholic presiding over a Christian ruling elite. But their friendship was shaken by the union of Tanganyika with Zanzibar.

The Chinese constantly seek to cultivate the world's 350 million Moslems. About 15 million of these live in Red China, many in zones claimed by the Soviet Union. Moslems from all parts of Africa, Asia and the Arab world are encouraged to make pilgrimages to Moslem shrines in China.

Peking's interest in Somali Islam as a militant "revolutionary" force in the Horn was shown in 1960 when the Red Chinese government invited Hagi Mohammed Hussein, President of the Pan-Somali League, to Peking. He is as known for his fanatical devotion to Islam as for his anti-Western ideas. At about the time of the invitation, Hussein and his Vice-President, Banafuri, quarreled and read each other out of the Party. Banafuri had publicly accused Hussein of selling out to the Chinese. It may have been Chang Yueh's minions that felt it necessary at this point to do something about these charges: leaflets suddenly appeared in Mogadishu's principal hostelry, the Hotel Giuba, accusing "American imperialists" of causing all the trouble.

For the first three years of its existence the Somali Republic lived largely from Italian, British and some Soviet and American economic aid. The break with this pattern came when Dr. Shirmarke accepted an invitation to go to Peking in August 1963, as part of a tour of several Asian states. A Somali-Chinese trade and payments agreement had already been signed in May 1963, by which China sold machinery, textiles, chemicals and tea to the Somalis. To China, Mogadishu supplied frankincense, myrrh, oil seeds, minerals and some "other goods." Published details of the accord went no further, and nothing at all was disclosed of an accompanying agreement on "technical and economic aid."

The Chinese granted the Somali Republic a $3 million loan, initially interest-free and with a low interest rate after ten years. Mogadishu has used this to balance its budget. The secret accord on technical assistance covered an early offer to build a state farm near Chisimaio, in the lower Giuba region. The Soviets had also backed two state farms of 13,000 acres, for raising oil seeds and cotton. The magnitude of these projects can be seen from the fact that there are barely 20,000 acres of arable farmland in the entire country. Later, the Russians sent more aid for another state farm at Hargeisa, complete with buildings, machinery, a school and other accessories. Another secret Chinese offer involved sending technicians. Dr. Shirmarke's government considered it compromising, and refused at first. But the troubles with Ethiopia, added to the economic dislocation already caused by a diplomatic break with Britain in 1963, changed Dr. Shirmarke's mind. He accepted several hundred Chinese technicians, mainly for agricultural activities.

In Peking, as is the custom with visiting heads of state, Dr. Shirmarke was received by President Liu Shao-chi and Chairman Mao Tse-tung. In the usual toasts and welcoming speeches, Chinese dignitaries emphasized the "Bandung spirit" of Afro-Asian unity against "outsiders," meaning of course people with white skins, including Russians. Shirmarke replied with noncommittal statements about African unity. In a joint communiqué issued August 10, both countries expressed satisfaction with their relations and support for anticolonialist movements and for the decisions of the Addis Ababa African Summit Conference.

After Premier Chou En-lai visited the Somali Republic in February 1964, Dr. Shirmarke announced that Peking would increase its aid. This would include rice and help in tobacco cultivation, leather and soap manufacture, the building of roads and perhaps airports. Shirmarke reasserted Somali "non-alignment" by stating that "Communism has no part" in his country and "is against the principles of the Somali people," Nairobi Radio reported on February 7, 1964.

The Chinese-Somali trade agreement is a fair example of the barter deals that Peking concludes wherever it can in Africa. The values of imports and exports are exactly balanced, so that Peking need not dip into its foreign currency reserves. The Chinese sell their goods in the Somali Republic and use the proceeds to pay for services of their aid missions and the operation of their big embassy in Mogadishu, which by 1963 had cut its staff from the original forty to about twenty. In 1964 about the only real Somali exports to China, despite the talk about frankincense and myrrh, were sharkskins, a popular ingredient of aphrodisiacs along the East African coast. Visiting Chinese trade delegations, in contrast to the frequent Russian and Western missions, usually travel long and widely inside the country. They concentrate heavily on the north, since the Somalis there control 95 per cent of the trade. In the southern part of the country, Europeans still largely run commerce. Here are also the permanent Asiatic residents, including a few Chinese who, since the establishment of diplomatic relations with China in 1961, have been actively making trading contacts among northern Somali merchants. Formerly the Somali trade channels ran from the northern part of the country to the outside world through the British crown colony of Aden. From the south, especially Mogadishu, they ran mainly to Italy. Now the country's trade is far more centered in Mogadishu. The Soviets built the northern port of Berbera with a view to cutting Aden, Britain's Arab stronghold, out of the normal Red Sea circuit, but this did not succeed. A seesaw, three-way competition between the Russians, the Chinese and the West developed for the privileges of trading with and aiding the Somalis in the herculean task of making a viable country out of their gritty deserts.

More dangerously for peace in the Horn, the same competition has been characteristic of aid for the Somali armed forces. On November 12, 1963, Foreign Minister Abdullahi Issa sent icy shivers down a few spines in Washington and London by announcing in Nairobi that the Somali Republic would accept military aid from the Soviet Union instead of from the West. The reason? "Unacceptable conditions imposed by the United States," said Mr. Issa. For three and a half years, he added, the government had been negotiating for arms offers of $18 million from the West. Then the United States had notified him that its help depended on agreement by the Somalis not to seek military aid elsewhere. Dr. Shirmarke's government would therefore take Russian aid of $30 million, or nearly twice that offered by the United States, West Germany and Italy.

Russia would send weapons to enlarge the small army, still equipped with World War II weapons, and would also outfit a small air force. Western diplomats were not able to verify reports that the army's total strength would be increased from 4,000 to 20,000. But arms deliveries began January 22, 1964, amid the border crisis with Ethiopia. By mid-1964 this Soviet-backed buildup of the army seemed to be underway. "America will understand our position," Issa said. The Somalis wanted "cordial and friendly relations" with the West and would maintain an attitude of strict non-alignment.

This launched the aid race in earnest. The United States offered to build fishing boats, donated three DC-3s to the infant Somali airline, and provided teacher training and construction work at the port of Chisimaio. Italy supplied an airline staff, and price supports for Somali bananas. Russia sent doctors, agricultural machinery and small industrial and food processing plants. Red China, after Dr. Shirmarke's trip, promised another $17 million for future development projects. Rice is an increasingly popular crop and food among the Somalis, and after experiments at Merca in growing the same kind of rice that has been successfully grown in Tanganyika, the government decided to build a new series of state farms, using army help. One of them was a large rice farm about twenty-five miles from Mogadishu, run along the lines taught the Somalis by the Chinese. To compete with this, the United States aid mission gave some advice on techniques of bread making, grain cultivation and soil conservation. United States and Italian oilmen investigated promising petroleum possibilities near Merca. The West Germans built a road, and the European Economic Community financed another. And so the competition went on. The Somali economy profited and showed real progress by 1965.

Red China devotes great attention to culture and information. Its effort largely centers on the fact that the Somali coasts are perhaps the most religious region in all Africa. The Koran is widely read and appreciated, so the Chinese have been quick to import Korans translated into Somali. One of the most interesting facets of Peking's effort is its exploitation of the Somali desire to shift away from Italian and increasingly toward English, a universal tongue in Africa, as the country's second language. The northern Somali politicians want to spread English, despite the break in diplomatic relations with Britain in 1963. But in 1964 there were only two good sources for books and magazines in English: Moscow and Peking!

In the Italian language the newspaper *Corriere della Somalia* in Mogadishu was subsidized by the Rome government, but had a Somali editor. Before that it had been a British newspaper. Its news sources were the Italian ANSA agency and the foreign embassies in Mogadishu, including the Chinese Embassy with its daily New China News Agency file. The *Corriere*'s presentation of the news could be called ethnocentric, and problems of race and religion, as in the

Chinese propaganda, are constantly stressed. It loses no opportunity
to discuss United States racial problems. The Italian Communist
Party planned to open its own bookstore, to propagate the Moscow
line.

As in other places in Africa, the United States Information Agency
has emerged second or third best. With its limited budget and
cramped and unimaginative approach to the African mind, the best it
could offer the Somalis was a series of subsidized paperback books,
many on stock anti-Communist themes, which interest few Africans.
The Soviet Union donated a new printing press to the government in
1964.

The story is the same in the field of films. Before independence, all
films came from Italy. Now there is a big demand for films in English.
English-language films are all coming from China and Russia, though
they are still distributed by Italians. One of the biggest hits of the
1963 season in Mogadishu was an English-language offering from
Peking, "Eagle in the Formosa Straits," a tale of evil doings of American imperialists who protect Chiang Kai-shek.

In 1964 an anti-American propaganda campaign in the Somali
Republic, largely Chinese-inspired, had reached such proportions that
United States Ambassador Horace G. Torbert Jr. and his staff were
seriously worried. It arose partly as a result of the crisis with Ethiopia, and partly as a by-product of the May elections, which returned
a substantial majority for the Somali Youth League, Dr. Shirmarke's
party, but which brought into temporary power a new Prime Minister, Dr. Hadji Hussein Abdurrazak, a strong and dynamic admin-
istrator who had less patience with the strong Eastward drift under
the previous government. In the period of instability that followed,
many broadcasts and editorials sounded as though the New China
News Agency file had simply been blue-penciled to substitute "an
imperialist power" for the "United States." The main targets were the
military aid to Ethiopia, and United States failure to support Pan-
Somali irredentism. The Soviets, despite their military aid, were
nearly as cautious as the United States in this respect. Only the
Chinese seemed willing to lend open propaganda support.

The Somali coasts are an increasingly important center of Sino-
Soviet competition for influence and power in Africa. Tactics are
highly flexible. For example, since neither Moscow nor Peking, each
for its own reasons, wishes to antagonize President de Gaulle, both
have been unusually reticent about public pronouncements calling for

the "liberation" of French Somaliland. Chinese contacts with the nationalist Somalis of the French enclave have been discreet and in 1964 apparently centered on one of Mohammed Harbi's successors, Mubarak Ahmed Mubarak, who was based in Cairo and who attended the Afro-Asian Solidarity Conference in Algiers in March 1964 as the representative of French Somaliland.

The crucial issue on the Horn remains the tension between militant Islam in the young Somali Republic and the proud Christian tradition of nearly two thousand years in Ethiopia. In a hastily scheduled "unofficial" stopover in Ethiopia just before arriving in the Somali Republic (an official visit was impossible since Ethiopia still recognized the Formosa regime) Chou En-lai seems to have tried to reassure Emperor Haile Selassie that China's intentions in the Horn were not aggressive. In a welcoming speech on February 1 the Emperor told his guest that two basic problems faced the world. One was to "raise the standard of living of those peoples who remain poverty-stricken, ill-fed, ill-housed, untaught." The second was the preservation of peace. This was indivisible and "as long as it is threatened anywhere on the face of the earth, so long as war is possible in any part of the globe—in India, in Vietnam, in Korea, in Berlin or in Cuba—not one of us is safe from destruction." This was a clear rebuke to Peking's uncompromising opposition to the Moscow-Washington nuclear test ban treaty of August 1963, and to Chou's advocacy of violent revolution to end Western influence everywhere.

On collective security between nations, Haile Selassie delivered another rebuke, this time to China's expressed view of the United Nations in Africa as a "tool of American imperialism." "Long ago," he told Chou, "we concluded that in the principle of collective security, embodied first in the League of Nations and today in the United Nations Organization, rests our best hope for peaceful survival." The New China News Agency did not quote these final words of the Emperor.

Only two days later Chou was in Mogadishu telling a news conference at the Chinese Embassy that "Ethiopia is controlled by foreigners and a foreign hand is over her, pressing down very heavily upon her. The Ethiopian people therefore want and wish to escape from this and be free." This aroused a storm of bitter comment in Ethiopia, though it may have somewhat encouraged the vague, amorphous Ethiopian opposition movement, which in December 1960 and several times before had attempted to revolt against the Emperor. It also probably delayed Ethiopia's recognition of Communist China for some months to come. Chou gave Morocco similar treatment at this news conference, during which he made his famous statement that "the revolutionary situation in Africa is excellent." A week later Chinese embassies all over the world issued a lengthy "corrected" text, with the insults to Ethiopia and Morocco expurgated, but it was too late. The damage had been done. This was Chou's major *faux pas*.

China's next important emissary was Hou Tung, who headed a successful Chinese trade fair in Addis Ababa in November 1964. Hou reminded Ethiopians that "friendly ties" between China and their country dated back to Chinese support during the war with Italy, and that they had supported Peking's entry into the U.N. Emperor Haile Selassie replied that he hoped China's power would not endanger the world, but would help to preserve peace "according to the principles of the Afro-Asian Solidarity Organization." Ethiopian newspapers and broadcasts showed the country was impressed with China's October nuclear explosion in Sinkiang, and noted that "even the United States government admitted that a disarmament conference without China would be of no value."

The New China News Agency claimed that 700,000 people had attended the fair and that an unnamed Ethiopian deputy minister had said: "Americans gave us one dollar but took away three. The peoples of Africa and Asia should cooperate to develop their countries."

The Chinese, like the Soviets, were prudent about direct interference in Ethiopia's domestic affairs. Haile Selassie was in a delicate position. In Melvin Lasky's words, he "lives like a man of the twentieth century and thinks like a monarch of the tenth century." It was clear to me from a brief talk I had with him in May 1963, during the Addis Ababa African summit conference, that he genuinely desires economic growth and modernization of his feudal country. Whether he can bring it about fast enough to keep ahead of Africa's winds of history is problematical. After more than thirty years' reign, other Africans, even the most rabidly socialist ones, respect him for his power and the tradition of leadership he incarnates as chief of the oldest independent state in Africa. This prestige seemed strengthened during his visits to the United States and to several Communist and Moslem states in 1963 and 1964. In the affairs of Africa as a whole, as leader of the OAU, the Conquering Lion of Judah was able to assume an anti-colonial role that tended to discourage African critics of his cautious policies at home.

He also appeared determined to keep Sino-Soviet rivalries, as well as American-Communist ones, as distant as possible from his country. The Soviets had made a determined diplomatic effort to mediate the Somali-Ethiopia border dispute. Jacob Malik, the Soviet Deputy Foreign Minister, visited Addis Ababa in March 1964. According to Western diplomats, Malik offered to reduce Soviet arms deliveries to the Somali army if Ethiopia "were prepared to make some concessions and offer some guarantees." The Emperor seems to have made a noncommittal reply.

Red China cannot allow Soviet ambitions in Ethiopia to prevail. Between them Ethiopia and the Somali Republic dominate the eastern approaches to the Red Sea and Suez. Control over either or both would give a strong vantage point in both the Arab world and Africa. Moscow has tempted Ethiopia by offering to discourage Somali designs and give massive military aid of the sort it gives Nasser. This, in the Soviet view, would end Ethiopian dependence on United States military aid. It would also end the danger of the Chinese moving in.

Over five centuries have elapsed since the ships of the Celestial Empire carried ivory and rhinoceros tusks from these countries of the Horn to the court of Peking. Now China is again busy opening this window at a Western extremity of its Sinocentric world.

CHAPTER FIVE

Zanzibar: Revolution and Race

THE REVOLUTION IN ZANZIBAR ON JANUARY 12, 1964, SCARCELY A
month after the island won independence within the Commonwealth
from Britain, focused world attention on East Africa as a new zone
where Chinese interests might collide with those of the West, and gave
Red China an important toehold off the East African coast. It provided a classic demonstration of Red China's skillful use of existing
racial, religious and social antagonisms to encourage a movement
calling itself both anti-colonialist and socialist at the same time.

Zanzibar seemed almost predestined for such an effort by Red
China. Its role as a gateway to East Africa, its direct sea contact with
not-so-distant Asia, and the prevailing trade winds of the Indian
Ocean had always placed it in contact with the peoples and civiliza-
tions of the East. Arab settlement began about A.D. 900. The Shirazi,
Moslem refugees from civil wars in Arabia and Persia, came from the
north. Negroid Bantu people moved up from the south. After long
struggles with the Portuguese around 1700, the Arabs of Oman finally captured the whole of the East African coast, including Zanzibar and its companion island of Pemba. By 1840, though they were a
minority, the energetic Arabs of Oman had effectively established
their rule over the conglomeration of African, Shirazi and other peoples. The Arab rulers introduced a plantation industry in cloves from
the Molucca Islands, and made Zanzibar the principal town in East
Africa, both commercially and politically. They controlled a vast
network of trading contacts around the world. From 1882 on the two
islands were united under one Arab ruler.

The attempt to suppress the flourishing East African slave trade, and the rival colonial designs of the Germans, involved the British in the affairs of Zanzibar and its sultans. In 1886 Britain, France and Germany reached an agreement on the extent of the Sultan of Zanzibar's dominions along the East African coast.

British control was largely vested in a new British East Africa Association, later called the Imperial East African Company. In 1890 the British proclaimed a formal protectorate over the island, divesting the Company of its control. The Sultan's mainland holdings were henceforth administered by the British government as the British East African Protectorate, or Kenya Coastal Strip, now part of independent Kenya, and the Uganda Protectorate, now the independent state of Uganda.

Responsibility for Zanzibar passed from the British Foreign Office to the Colonial Office in 1913. The island got a constitutional government in 1926, with an executive and legislative council. Africans began to serve effectively in the Sultan's government in 1946. By 1956, when new constitutional changes gave larger self-rule, the Legislative Council included three Arabs, two Africans, two Asians and one European in addition to the British Resident. Five of these seats went to the Afro-Shirazi Party (ASP) in a rout of the predominantly Arab Zanzibar Nationalist Party. This defeat signaled the coming decline of Arab power. In 1959 the ASP split wide open with the formation of the Zanzibar and Pemba People's Party (ZPPP). The first elections under a new constitution in January 1961 brought deadlock between the ASP and the Nationalists. In June new elections brought victory for a coalition of the Nationalists and ZPPP. There were bloody riots, which, according to official figures, killed sixty-eight people. In a compromise, Sheikh Muhammed Shamte of Pemba, head of the ZPPP, was made chief minister, while Sheikh Ali Muhsin, a Nationalist leader who had visited both Cairo and Peking, was given a lesser post.

After full independence came on December 10, 1963, events moved very swiftly indeed. The exact role that Red China, its agents and its friends played in the revolution of January 12, 1964, may long be argued by journalists and historians. But certain facts have been established by Western and neutral observers. There can also be no argument about the great amount of interest that Peking had always shown in Zanzibar, and especially since its revolution.

The Sultan's government, recognizing this, had already decided to open diplomatic ties with Peking before hundreds of determined

armed men crushed the Sultan's security forces, massacred and imprisoned many Arabs, and brought the ASP to power on the night of
January 11-12.

Sheikh Ali Muhsin had been careful to keep in touch with both
Cairo and Peking, even as he purged his Zanzibar Nationalist Party
of its leftist radicals. Peking's envoys had been among the guests at
the Independence Day ceremonies on December 10, and Ali Muhsin
had announced the opening of diplomatic relations at that time. On
December 12 he signed an agreement to this effect with Ho Ying,
who became Chinese Ambassador, and who was then already accredited to Tanganyika and Uganda.

The rising curve of Peking's interest is shown by the fact that the
four Zanzibari delegations invited to Red China in 1962 increased to
twelve in 1963. Peking gave great publicity to the independence celebrations. On December 10 Radio Peking hailed the "glorious traditions of heroic struggle against colonialism and imperialism," and
reported a message from Ali Muhsin thanking China for "moral and
material support" in the fight for independence.

Sheikh Mohammed Abdul Rahman, called "Babu," is the Zanzibari singled out by most Western observers as the chief liaison man
with Peking. He is a charming, clever man, described by one Briton
who met him as "a veteran of Chelsea cocktail parties and [Labor
M. P.] Fenner Brockway's Movement for Colonial Freedom in London." He headed the Umma Party, which attracted little attention
before the January 12 revolt. This is what Babu himself said about
the role of the Umma in an interview with *Révolution* (No. 9, 1964),
a glossy illustrated monthly, financed by Red China and published in
Paris:

> The reality is that there was a true revolution in Zanzibar. Its objective
> was to destroy the old order and to install a new society. It is certainly
> difficult to affirm that all those who took part in the revolution were
> socialists, but they had a socialist orientation. The Marxist organization
> of Zanzibar, the Umma Party, took a leading role in the national and
> democratic revolution. From now on and finally, this has taken the path
> of the socialist revolution.

Babu was a regional editor of *Révolution*. He had visited Peking,
served as Zanzibar correspondent for the New China News Agency,
and had also been editor of a leftist newssheet called *Zanews*. Since
1960 he had held several offices in the Zanzibar National Party, for
which he organized youth and labor wings.

Babu contacted the Communist-directed World Federation of Trade Unions (WFTU) in Prague, and succeeded in winning WFTU grants and Communist-bloc scholarships for his protégés, who became known as *Makomred,* in most Communist-bloc countries, including Cuba. He is a close friend of Fidel Castro and Castro's right-hand man, Ernesto ("Che") Guevara. He helped set up a "Zanzibar office" in Havana and a training program in Cuba for guerillas. An Arab named Ali Mahfoud and a native of the French-ruled Comoro Islands named Foum were trained in Cuba, and both were among the guerillas who took over Zanzibar in January 1964.

In March and April 1962, Babu, as Secretary-General of the Zanzibar National Party, was one of the Zanzibari delegates at a constitutional conference in London, so he was well familiar with British thinking on the island's and East Africa's future. This must have made him useful to his Chinese contacts. After riots that followed the unsuccessful outcome of the constitutional talks in May 1962, Babu and a number of other Zanzibari politicians were arrested by the British under emergency regulations. By the end of 1962 all were released and the state of emergency ended. This gave Babu a short period of "martyrdom," which made him even more valuable from the Chinese point of view. Shortly after the final conference on independence, held in September 1963, Babu went to London. He did not return to Zanzibar until after the independence celebrations. Probably sniffing potential subversion, the Sultan's government banned the Umma Party. Babu went to Dar es-Salaam, Tanganyika, where he spent the evening of the revolution, January 11.

Babu returned to the island as soon as the revolution had been successful, to become Foreign Minister of the revolutionary government. In an interview with the New China News Agency he said: "The victory of the Zanzibar revolution was only a step in the revolution in Africa, Asia and Latin America. The Zanzibar people send greetings to Chairman Mao because they learned a lot from his works."

In 1964, while Tanzanian Minister of Planning and Cooperatives, he visited New York. He lectured Negroes in Harlem on the need for "revolutionary discipline," and conferred with Black Nationalist leader Malcolm X, who had visited African statesmen during the preceding summer, shortly before being murdered. Early in 1965 Babu went to Peking and prepared the visit, in February, of President Julius Nyerere of Tanzania.

Plans for the Zanzibar revolt, it appears, were actually laid in discussion among agents of various Communist-bloc states during 1962—the very year in which Babu was attending the meetings in London—in Leningrad, Prague, Sofia and Warsaw. One of those who participated was Ali Sultan Issa, secretary of the Zanzibar Federation of Progressive Trade Unions, who gradually swung the Federation away from the Moscow-directed WFTU pattern and toward Peking.

Ali Sultan Issa was among several Zanzibaris studying trade union-ism under WFTU auspices. Another was his wife, Aissha Ali Sultan, who had lived in Peking since 1962. Aissha called herself "Secretary-General of the Democratic Women of Zanzibar," and representative of the "Zanzibar Peace Movement," though no one on the island appears to have ever authorized her to use such titles.

Still another Zanzibari training in Peking was Miraji Ali. Ahmed Said Kharusi, a pro-Moscow Zanzibari who spotted the two Chinese protégés at the Ninth World Conference at Hiroshima Against the Atomic and Hydrogen Bombs, wrote an indignant letter, which *Izvestia* published on August 17, 1963:

> They do not live in Africa but in Peking. . . .
> Who are they really? Miraji Ali was a hospital attendant in Zanzibar. Sometime at the end of 1959 or early in 1960, he turned up in Peking as a Peking Radio announcer. No responsible Zanzibar organization had sent him to Peking or authorized him to speak at international confer-ences. Nobody knows him as a political leader in our country.
> As to Aissha Ali Sultan, nobody in Zanzibar knew her as a political or public leader. In his time, her husband had been a leader of the Zanzibar National Party. But in June 1962, the Party's Executive Committee ex-pelled him for his splitting and subversive propaganda activity. Sometime last October he sent his wife to Peking to "teach Swahili. . . ." Very little time passed and she left Peking for the World Congress of Women in Moscow and then to the recent conference in Hiroshima. In Peking, Aissha Ali Sultan was "helped" to prepare her speeches. . . . She has been given a private house in one of the finest districts of Peking.

Ali Sultan Issa had been spotted early by Western intelligence agencies as one of China's main agents for East Africa, and possibly for South Africa as well. In 1961 he was finding students in East Africa to study in China.

Other Zanzibaris acted as liaison agents between Peking and the island. One was called "Pink-Eye Moyo," a youth leader. Another, Salim Ahmed Salim, once political secretary of Babu's Umma Party, took training in Eastern Europe, then for a time ran the Zanzibar bureau in Havana. At the time of the Zanzibar revolution he was in China translating political books from English into Swahili. Before the Sino-Soviet split forced the New China News Agency and other Chinese offices to leave Prague, a student there named Habib Suleiman acted as go-between for Peking and the Umma Party.

One result of these various contacts was that independent Zanzibar, even before the revolution, was quickly recognized by all the Communist countries. The Soviets lagged somewhat behind the Chinese in sending their diplomats, something they probably regretted later when Peking's influence began to grow. An unprecedented flow of congratulations came in from the labor unions and front organizations throughout the Communist world, including China's three satellites, North Vietnam, North Korea and Albania.

"Field Marshal" John Okello was a twenty-seven-year-old, relatively unschooled native of Uganda, who had learned military tactics from the anti-British Mau Mau guerillas in Kenya. He had joined the Havana guerilla-warfare school and returned in 1963 to organize a "revolutionary command." In the revolution he took military command of the insurgents who stormed government buildings and installed the "Republican Government." This government was led by Sheikh Abeid Karume, a former longshoreman who lived in a simple native house in the African quarter of Zanzibar town, and who was now President of the Afro-Shirazi Party. The Prime Minister was Sheikh Abdullah Kassim Hanga. He was the first student to graduate from Moscow's Friendship University, with a degree in political economy. His wife, an American-born Soviet citizen, worked as an expert on Zanzibar at Moscow's African Institute. The Foreign Minister was Babu.

Formation of the People's Republic of Zanzibar and its immediate recognition by Red China were given maximum publicity throughout the Communist world. Radio Moscow, while admitting that threats of possible British intervention had not materialized, warned African listeners that Britain and the United States "have sent warships to Zanzibar that are ready to disembark landing parties to suppress the revolutionary movement on the island." Babu was quick to announce that Red Chinese aid was on the way.

On January 26, after Britain had intervened to halt army mutinies in Kenya, Tanganyika and Uganda, which some observers were at first tempted to link with the Zanzibar events, the Soviet Foreign

Ministry reacted. Without mentioning Britain by name, it warned "those who do not wish to abandon their former colonial privileges" that any "forcible acts" toward the new Zanzibar People's Republic would be "fraught with dangerous consequences." Zanzibar was included with Tanganyika in a promise of Chinese help of nearly $40 million.

The Soviets had announced recognition on January 18, a day after the Chinese, and Khrushchev's first message had been rather cautious. He had merely expressed hope that relations would develop along lines of peaceful coexistence—in Communist diplomatic parlance, this is a phrase reserved for Western and Western-aligned countries; "fraternal" is the word used for special friends.

The Chinese message offered to "maintain and develop friendly relations," something Peking immediately set out to do. After January 16 correspondents for Pravda and the Czech and Polish agencies were allowed to join a New China News Agency correspondent already on the island. Their reports avoided mention of the killing and imprisonment of hundreds of Arabs by the new regime. They insisted that law and order prevailed. They branded the presence of Western warships off Zanzibar—one British unit was there to evacuate British subjects who wanted to leave—as "intimidation."

There was at least accidental collaboration between Moscow, Peking, Havana and other Communist capitals in preparing the revolution. Africans taken aboard Soviet ships to Cuba were given military and political training in Cuba under the direction of the Haitian Communist leader, René Depreste, for work in both Africa and Haiti. The number of Zanzibaris, if any, who studied guerilla tactics at the Chinese training schools near Peking and Nanking was probably smaller, for example, than those trained for the Cameroon, Portuguese Guinea or Niger. What Peking clearly gave, as can be seen from even a casual monitoring of Radio Peking broadcasts and reading of New China News Agency releases, was incitement and encouragement. It was also extraordinary to observe the degree of temporary cooperation between elements as diverse as Babu, the suave and self-sure diplomat, and "Field Marshal" John Okello, with his rude ways and references to "Mungu," an avenging god of the African bush. Certainly Okello's blustering on the radio about his "ninety-nine thousand nine hundred and ninety-nine partisans," about the vast casualties inflicted on the "enemy," helped to speed his downfall and his return in disgrace in March to his native Uganda.

It is clear that Babu and his Chinese friends found Okello highly embarrassing, and were anxious to get rid of him as soon as possible. New China News Agency dispatches spoke with obvious relief of his decline. Okello had seemed likely to take a pro-African stand against Babu's supporters, most of whom were part Arab.

Moderate politicians like Education Minister Othman Shariff and Finance Minister Hasnu Makame were sent away to the London and Washington embassies respectively. This made way for the promotion of Abdelazziz Twala and Hassan Moyo, pro-Communist Arabs. Key British civil servants were dismissed for the same reason. An East German, for example, took the place of a Briton as permanent secretary at the Ministry of Finance.

Zanzibar's once feudal society raced into socialism. On March 8, at a mass meeting, President Karume proclaimed the "Zanzibar Manifesto." This nationalized all land and redistributed it to the peasants. It proclaimed the People's Republic of Zanzibar as a one-party state, with the Afro-Shirazi Party as the sole party, "to be organized so as to apply progressive theses." Karume promised that the old system, under which 80 per cent of the land was said to have belonged to the Arab 13 per cent of the population, was dead forever. The New China News Agency quoted him as saying: "The government will give the poor peasants financial aid and technical assistance so that they can undertake agricultural exploitation in a modern and scientific manner, on the basis of collective and cooperative principles. But at the beginning, all lands must be redistributed to the masses, who will be encouraged to adopt new methods to increase production." Unemployed and old people were promised help. The exclusive British clubs were nationalized. All racial bars were supposed to be lowered.

Other features of a racial socialist state, including "volunteer" labor brigades, were soon added. On April 5, 1964, the New China News Agency reported under a Zanzibar dateline:

Some 15,000 inhabitants of the capital of Zanzibar took part today in volunteer labor on the farm administered by the government at Kizimbani. Beginning at dawn, the inhabitants of various quarters of the capital, carrying hoes and pails, singing revolutionary songs, beating drums and dancing, marched enthusiastically toward the fields. President Karume, Vice-President Kassim Hanga, Cabinet ministers, members of the Revolutionary Council, and numerous officials of the government worked together with the inhabitants. The interim chargé d'affaires of China [Ambassador Meng Ying was to arrive two days later], Lieou Kan, and other diplomats also took part.

Abdullah Said Natepe, General Secretary of the "Federation of Revolutionary Trade Unions of the Afro-Shirazi Youth League," saw a "new era" opening where "all inhabitants would enjoy equal rights and privileges." Said Saleh, Treasurer of the League, found the redistribution of land to be a "good thing, since a handful of people had unjustifiably occupied the land in the past."

Illiteracy was an early target of the government. A national illiteracy drive opened in April. Cadres of the Afro-Shirazi Youth League and the Students Union took special courses from professional teachers, then conducted literacy training themselves for illiterate adults and children unable to attend primary school. The Chinese news media reported enthusiastically that such institutions as the Homwood Boys' School and the new adult education center at Darajani were teaching the Swahili language. Under the old regime, this had been less respectable than either English or Arabic. To the Chinese Swahili is a useful "underdog language," which they are encouraging in their radio broadcasts and in the instruction materials they send to East African states.

The Zanzibar electricity enterprise and other utilities were nationalized. Economic distress appeared to be increasing. Thousands of Arabs, Africans and Shirazis fled the islands for Oman, as for Kenya and other East African regions. Some of the Muscat Arabs were repatriated to that sheikhdom. Kenya barred further Zanzibari immigrants, pleading its own unemployment problem. Bank deposits fell close to the zero point in a wave of withdrawals. The government asked the United Nations urgently to find replacements for hundreds of key British officials who were leaving.

In spite of these difficulties, there was no doubt about the direction taken by Zanzibar and Pemba. In March 1964 "counter-revolution" was proclaimed a crime punishable by death.

CHAPTER SIX

Tanzania: Storm and Stress

BOTH THE UNITED STATES AND THE SOVIET UNION, LIKE BRITAIN, took early alarm at the pro-Chinese drift of Zanzibar. But they reacted in basically different ways.

The initial American reaction bore some of the earmarks of panic. The United States chargé d'affaires and several American newsmen had been expelled soon after the revolution in January 1964. On April 2, William Attwood, United States Ambassador to Kenya, who had long experience of Sino-Soviet penetration in Guinea, said in New York that China and East Germany were attempting to turn Zanzibar "into a kind of non-African state to be used as a staging base for political maneuvers" in Africa. The fifteen-man Chinese mission was obviously there for "a political purpose," he added, but the United States could do nothing about the problem, which "should be a source of concern of Africans."

Abeid Karume called Attwood's remarks "insulting." He ordered the United States satellite tracking station on the island closed by the end of April. The State Department agreed, noting that this was the first time a country had voluntarily left the world-wide space program. Peking proclaimed a new victory for the "popular forces" on Zanzibar against the "American military clique."

The Soviets were working as hard as the Chinese, but perhaps with less visible result. They and their satellites, especially the Czechs, offered to buy up Zanzibar's entire production of cloves, about 11,000 tons a year, at preferred prices. A Czech diplomat told me with amused cynicism: "Cloves cost us nothing. In Zanzibar, both we and the Chinese can *cheaply* win good will." The first Soviet Ambassador, Dimitri Stepanovich Chuvakhin, was one of Moscow's top Communist-bloc specialists. He had served in Albania, in Canada as Ambassador, and then had worked as a deputy director of the Southeast Asia Department of the Soviet Foreign Ministry.

Moscow evidently managed to get arms into Zanzibar before Peking did. On March 17, 1964, the Soviet freighter *Faisabad* arrived, ostensibly to pick up cloves. In the dead of night the *Faisabad* unloaded some forty military trucks, track-mounted artillery mortars and some other equipment. The vehicles had low-pressure tires, like those intended for desert use, and it seemed likely that the shipment had been diverted from one intended for the Somali Republic. The artillery in the shipment appeared to date from World War II. Zanzibar Radio reported on April 24 that Chinese experts had begun building a road between Maziwangombe and Wete.

The 1964 May Day military parade in Zanzibar disclosed how closely the new Zanzibar "People's Army" of 300 men was being modeled along Chinese lines. It proudly displayed Soviet weapons: submachine guns, eighteen trucks, six heavy machine guns and four each of heavy mortars, anti-aircraft and anti-tank artillery. The army's Commander-in-Chief, Yusufu Himidi, appeared in a jeep with no other than Ali Mahfoud, who, as we saw, was trained in Cuba. The Associated Press reported that the army units were followed by 10,000 civilian "volunteers," singing, clapping their hands and carrying banners proclaiming "Long live the solidarity of the working class" and "Death to imperialism and neo-colonialism." To celebrate the occasion, President Karume released about one thousand political prisoners, mainly Arabs.

Peking appears to have waited until June, after the April union with Tanganyika, to begin its own arms deliveries. Almost simultaneously, *Révolution* in Paris released an interview with Babu in its No. 9 issue. The interviewer, Richard Gibson, asked Babu whether he considered that armed struggle was necessary for the establishment of a "socialist order." Babu replied with a classical statement of Red Chinese dogma, which he was to repeat almost word for word to American Negro audiences in Harlem later:

Yes, it is a necessity. There may be possibilities of a peaceful transition to socialism, but up to now, there has been no precedent in history. . . . From the moment where the people take arms, it is most difficult for a leader to moderate the ardor, the allure and the rhythm of revolution. I believe that armed revolution itself compels a country to transform itself sooner or later into a socialist country because of the very intensity of popular demands. . . . We know nothing else but either socialism or capitalism. There can be two roads, and only two roads, and we have chosen scientific socialism. An African revolution can transform itself into a socialist revolution. This is exactly the process that is going on in Zanzibar.

In London the Commonwealth Relations Office was "deeply concerned" at the trend of events in Zanzibar. Early in April, Foreign Minister Babu seemed to be consolidating his power and that of Peking. Besides controlling the Foreign Ministry and thus all contacts with Ambassador Meng Ying and his sixteen-man staff, Babu had a strong hand in the police, and controlled a majority in the National Revolutionary Council. Perhaps most important, he had a grip over Zanzibar's new "People's Militia" or "freedom fighters."

While Babu was away in Jakarta, Oskar Kambona, the energetic and imaginative Defense Minister of Tanganyika, began a series of visits and return visits between politicians of Tanganyika and Zanzibar. President Julius Nyerere of Tanganyika made a rapid trip to Zanzibar. After talks with President Karume, the two leaders announced on April 26 that they had decided to merge their countries into the United Republic of Tanganyika and Zanzibar.

The Soviet, British and American embassies had been informed ahead of time. Zanzibar Vice-President Abdullah Kassim Hanga had taken part in the secret talks that preceded the merger, shortly after a visit to Moscow during which he may have received Soviet blessings for the move. Gordon Brook-Shepherd, *Sunday Telegraph* diplomatic correspondent, wrote that Britain had prepared in advance and *cleared with the Zanzibar Revolutionary Council* plans for the British forces to land in Zanzibar, if needed, to ward off any armed leftist counter-blow against the merger. A "contingency plan" had been developed that would be put into action if Presidents Karume and Nyerere made a joint written request for help.

These plans were worked out after it was learned that Babu and his followers had ordered twelve aircraft from East African Airways to remove 300 Tanganyikan police. The police had been sent to Zanzibar at President Karume's request at the time "Field Marshal" Okello's revolutionary irregulars were being disbanded. President Karume had managed to stop the order. Kenya and Uganda, which like Tanganyika had suffered army mutinies only a few days after the January revolution, promised their support too.

Many Western commentators concluded that this was a victory of secret British diplomacy. They thought it had at least momentarily stymied the Chinese threat and was therefore approved by the Russians. Initial Soviet comment was favorable. The Chinese were cautious at first, then Mao Tse-tung congratulated President Nyerere. Babu was in Pakistan on the way home when the announcement was made. He claimed to have known about it all the time.

Julius Nyerere became President of the United Republic, later christened Tanzania. Karume was named first Vice-President, and chief executive on Zanzibar. President Nyerere had the right to repeal or revoke existing laws on Zanzibar by decree. The Zanzibar legislature kept its control, under Karume, over such internal matters as roads, public health and utilities.

President Nyerere found two new jobs for Babu and Kassim Hanga. Babu became Minister of Planning of the Tanzania government, while Hanga was given the post of Minister of Industry and Mines. The 300-man People's Army was supposed to be absorbed into Tanganyika's forces. President Nyerere disclosed on August 31 that China would send seven military instructors and four interpreters to train troops for not over six months. Other instructors were to come from Israel, Canada and West Germany. The Ethiopian and West German air forces sent several planes.

Babu and his friends prepared their comeback. The Chinese labor, student, women's and cultural organizations helped out by multiplying their invitations to Zanzibar delegations and sometimes patently ignoring those from Tanganyika. A Zanzibar News Agency, or Zanews, was set up in May under the direction of one of Babu's protégés, Said Salim Abdullah. "The armed struggle is a means of facing up to the obstinate attitude of the colonialists," he told the New China News Agency just before a visit to Peking in May, during which he planned coordination of Zanews activities with the New China News Agency.

China saluted Zanzibar by sending the 6,100-ton freighter *Ho-Ping* (Peace) to Zanzibar harbor on May 15. This was the first Chinese ocean-going ship to visit East Africa since the fifteenth century. Meng Ying, Chinese ambassador in Zanzibar, and Vice-President Karume marked the occasion with pomp. The captain, Pao Hao-hsien, gave a dinner aboard for Karume and the Zanzibar Revolutionary Council to commemorate the reestablishment of China's ancient links with Africa across the Indian Ocean. Captain Pao then sailed on to deliver the makings of a big Chinese trade fair at Dar es-Salaam and to pick up Tanganyikan cotton for the mills of China. The *Ho-Ping*'s maiden cruise in African waters symbolized another Chinese triumph: it was one of the more recent products of mainland China's shipyards built without Soviet aid.

Tanzania's other Zanzibari Vice-President, Rashidi Kawawa, visited China in June. He saw Mao, President Liu Shao-chi and other Chinese leaders, and returned with loans and gifts totaling $38 million. Kawawa promised to back Chinese policy in Southeast Asia, in return for which Peking expressed support for the second African Chiefs of State Conference in Cairo on July 17. "China," said Kawawa upon his departure, "is not only a good friend of the United Republic but also of all Africa . . . I share the views expressed by Comrade Mao Tse-tung when we called on him, that the imperialists are like dirt that will not move until it is swept out."

In July, Peking named Ho Ying Chinese Ambassador to Tanzania. This was a promotion: he was simultaneously relieved of the lesser post in Tanganyika. Meng Ying, in his turn, was pulled out of Zanzibar—Peking had other assignments in store for him, which we shall examine later. Ho Ying now became Peking's senior diplomat in East Africa.

East Germany competed with China and the Soviets for a leading role in Zanzibar. Though the Zanzibaris recognized East Germany before the union, Tanganyika had recognized the Bonn government of West Germany. On May 17 the union government signed a friendship and "mutual assistance" accord with Guenther Firtsch, the East German Ambassador. The Pankow regime promised hospital and nurse training and set up a medical school. East Germans were sent to teach nearly 3,000 Zanzibaris at the new Lumumba College, for which China supplied two new transmitters. East Germans also ran the nationalized Zanzibar Radio. Bonn tried to persuade President Nyerere's government to throw out the East Germans, indicating that they might cut off West German economic assistance.

Tanzania devoted attention to building up its military forces. The Ethiopian Air Force, which is American-supplied, sent six T-28s and two Dakota transport aircraft, forty pilots and ground crew, in line with OAU decisions taken in March 1964. West Germany sent Nordatlas transports and a squadron of Dornier 27 trainers with instructors and technicians. One hundred and twenty paratroopers were sent to Israel for intensive training.

Russian and Chinese weapons streamed in. The *Ho-Ping* delivered rifles and automatic arms to Dar es-Salaam on September 2, as part of the Chinese military aid promised to Kawawa. At Mtoni, outside the town of Zanzibar, the camp of the Zanzibar People's Liberation Army was staffed by Chinese military advisers. "There are only seven Chinese and they are no menace. We had to take arms from wherever we could get them," said President Nyerere in a broadcast November 15. A Soviet training camp was at Chukwani, five miles from Mtoni.

Tanzania's drift into pro-Communist alignment in 1965 had complex roots. Fortunately for its economy, heavy British aid subsidies, especially to Tanganyika, continued under existing Commonwealth agreements. The country had the added benefits of Eastern economic help. The Chinese contribution was largely agricultural. Chinese experts of a state farm and planning team led by Hsu Chao went to Zanzibar to study the possibilities of silkworm cultivation and other crop diversification so that the island could escape its sole dependence on clove cultivation.

Tanganyika lives largely from subsistence farming and has a per capita national income of less than $50 yearly. Under British rule its larger farms were limited to production of sisal hemp, coffee or tea. Sisal accounts for about one-third of export income and it tended to remain controlled by white settlers after Tanganyika become independent in 1961.

Chinese agricultural teams visited Tanganyika. Professor Huang Chi-fang and an assistant afterward told a New China News Agency correspondent in Dar es-Salaam that there were "vast stretches of fertile land with immense water resources" that could be used for growing rice. Another Chinese team traveled nearly to the foot of Mount Kilimanjaro in the northeast, to the Lake Nyasa basin in the southwest, and along the coast. In their report they stressed that pasture lands and forests, as well as "aquatic wealth," might be put to better use, which of course British experts and United States aid missions had long known. But Peking was given credit for wanting to help.

Chinese and other Communist influence in Tanzania had political and social roots as well as economic ones. With 363,688 square miles and over 9 million people, Tanganyika is the largest East African state. Before it became independent on December 9, 1961, the United Kingdom had administered it under the international trusteeship system of the United Nations. Upon independence it joined the Commonwealth and continued to participate in the economic and technical activities of the East African Common Services Organization, along with Kenya and Uganda.

Tanganyika was once considered a multi-racial country. By 1965 this was no longer true. Asians, Arabs and Europeans comprised only about one per cent of the population. None of the 120-odd tribes is large enough to dominate the others. The country has the advantage of a *lingua franca* understood widely in other parts of East and Central Africa: Swahili. Pagans, Moslems and Christians occur in that order of strength, but the ruling elite since independence has been divided between Christians and Moslems.

Like Zanzibar, Tanganyika has a history of outside domination and conquest, with Arabs and Portuguese figuring prominently. Germany occupied the territory during the general European scramble for Africa, in 1885. Only persistent, ruthless repression, notably that of the "Maji-Maji Rebellion" in 1907, permitted the Germans to build two railroads, the Tanga-Moshi and the Dar es-Salaam–Kigoma line (of strategic importance in sending supplies to rebels in the Congo). After heavy fighting in World War I, Tanganyika was placed under a League of Nations mandate. Britain was the administering power. Economic development slowed to a halt during World War II. Nearly 100,000 Tanganyikans served in Commonwealth armies. Tanganyika then became a United Nations Trust Territory.

Uhuru na Kazi (Freedom and Toil) was the motto of the leading Nationalist party, the Tanganyikan African National Union (TANU), formed in 1954. This dominated a multi-racial legislative assembly by 1960. TANU's leader is President Julius Nyerere, a dynamic, warm-spirited and politically skillful man. Before Tanzania's strong Eastward swing, and his visit to Peking in February 1965, he was looked upon as a friend of the West. He believed in a leading role for foreign private capital investment. As a Roman Catholic he mistrusted Communism. He became first Prime Minister, then, after independence, was elected President. He has always believed in and worked for a Federal Union of Tanganyika, Zanzibar, Kenya and Uganda, with Central African countries possibly coming in too.

The new republic quickly recognized Red China. Ambassador Ho Ying arrived in Dar es-Salaam on February 2, 1962. He was an African expert who had set up the African Affairs Department of the Ministry of Foreign Affairs in Peking. He had cultivated the governments of Uganda, Zanzibar and Kenya immediately, before those countries were free to recognize Red China on their own. Ho Ying also made friends with King Mwambutsa IV of Burundi, which had far-reaching consequences for the Congo, as we shall see when we consider that unhappy country.

Ho Ying ceased to hold the post of Ambassador to Uganda concurrently with his Tanganyikan position when another Red Chinese Ambassador was appointed to Uganda in April 1964.

The Soviet camp was active too. In the period 1960-62, Soviet-bloc commentators classed Tanganyika, along with Nigeria, Togo and Senegal, as a state that leaned toward a "capitalist path" and followed "bourgeois democratic" models. The Moscow-directed World Federation of Trade Unions (WFTU) was by 1962 pressuring Nyerere through small opposition groups. Moscow made great efforts to attract students and other Tanganyikans to Russia and Eastern Europe. The WFTU and the Women's International Democratic Federation (WIDF) were active in these efforts. But the Soviets were not very effective in Tanganyika.

Chou En-lai had been scheduled to include Tanganyika and its East African neighbors in his African tour of 1963-64. President Nyerere had accepted an invitation to Peking in February 1964. All this was postponed by the army mutinies in Tanganyika, Kenya and Uganda just after the Zanzibar revolution in January.

One of Ho Ying's most important missions in Dar es-Salaam was to maintain a liaison for Peking with the "Committee of Nine" that the May 1963 African Summit Conference at Addis Ababa had established for aid to African liberation movements. Many South Africans and those from Portuguese territories expressed dissatisfaction with the Committee. Its members were at first simply African ambassadors accredited in Dar es-Salaam who were handling "liberation" business—especially collecting and supposedly distributing money collected for arms and paying agents—in their spare time. The Committee, in fact, was accused by Ghanaians and others of sometimes simply pocketing the money.

The outbreak of armed uprisings against the Portuguese in Mozambique, on Tanzania's southern frontier, in October 1964 further added to Tanzanian nervousness. Nearly 10,000 Mozambique refugees from the fighting streamed across the swampy frontier lands. Tanzania feared Portuguese counter-attacks for guerilla raids from Tanzanian territory. On several occasions the good ship *Ho-Ping* brought Chinese arms to the Tanzanian coast, some of them probably for Mozambique, but many doubtless for the rebel operations in the Congo. Malawi, which opposed Chinese influence and sought to keep on good terms with Portugal because it needed Portuguese railroads and ports in Mozambique, accused Tanzania of plotting to invade it. Tanzania denied Malawi charges that Malawians were being trained in Dar es-Salaam to "liberate" Malawi from Dr. Banda's rule.

Western influence was first placed in jeopardy when Britain, acting on the request of President Nyerere, President Kenyatta of Kenya, and Prime Minister Obote of Uganda, sent troops to quell the mutinies in January 1964. Moscow joined Peking in a chorus of protest against "Western imperialist intervention." Radio Peking in April beamed to East Africa a long tirade about entry of the United States Seventh Fleet into the Indian Ocean. The United States Ambassador to India, said Peking, had tried to cover the whole thing up, but his slip was showing, and his mention of the need to provide stability for Asia and security for India had only shown that strategic objectives were also involved.

The discovery of two "American plots" against Tanzania in the winter of 1964-65, which finally led to a break in United States–Tanzanian diplomatic relations, had a long prelude. This was a period in which President Nyerere was showing mounting irritation and sensitivity to Western criticism, especially from the press.

On August 31, 1964, Nyerere in a news conference chided Western correspondents. The West, he said, should respect Tanzania's decisions and not try to pressure the country. When asked about risks inherent in accepting Chinese aid, he replied: "The maximum risk is that the army will revolt. My army revolted in January. It was not trained by the Chinese." The Zanzibar revolution, he pointed out, was nationalist, not Communist. "Is a government [faced with possible counter-revolution] expected to sit down like a pack of damn fools and do nothing? They accepted military aid from Russia and China. They had no choice."

On November 15 President Nyerere announced he had seized letters proving that the United States was plotting to help Portugal make retaliatory air attacks on Dar es-Salaam. The Tanzanian press and all the Communist information media, especially of Peking, took up the chorus and accused the United States. When U. S. Ambassador William Leonhart first offered proof to Nyerere that the "letters" were forgeries, Nyerere appeared to accept it. But Tanzanian skepticism remained. The Tanzanian Ambassador to the United Nations said in New York on December 8 that the government would be convinced that the documents were authentic until "shown otherwise." "Why," he asked, "if they are a forgery, did the U. S. Embassy in Dar es-Salaam have experts come from Washington to prove it?" At this point, Ho Ying and his staff, who perhaps prepared the letters themselves, must have laughed heartily.

In December President Nyerere made a visit to Zanzibar and Pemba, which helped to establish his popularity there.

The forty British businessmen, officials and cable personnel remaining on Zanzibar were said to view the union as a restraint on such politicians. The remaining Arabs, Indians and other racial minorities also looked upon Dar es-Salaam's influence as healthy. Meanwhile the power of the extremist Revolutionary Council remained strong, as did a spirit of Zanzibari separatism.

President Nyerere's government, of course, badly wanted good newspaper publicity for the visit. On January 4, 1965, it charged that *Time* magazine had "ridiculed" Tanzania: it had used "bad" and "degrading" language and had not covered the visit. On January 15 Tanzania expelled two American diplomats accused of a new "plot." Evidently the charges were based on a monitored phone conversation. The two had mentioned "ammunition." The "ammunition," it turned out, was the word "ammunition" used in the American sense of "arguments." They had hoped to persuade the State Department to send friendly greetings to Abeid Karume, and had said "I think we've got enough ammunition . . . to convince them now."

This pathetic affair led to a total break. After a few days the State Department withdrew Ambassador Leonhart, and the Tanzanian Embassy in Washington closed down. President Nyerere was triumphantly received in Peking. Ho Ying's Chinese Communist Embassy had become one of the most active of Peking's missions in all Africa.

Chou En-lai paid his long-delayed visit to Tanzania June 4-8, 1965. He was accompanied by a large delegation that included Deputy Foreign Minister Chang Han-fu, the deputy secretary-general of the State Council, Lo Ching-chang, and Ko Hua, director of the Department of African Affairs of the Foreign Ministry. His reception in Dar es-Salaam, and especially in Zanzibar was warm and even enthusiastic. It was clear that he sought Tanzanian support for China's attempt to bar the Soviets from the second Afro-Asian Conference in Algiers, later postponed. He also argued in favor of a united African front against the United States war effort in Vietnam.

In a speech broadcast by Dar es-Salaam Radio June 4, Chou added a picturesque postscript to remarks he made during his first African voyage:

An exceedingly favorable situation for revolution prevails today not only in Africa but also in Asia and Latin America. The national liberation movement in Africa, converging with that in Asia and Latin America, has become a mighty torrent pounding with great momentum at the foundation of the rule of imperialism. . . . The revolutionary storms in those areas are vividly described in Chairman Mao Tse-tung's famous verses: "The four seas are seething, clouds are lowering and waters raging, the five continents are rocked by storm and thunder."

President Nyerere, while warning against all forms of foreign interference in Tanzania, endorsed Chou's remarks about revolution, adding that "We are also determined to eliminate capitalism and I can assuredly say that this process has already started." But he gave Chou a stiff reminder: "Tanzania is not a puppet of East or West . . . We will accept aid from anybody as long as it does not interfere with our policy."

The reaction elsewhere in East Africa was chilly. The Kenya government retorted that it wished to avoid all revolutions, whatever their origin. If Chou had been fishing for further invitations in East Africa, he was unsuccessful. East African leaders were preoccupied by the impending breakdown of the East African Common Services Organization, a breakdown which the Chinese were encouraging. Chinese propaganda references to "relics of colonialism" at the moment of Chou's visit were intended as part of this encouragement. On May 21, the Organization's Central Legislative Assembly suspended its proceedings. No more budgetary means were available for the common administration of ports, railroads, telecommunications or posts. Even the common currency and tax structure was to be abandoned. Tanzania was making preparations to issue its own currency and to employ funds, which could have been used for the Organization, to finance a growing number of Chinese imports flooding the country with cheap consumer goods under expanded trading arrangements.

There was another source of tension at the time of Chou's visit. On May 15, Kenyan police had intercepted a convoy of 75 tons of Chinese weapons bound for Uganda and detained 57 Ugandan nationals traveling with the convoy. This produced great embarrassment in Kampala, hasty trips by Ugandan envoys to Nairobi to smooth things over, and a telephoned apology from Ugandan Prime Minister Milton Obote to Prime Minister Kenyatta.

CHAPTER SEVEN

Kenya: An Uneasy Society

"WHAT IS MOST STRIKING IN CONVERSATIONS HERE IN EAST AFRICA," reported a Swiss correspondent from Nairobi, "is that the term 'Chinese' has almost completely supplanted that of 'Russian' or 'Soviet.' . . . Actually, it is less as Communists than as . . . Chinese that Mao's envoys here are feared. One suspects that they are here to prepare the ground for a massive immigration which would soon enough become a new form of colonization."

This sort of feeling has been occasionally noted from Kenya and all the way southward to South Africa. It is often compounded by local economic jealousies when Chinese laborers, as in South Africa, at one time seemed to threaten the expansion of white colonization. In Madagascar, which has East Africa's largest Chinese community, this has had political consequences, which we shall see later on.

Red China's interest in East Africa is linked strongly to its even greater interest in the Congo. Some of Peking's first commercial contacts in Africa were made along the littoral after its Cairo Embassy had been opened. In seeking to penetrate this region, Peking directly challenged British and Commonwealth interests in Africa for the first time.

Strained and complicated race relationships in Kenya have made that one-party independent republic of 224,960 square miles and 9 million people attractive to Peking. The African tribes come from four major linguistic groups: Bantu, Nilotic, Nilo-Hamitic and Hamitic. Of Kenya's forty-eight tribes, the two largest are the Kikuyu with nearly 1 million Bantu, and the Luo, including some 750,000 Nilotics. There are about 35,000 Arabs, nearly all Moslems, living mainly in the Kenya Coastal Strip. This was handed over to Kenya in 1964 after having had special protectorate status under a lease from the former Sultan of Zanzibar.

Asian immigration began around 1900 when Moslem, Hindu, Sikh and Goan workers were brought from India to work on the Uganda Railway. Asian traders, including some Chinese, had already lived along the coast for generations. In 1965 they numbered about 183,000, and through their skills and education controlled key sectors of commerce, industry and the civil service. Africans wanted, and were taking, control of these themselves. All this led the Chinese to tone down their propaganda about "Afro-Asian solidarity" where Kenya was concerned.

Kenya became a British Protectorate in 1892. A great smallpox epidemic in 1888-89 was an important factor in Kenya's history. It combined with rinderpest, locusts and a drought to drive the Kikuyu out of their traditional tribal homes and into the Kiambu region, near Nairobi. Lord Delamere, the British Governor-General, persuaded Europeans to move in and farm the empty country. This aroused the indignation of the Kikuyu. African politicians ever since have concentrated on convincing the Kikuyu that all their land was stolen from them by the white settlers. The Highlands had been reserved for the whites, and it was not until 1960 that Africans were allowed to resettle there.

The first real nationalist organization was the Kikuyu Association, formed in 1922. The name was changed to Kikuyu Central Association, and in 1928 Jomo Kenyatta became its General Secretary. Eventually it split into moderate and radical wings: the latter became the tribalist, anti-European, primitivistic society called the Mau Mau. In 1946, the Kenya African Union, now the Kenya African National Union (KANU) and Kenya's ruling party, grew out of an earlier club called the Kenya African Study Union.

In 1952, the Governor, Sir Evelyn Baring, announced the beginning of the Mau Mau Emergency. Mau Mau began as a Kikuyu secret society aiming to overthrow the British Protectorate authorities and drive out the whites. It dominated the Kikuyu by exploiting their tribal spirit and their atavistic fears and superstitions. Its oaths sworn in blood, its savage massacres of Africans and Europeans, and its unholy rites made it notorious. The Emergency ended two years later, and it affected Kenyan life profoundly. When it did end, political parties were banned, so that the development both of KANU and of its chief opponent, the Kenya African Democratic Union (KADU), was retarded by a number of years.

Jomo Kenyatta, Prime Minister of Kenya since the government was formed June 1, 1963, and again after full independence in December 1963, is of the senior Kenya leaders probably the least inclined toward Communism. He was born of Kikuyu parents and educated by Scottish missionaries. Supposedly he got his name from the beaded belt—in Kikuyu, *mucibi wa kinyata*—that he wore while a government water inspector.

Kenyatta lived in England for fifteen years, studying at the Quaker College in Woodbridge, Selly Oak, and sharing a flat in London with American singer Paul Robeson and the Negro South African writer Peter Abrahams. He worked at the Institute of Oriental and African Studies in London and the London School of Economics, under Professor Malinowski, the distinguished anthropologist. He married an Englishwoman, Edna Clarke, studied at Moscow University, campaigned with George Padmore, Kwame Nkrumah and others for African rights, and championed the Kikuyu in his book, *Facing Mount Kenya,* published in 1938.

Kenyatta denied that he directed Mau Mau activities. But in April 1953 he was convicted, with five other leaders of his party, the Kenya African Union, of managing Mau Mau operations. He was sentenced to seven years' imprisonment. These were years of slow progress toward Kenyan autonomy. Kenyatta was freed from prison in April 1959, but indefinitely restricted to Lodwar in the Northern Frontier District. By January 1960 his detention had become the most dramatic issue of Kenyan politics. In March 1960 the Kenya African National Union (KANU) was formed. Kenyatta was elected as party president. After general elections in February 1961 brought a KANU victory, the party refused to form a government until Kenyatta was freed.

Kenyatta was finally released from restriction only in 1961, and he emerged clearly as the leader of the African majority in Kenya. He entered the Kenya Legislative Council in January 1962 as leader of the opposition. In March he became Minister of State with responsibility for constitutional affairs and planning. Finally, when the autonomous government of June 1963 was formed, he was chosen Prime Minister and was confirmed in this office when full independence came at the end of that year.

Kenya became a Republic within the Commonwealth on December 12, 1964, the first anniversary of independence. Kenyatta, now President, replaced the Queen as constitutional chief of state. The new constitutional framework was the result of the interplay of many racial and regional forces, chiefly those of *majimbo* (regionalism) against *harambee* ("working together," or centralism). Though *harambee* prevailed, Kenyatta had shown concern for the smaller tribal rivals of the Luo and Kikuyu by creating seven regional assemblies.

On November 11, 1964, Ronald Ngala, leader of the KADU opposition, dissolved his party voluntarily. He crossed the floor of the House of Representatives to join KANU. Kenya had become a one-party state. In this the smaller tribal leaders backed him. Kenyatta had shown great patience and statesmanship in waiting for the opposition leaders voluntarily to accept one-party rule.

In December, President Kenyatta warned against subversion. "It happens in many young countries," he said, "that members of Parliament may become the target of some foreign government or subversive institution. Forces may become unleashed, spurred on by external pressures. The Government of Kenya will meet any threat of subversion with the fullest rigors of the law."

Kenyatta may have been referring particularly to his shrewdest and most Eastward-leaning rival, a serious contender to succeed him, Ajuma Oginga Odinga. In 1964 Odinga was Home Affairs Minister in the Kenya Government, and the man in whom both Moscow and Peking, but especially Peking, have shown the most interest. He is a Luo, with a strong tribal following among the Luo of the Nyanza region. Born in 1912, he was educated in Uganda. In 1948, while in business in Maseno, Kenya, Odinga met and attached himself to Kenyatta. He took office in the early Kenya African Union, and visited India in 1963. Though arrested and questioned during the Mau Mau Emergency, Odinga never served a jail sentence. In May 1959, with Tom Mboya, the West's most prominent Kenyan supporter, he formed the Kenya Independence Movement in London. After becoming Vice-President of KANU and paying his first visit to the Soviet Union and Red China, his passport was withdrawn. In 1962 he nearly split KANU and the labor movement over a dispute with Mboya. Though he is a Luo, the Kikuyu respect him.

Perhaps in part to counter the pro-Eastern propensities of Oginga Odinga, who moved from the Home Affairs Ministry to become Vice-President and Minister Without Portfolio, Kenyatta appointed Tom

Mboya Minister of Economic Planning and Development. Mboya, whose contacts with the West, and the United States in particular, were at least as good as those of Odinga with Russia and China, had become a prime mover in African labor movements and was chief of Kenya's trade unions. He had already served in previous Cabinets as Minister of Labor and Minister of Justice and Constitutional Affairs.

A European, Bruce MacKenzie, remained as Minister of Agriculture, symbolic of the important role of European farmers. A new scheme of National Youth Service, organized by KANU, was intended to increase knowledge of agriculture and therefore productivity, while providing useful work for the large number of unemployed young people. During the first year of independence landless Africans had been settled on two-thirds of the projected 1.1 million acres of the former "White Highlands" of the Kikuyu. But most African farmers still existed on a subsistence economy. They grew corn and beans on small plots. As in all other countries of Africa, Asia and Latin America, rural people streamed into the towns in search of work and food.

Not only land but also the jobs and economic status once held by 45,000 Europeans and 183,000 Asians were passing under African control: an economic and a social revolution were under way simultaneously. To accelerate it, President Kenyatta established, with Soviet financial aid, a "Lumumba Institute" outside Nairobi, and said he hoped that it would become an African center for academic study in culture and anthropology. However, the chairman of its board of management, Bildad Kaggia, a supporter of Odinga, called it primarily a "party militants' school." Over 100 students each year would be taught African socialism, and journalists, civil servants and others were invited to attend.

Chinese interest in Kenya had started earlier and had been more sustained than in most other African countries. Peking's propaganda supported the Mau Mau movement in the early 1950's. This foreshadowed later support for tribal revolts in the Cameroon Republic and the Congo. Peking repeatedly lauded the Mau Mau as a "patriotic and anti-imperialistic organization" and vaunted its violent, bloody history.

When Kenya finally won independence, Marshal Chen Yi, Red Chinese Vice-Premier and Foreign Minister, attended the celebrations in Nairobi on December 12, 1963, with great fanfare. China was first among the Communist countries to announce diplomatic relations. The U.S.S.R. and Czechoslovakia were close seconds. The other

Soviet-bloc countries quickly followed. The first ambassadors President Kenyatta appointed were Adala Otuko to Moscow and Henry Mulli to Peking. East European newsmen arrived for the independence ceremonies and stayed on afterward. Communist China sent a bevy of New China News Agency reporters, television and radio operators, and cameramen.

The army mutinies of January 1964 delayed the progress of Chinese influence. The Chinese diplomats holed up in their Nairobi hotel. Chou En-lai canceled his scheduled visit. As in Tanganyika, the government found itself forced to call for British help and virtually disbanded the army. The British Army was withdrawn during 1964. Only British-trained police units remained in 1965, together with the new Kenya army. Oginga Odinga, as Home Affairs Minister, rooted out several British officials whose zeal or old-time connections disconcerted Communist supporters.

Ambassador Wang Yu-tien, one of Red China's most seasoned career diplomats, presented his credentials on April 20, 1964, to the Queen's representative, Governor-General Malcolm MacDonald. Wang had been director of the West Asian and African Department of the Chinese Ministry of Foreign Affairs.

The New China News Agency abandoned its earlier prudence about Kenya, displayed since the end of the Mau Mau Emergency. It gave large play to remarks of Bildad Kaggia denouncing white settlers for discharging Kenyan workers. He urged immediate nationalization of the larger plantations and their transformation into state farms. Parliamentary Deputy Duya Oprong, a KANU regional secretary, visited Peking in April as guest of the Chinese Afro-Asian Solidarity Council. On returning to Nairobi, Oprong announced that the "presence of the United States Seventh Fleet in East African waters is a threat for this part of the continent." The successful United States Peace Corps contingent in Kenya, and another group of pioneer-minded Americans called the "Crossroaders" working in Kenya, came in for Chinese attack, through Oprong. He also suggested opening an AAPSO branch in Nairobi.

The Chinese probably considered Oginga Odinga their man in Nairobi. As exchanges of visits with China increased, they openly and increasingly used him as the recipient of their funds in Kenya. In September 1963, Ho Ying, Chinese Ambassador to Tanganyika, offered a period of training in China to twenty Kenyans. Home Affairs Minister Odinga was asked to choose the Kenyans and to decide whether their training would be in engineering or in military subjects. He was reported to have chosen the latter.

Odinga opposed British intervention during the mutiny of the Kenya Rifles in January 1964. When Commonwealth Minister Duncan Sandys came to Nairobi in March to sign new military agreements for the British defense of Kenya, Home Affairs Minister Odinga again disapproved. After the agreements were signed, the succession question was debated as a major issue. KANU and younger trade union leaders opposed Mboya and Foreign Minister Joseph Murumbi, whom they also considered too pro-Western. They preferred Odinga. And Odinga looked like Peking's candidate. This lent extraordinary interest to his visit to Peking in May 1964.

Odinga and his delegation saw Liu Shao-chi and Mao Tse-tung, denounced white imperialism, said the other things that are said during the thousands of visits by African leaders to Peking, and on May 10 signed an accord for economic and cultural "cooperation." What also happened gradually leaked out after Odinga returned to Nairobi. Along with the stock phrases about "colonialism" and "imperialism," Odinga insisted on calling for a virtual Red Chinese declaration of war against the Republic of South Africa, to aid in throwing off white rule there. This was highly embarrassing both to Peking and to the main South African nationalist group, the African National Congress, whose principal leader Nelson Mandela and a number of other persons were at that moment on trial for their lives in Pretoria. "It was," as one Western official commented, "as though someone had put on a wrong record—and could not stop the gramophone."

Odinga hit out at people who passed resolutions condemning South Africa but did nothing more. "We have come to the conclusion," he said, "that those who pass resolutions on such serious questions merely find this the best way to avoid the problem." Odinga, like other African leaders, undoubtedly knew of Red China's trade with South Africa. In 1963, as Communist representatives and others the world over called for a boycott of Dr. Verwoerd's government, International Monetary Fund statistics showed China-South Africa trade steadily increasing.

This sally on South Africa by Odinga was so unwelcome that the New China News Agency cut all reference to it from their report on his speech. When Gitu Kahengeri, Chairman of the Kenyan Writers' Union, and his secretary arrived in Peking on May 14, the Chinese were more careful about allowing their African guests to speak impromptu in public.

Under the Kenya constitution in 1965, Vice-President Odinga had no power to appoint or dismiss ministers. He would not automatically succeed President Kenyatta if Kenyatta died in office. His responsibilities included the parliament, Africanization and training, elections and the national development fund. Odinga was thus in a good position to use his considerable financial and persuasive ability in organizing more exchanges of all kinds with the Communist countries. He is one of the few Africans who refuse to admit to Marxist persuasions, and who yet manage to remain on good terms with both the Russians and the Chinese. At the Republic celebrations in December 1964, Ambassador Wang and other Chinese present presented Odinga with gifts from Tung Pi-wu, Vice-Chairman of the Chinese People's Republic. Shortly thereafter, Mrs. Odinga visited Moscow, where their son is a student.

On November 30, 1964, the London *Daily Express*, never noted for excessive sympathy for African regimes or politicians, reported that large quantities of medicine, guns, rifles, ammunition and radio sets were being flown into Nairobi airport in unscheduled and unidentifiable transport aircraft, including some from Prague. These were moved in trucks of the Prisons Department, then controlled by Odinga, to a secret destination. The *Express* thought this was being done without the knowledge of Prime Minister Kenyatta and the rest of his Government. To other observers on the spot, it seemed just as likely that these were arms destined for the Congolese rebels: similar shipments were then moving south into Uganda and the Sudan.

The Congo crisis, especially the November 1964 rescue at Stanleyville of white hostages by Belgian paratroops ferried by United States aircraft, put a severe strain on Kenyatta's prestige in the country, and on relations between Kenyatta's supporters and those of Odinga. Kenyatta headed the African Unity Organization's Congo conciliation commission, which had been ineffectual in the crisis. Under his auspices United States and Congolese rebel representatives met in attempts to find a formula to save the hostages and end hostilities between Premier Tshombe's government and the rebels. Just as the talks broke down, the paratroops and the Congolese national army both arrived simultaneously at Stanleyville. There was a wave of anti-American feeling throughout Africa, reported exultantly by the Communist information media. Visibly discouraged, Kenyatta evidently authorized a big anti-American demonstration in Nairobi. This got out of hand and gasoline bombs were thrown. U.S.-Kenyan relations began to deteriorate.

Richard Beeston, London *Daily Telegraph* correspondent who was expelled for his reports on mounting Communist influence in Kenya, wrote that the Congo affair arose just as Kenyatta was preparing to act against Odinga, but that the new turn of events had stopped this. Beeston reported growing tension between the Luo tribal supporters of Odinga and Kenyatta's Kikuyu ministers. He also wrote that an initial group of about forty Chinese-trained Luo guerillas and saboteurs had returned from China and were thought to be at a training camp near Kakamega, near Lake Victoria, in the extreme west of the country near Uganda and the Sudan. The Hamburg newspaper *Die Welt* reported a short time later that eighteen Kenyans were in training at Wuhan Military Academy, in Central China: these were very possibly the original contingent agreed upon by Ho Ying and Odinga back in September 1963.

The Soviets, the Chinese and the West engaged in their usual foreign aid competition. Odinga and Foreign Minister Murumbi, on the way home from Peking in May 1964, had secured sizable promises: a 200-bed hospital, a technical school for 1,000 students, credit financing for a chain of food processing plants, and a radio station. It looked as though the radio station would serve for short-wave broadcasts, since Kenya already had a good, British-built domestic radio and television service.

In September, a Kenya government official calculated that the total value of assured aid to Kenya from the Communist bloc was slightly less than that of two relative newcomers to the foreign aid business—Japan and West Germany—together. The Chinese contribution, despite the large publicity it got, amounted by early 1965 to about $25 million in interest-free loans for technical aid and equipment, and a gift of $2.8 million to balance the budget.

The West had done far more. Britain alone had supplied nearly $300 million since 1945, half in outright gifts. The Commonwealth Development Corporation in 1964 was supporting thirty-two projects in East Africa, including agricultural and forestry projects, processing plants and factories, housing and water supply plants in Kenya. United States post-independence economic and technical assistance to Kenya had totaled more than $32.2 million. To achieve the goals of its six-year development plan by 1970, Kenya would need $887 million more in new investments—$526 million from private business and $361 million in governmental funds. Most of this would probably come from the Commonwealth, though the Chinese and the Soviets are certain to seek to increase their share.

Internally, from Peking's viewpoint, Kenya's vulnerable points are its army and the smoldering resentment of the Kikuyu and other Africans against the whites and the Asians, as well as the Kikuyu-Luo rivalry and occasional friction. The Chinese training and equipping of Luo guerillas, if actually taking place on any appreciable scale, would be a development to alarm the Nairobi government. During the army mutiny in January 1964 there had been communal strife—as there had been in Zanzibar during the revolution, and in Dar es-Salaam during the army mutiny there—between Africans and Asians. In December 1964 the Information Minister warned that non-Africans who stirred up trouble in Kenya would be given twenty-four hours notice to leave the country "no matter how rich they are." A seminar on racial and communal tension in Nairobi recommended that all non-Africans who wished to live in East Africa should become citizens; that the educational system should be fully East African; and that expatriates coming to serve the three East African countries should be given accurate and relevant instruction about "the East African way of life."

It is conceivable that in a new time of emergency, Peking would do what it had been doing successfully in the Congo: broadcast barefaced racist propaganda to encourage the Africans to rise against "white oppressors," perhaps appealing to remnants of the Mau Mau who still haunt the Kenyan bush.

The Kenyan economy, as Peking is well aware, faces the same two major hazards that most other African economies face. One is the flight of capital and the decline of trade since independence. Western businessmen hesitate to put their money into the country. The Chinese make every effort both to discourage such investments and to deprecate both Soviet and Western aid, while urging the virtues of their own "disinterested" programs.

The second great danger is that the African population is increasing while wages are tending to drop. The departure of white settlers and Asians has resulted in a declining demand for goods and services, to say nothing of the decline in the number of paid jobs that this departure means. With the advent of Kenya's one-party state, and its sharing of the almost Africa-wide disapproval of Western policies, especially those of the United States, in the Congo, Southeast Asia and elsewhere, Peking might secure all the support and sympathy it seeks in Kenya without making any major effort to disrupt the existing order, or even of Kenya's policy of non-alignment.

CHAPTER EIGHT

Uganda and the Watusi

UGANDA, LYING BETWEEN LAKE VICTORIA, THE SNOW-CAPPED Ruwenzori Mountains and the blistering northern desert, might not at first hand appear likely as a prime target for Peking. However, it links Kenya with the Congo, which most certainly is one.

From 1959 to 1964, Uganda became the largest haven for the Watusi refugees fleeing massacres by the Bahutus in Rwanda. In 1965, Congolese rebels opposing the legal government of the Congo (Leopoldville) began to use Uganda, as well as Burundi and Congo (Brazzaville), as a staging area. Retaliations against Ugandan territory led to growing Ugandan hostility toward Tshombe and his American backers.

Uganda is small. It has 94,000 square miles and a population of about 7 million, including about 11,000 Europeans and 78,000 Asians, mainly Indians but also including a few Chinese merchants. The Africans are of mixed origin, both Bantu southerners and Nilotic northerners. British protection was established in the 1890s. The British soon found they had to deal with four well-defined kingdoms, of which the largest was headed by the Kabaka, or King, of Buganda.

The central political problem has been Buganda's determination to remain as independent as possible of the central authorities and the rest of the country. The towns are largely European and Asian in tone, since they were built almost entirely by the immigrants.

Uganda achieved independence on October 9, 1962. Red China

recognized it soon afterward. During the Congo crisis of 1960, the Chinese propaganda media reported disturbances in Uganda. The Chinese, like the Soviets, began to buy Uganda's cotton in 1962. Nairobi Radio reported on January 10, 1964, for example, that Uganda had sold 20,000 bales to China for $1.8 million and hoped to sell 80,000 more bales. The chairman of Uganda's Lint Marketing Board, Elizaphan Ntende, was frequently invited to Communist-bloc capitals, including Peking, to talk business.

Uganda has something else the Communist bloc wants: strategic minerals. Since 1953 it has tried to escape the bounds of its agricultural subsistence economy by developing mineral veins, especially the Kilembe copper mines. It has sold copper ore to the Soviet Union regularly since 1962. There is also cobalt, which Red China has sought eagerly for its atomic weapons tests, which began in October 1964. This cobalt, as far as can be determined, has so far only gone to the West. Another highly strategic metal, beryl, used to produce nuclear-energy, high-speed aircraft and guided missiles, was regularly bought up by the United Kingdom's Atomic Energy Authority.

Especially since the African Summit Conference of May 1964 in Addis Ababa, and the establishment of the "Committee of Nine" in Dar es-Salaam to aid African liberation movements in the Portuguese colonies, Southern Rhodesia and South Africa, there have been persistent reports that guerilla fighters were being trained in Ugandan camps. Prime Minister Milton Obote, who made one of the most militant speeches about liberation of all the African Chiefs of State at the Addis Ababa Conference, gave assurance that he would cooperate discreetly. This has given the Chinese some opportunities to use Uganda territory for occasional clandestine operations aimed against the white supremacy governments of the South.

It is interesting that the Ugandan whom Peking apparently counted on most at an early date remained aloof. This was Joseph William Kiwanuka, chairman of the Uganda National Congress Party. His career is interesting because he is an African politician who remained truly "non-aligned," despite considerable experience of both Eastern and Western "camps." The son of the Finance Minister of the Kabaka, he was educated in good schools and colleges in Uganda, then served with the British Army in World War II. He became editor of the newspaper *Matalasi* (The Messenger), which was European-owned and favorable to the British administration.

During anti-British riots in 1949, Kiwanuka was attacked by a mob and nearly killed because of his reputation as a collaborator. He went to Britain to study journalism, then returned to Kampala to start his own newspaper, the *Uganda Post*. After his visit to Peking the Chinese sent printing presses for the city of Kampala.

Before his visit Kiwanuka had already served alternating terms in the parliament of Buganda and in jail for sedition and other political offenses. The Kabaka's government charged him in 1958 with an attempt to assassinate the Kabaka, but the British authorities quashed his fifteen-year sentence when his lawyers appealed. In 1959 the Uganda National Congress was weakened by the defection of several leaders, notably Milton Obote, who formed what became the ruling Uganda People's Congress.

Partly through his Peking contacts, Kiwanuka became a member of the All-African People's Conference and served on the executive board of the Afro-Asian Solidarity Council. Despite this he never gave the appearance of compromising himself with either Peking or Moscow.

Peking's first ambassador to be accredited, on January 7, 1964, was Ho Ying, who at that time was also accredited to Zanzibar, Kenya and Tanganyika. Li Tchouen was chargé d'affaires and also a sort of super-consul dealing with the affairs of the Chinese community in Uganda. Finally, on May 17, 1964, Chen Che-fang presented his credentials to President Edward Mutesa: he was accredited solely to Uganda.

Lacking any promising stooges or friends in Uganda, Red China's diplomats sought a promising issue. They had already established a reputation for meddling in Uganda's biggest problem: refugees. According to a dispatch of Robert Hallet, *Christian Science Monitor* correspondent, on June 5, 1964, the country was caring for some 47,000 refugees. Ten thousand came from the Southern Sudan, victims of the repression of a revolt of Southern Sudanese Christians by the Moslem government in Khartoum. Luo tribesmen from Kenya looking for work were another group. But by far the largest and most tragic group were the lithe, long-limbed Watusi, the one-time aristocratic rulers of Rwanda, on whom the Belgians had depended heavily during their administration of Rwanda and Burundi.

Their inferiors were the simple Bahutu people. The Watusi, a minority, were determined when independence approached that "democratic" rule would not mean rule by the Bahutu majority. A few politically conscious Bahutus were equally determined that it would.

For various reasons the Belgians and the Catholic Church switched their support to the Bahutu political movement as it emerged. When the civil war broke out in Rwanda in November 1959 the Watusi were outnumbered six to one, though they had the support of pygmies called Batwa who fire poisoned darts. The Watusi were routed. They fled into Uganda and Tanganyika. Thousands were killed on both sides. We shall examine later the sequel of the Watusi exodus in Rwanda, Burundi and the Congo, and the Chinese role in it.

Uganda, with the vast potential fifth column that the Chinese-influenced Watusi represented, was in somewhat the same position as Jordan, Lebanon or the other Arab countries where there are large colonies of discontented Palestinian Arab refugees. The fugitives did not integrate into Ugandan life easily. They listened to the Peking radio broadcasts in their native language. Some could read the French-language Chinese propaganda brochures that told them that some day they would return.

And another dangerous African fuse was kept smoldering.

The Red Chinese diplomat appointed to keep it burning is worth a second glance. Ambassador Chen Che-fang's career offers a fair example of the background of solid domestic service to the Chinese revolution that Peking nearly always demands of its envoys before sending them abroad.

Chen Che-fang's first foreign post was the ambassadorship to Syria, which he received in 1956 at the age of fifty. Before this he had held many public positions in Canton, chief city of his native province of Kwantung. When the Communist revolution was victorious in 1949, Chen was acting general secretary of the Canton Municipal People's Government and at the same time Director of the Public and Enemy Property Administration Office. After other high Cantonese posts, he was Vice-Mayor of the city from January 1955 to April 1956.

Chen was relieved of his Syrian post when Syria and Egypt were joined under Nasser's leadership in the United Arab Republic in February 1958. Shortly afterward he was appointed Ambassador to Iraq, where he served until being called home to research duties as Vice-President of Foreign Affairs. When Chen was appointed to Uganda in April 1964, Ho Ying was relieved of his responsibility for that country and was able to concentrate entirely on Tanzania.

Prime Minister Obote's government, to the great satisfaction of the Communist world, contributed its share to the wave of anti-American feeling that swept over much of Africa in the wake of the American and Belgian rescue of white hostages held by the Congo rebels in Stanleyville in November 1964.

In mid-January 1965, Congo rebel leader Christophe Gbenye came to Kampala, after traveling disguised as a Nigerian. He met Prime Minister Obote, President Nyerere and President Kenyatta. Gbenye seems to have had some success, though Kenyatta was not impressed by the rebels' popular support. Obote was quoted as declaring that the United States was concerned only with the Congo's uranium. Washington, said Obote, was prepared to wipe out "all black men in the heart of Africa," a quotation eagerly picked up from Western agencies by the New China News Agency. A few days before, Ugandan authorities had arrested *Time* magazine's Nairobi chief, Peter Forbath, when he visited the Ugandan town of Arua, near the border of Congo rebel territory. Forbath found it to be a main supply point for the rebel troops, who called themselves "Simbas," or lions. Unmarked Soviet Ilyushin-18s from Algeria—part of Moscow's bid to match Peking's effort in the Congo—had been arriving from Juba and landing on Arua's tiny airstrip with arms cargoes. Forbath was accused of spying by authorities in Kampala, and expelled from both Uganda and Kenya.

Uganda was drawn more deeply into the Congo war. In February Premier Tshombe accused Kampala of sending regular Ugandan troops into Congolese territory in support of the rebels. Prime Minister Obote denied this and made the counter-charge that American T-28 aircraft flying for the Congolese air force had bombed two Ugandan border villages. At a meeting of the United Nations Economic Commission for Africa on February 16, the chief Ugandan delegate accused the United States of mounting "a campaign of genocide against the black populations of Africa." This had become one of Peking's favorite themes.

In looking over Peking's East African prospects, Western diplomats seemed to be satisfied, first, that the Zanzibar revolution had no direct connection with the army mutinies in Tanganyika, Kenya and Uganda that followed. The army risings were due to dissatisfaction with pay and conditions of service. But the mutinies shook the stability of all East Africa, as did events in Zanzibar itself. Supporters of an early East African union, such as Zanzibar's Abeid Karume, saw prospects fading further into the distance. Uganda's Milton Obote rejected the idea outright.

Peking's strategy evidently was to penetrate from Tanzania through Kenya and Uganda directly into the Congo and southward along the coast. Western diplomats did not overlook the Communist threat. But they realized that it would be a fatal mistake to antagonize East and Central African politicians in areas not yet touched by the guerilla flames fanned from Peking, by making them think that every move Washington or London made was motivated by cold war considerations alone. This would be one of the surest ways to help Peking accomplish some of its most cherished hopes.

CHAPTER NINE

Some Islands, Large and Small

SINCE THE THIRTEENTH CENTURY, WHEN THE GREAT KHAN SENT messengers to Madagascar, this giant among islands, nearly as large as the state of Texas, has appeared as a natural steppingstone between Asia and Africa. From its highly strategic vantage point a few hundred miles off the coast of Portuguese Mozambique, the Malagasy Republic, as it has been called since it won political independence from France in June 1960, could become a dagger aimed at East and South Africa.

No one is more aware of this than President Philibert Tsiranana, Malagasy's founding father, President, Prime Minister and Minister of Defense. He is so saturated with French culture and French traditions that his name causes chuckles among Africans less oriented toward Paris than he is. But President Tsiranana announced that his country would not follow President de Gaulle's lead in recognizing the Peking government in January 1964. "It would be contrary to Malagasy interests," he said.

President Tsiranana and his government were shocked and a bit frightened by the army mutinies in East Africa and by the pro-Chinese drift of the revolution in Zanzibar. Their attitude may also have been due to the colony of 9,000 Chinese living in the Republic, the largest such colony in Africa, which Tsiranana has several times warned against political activity.

President Tsiranana gave Malagasy's official reaction to the events in East Africa in these terms to Phillip Decraene, a writer for *Le Monde*:

Whatever comrades Khrushchev and Mao Tse-tung may say, they have something to do with this affair. They have, each of them, trained men in their methods and we know from now on these men are at work in Africa.

President Tsiranana indicated his willingness to back Premier Tshombe of the Congo (Leopoldville) in his fight against Chinese-supported subversion. At a conference of thirteen French-speaking African states and Malagasy in Nouakchott, Mauretania, in February 1965, Tananarive was chosen as the first meeting place in January 1966 of a new Common African and Malagasy Organization (OCAM). The conference resolutions strongly condemned outside subversion and indicated that the new grouping, which replaced several earlier ones of the former French African Community, would strongly fight against it.

Madagascar's history and background make it a logical target of Red China's "Afro-Asian Solidarity" propaganda. Madagascar is thought to have been unpopulated until shortly after the birth of Christ. Between then and the twelfth century A.D., during the time it was discovered first by the Arabs and then by the Chinese, it was populated by waves of immigrants from Southeast Asia. Arabs from southern Arabia followed them, and Europe's first contacts began in the time of the Portuguese seafarers, after 1500.

During the period of nineteenth-century empire-building, France and Britain both eyed the island. France won out, after a brief colonial war in 1822-23, and it became first a French protectorate, in 1885, then a colony in 1895. There was always at least sporadic resistance to French rule, and a nationalist political underground existed at the unusually early date of 1917.

Some self-rule was granted after the French African Conference of Brazzaville in 1944. Three years later one of the most bloody and terrible colonial revolts of all time was suppressed by massed French military might: official French figures admitted 11,000 killed; some estimates ran as high as 80,000. More than 10,000 others were imprisoned.

In 1958 the country voted in the French constitutional referendum for independence within the French African community. It became one of the leaders of the Union Africaine et Malagache, or African and Malagasy Union (UAM). Its leaders always take great pains to insist on the non-African, quasi-Asian cultural heritage of Madagascar. At the African Summit Conference in Addis Ababa, Ethiopia, in May 1963, the Malagasy delegates stubbornly insisted that the African Charter drafted and signed at the conference should be an "African and Malagasy Charter." They won their point.

The Malagasy Republic is about 40 per cent Christian, divided almost equally between Roman Catholics and Protestant churches, and 60 per cent pagan. There is little parliamentary opposition to President Tsiranana's ruling Socialist Democratic Party (PSD). However, there is hostility between the traditional rulers of the country, the Hova people, from which the queens of Madagascar traditionally came. From this group emerged the chief opposition party, the AKFM, or Congress of the Independence of Madagascar, which advocates a far more militantly neutralist and less pro-French policy. As is true with so many other former French colonies, Malagasy students in Paris are exposed to Communist teachings in all their forms.

French and native Communists infiltrated the AKFM to some extent. The Chinese have made some discreet overtures to the Reverend Richard Andriamanjato, a mayor of Tananarive and a Protestant minister of strongly leftist views. Another key AKFM militant whom both Moscow and Peking have had their eye on is Dr. Joseph Raseta. He is a Protestant who served in cabinet posts after returning from exile in France (the French authorities once turned him back in Djibouti in 1959).

Communist nuclei exist in the Comité Social Malagache, and in the FISEMA, an extreme-left-wing labor federation. When President Tsiranana visited France in 1964, the Paris press reported that he had handed President de Gaulle a voluminous dossier on Red activities on the island.

President Tsiranana has developed his foreign policy partly as a function of his apprehensions about subversion from the outside. Since there is a strongly Pan-Arab party in the Comoro Islands (the "Comoro Liberation Front," with an office in Algiers and contacts with the Red Chinese Embassy there), he developed relations with Israel. Most important, Tsiranana has cultivated relations with Nationalist China and other anti-Communist Asiatic countries.

In April 1962 he was the first African head of state to visit Formosa as the guest of General Chiang Kai-shek. President Tsiranana called his visit "very rewarding," and said Malagasy "had much to learn from Nationalist China in economic development, land reform and modernization of armed forces." He invited General Chiang to Malagasy. A Malagasy mission to Taipeh in September 1962 bought fish, and agreed to send fishing trainees to Formosa.

In 1963 President Tsiranana received visits from President Maca-
pagal of the Philippines and from Federal Prime Minister Lee Kwan
Yew of Singapore. Lee was one of the principal architects of the
Malaysia Federation and a leading Asian opponent of Red China.

A 1964 estimate of the island's population showed 9,000 Chinese
and 15,000 Indian residents. According to a Nationalist Chinese
source, there were four Chinese-language newspapers on the island,
three of them Nationalist in orientation and one that showed some
propensities to Peking.

Chinese merchants were first reported in the town of Tamatave in
1862. Seven years later the French General Gallieni brought 3,000
Chinese coolie laborers from the frontier of Tonkin, Indochina, to
build the island's highways and railroads. After the Sino-Japanese
war of 1932-34, several hundred Chinese, mainly from Canton, came
to live in Tananarive, Tamatave and Finarantosoa. Many assimilated
well with the natives, but preserved their national customs. Some are
Roman Catholic. They are chiefly merchants and have a virtual
monopoly of the food and spice trade on the east coast. A few are
planters or run transport businesses.

Their great economic power and strategic situation in the community, with the ability to conduct arms traffic, for example, with the
East African coast, could make the Madagascar Chinese excellent
tools for Peking. It is interesting that when Radio Peking first began
transmissions to Africa in 1956 one of its original daily programs was
a transmission in Cantonese beamed directly to them.

The Chinese of Malagasy, like those of the Eastern islands and the
African countries, are regarded by Peking as possible allies. Fang
Fang, Vice-Chairman of the Chinese State Commission for Overseas
Chinese Affairs, laid down guidelines for Peking's policy toward these
Chinese in an article in the *Overseas Chinese Affairs Journal* in October 1964. He urged them to maintain "a patriotic united front" in
support of Communist China and to support "national democratic
revolutionary movements of the local peoples." The *Fukien Overseas
Chinese Hometown News* enumerated tasks for the overseas Chinese
community in the "socialist education" movement. Among these
were:

To learn from Chairman Mao's thinking, from the "three-eight" work
style of the People's Liberation Army and from the revolutionary spirit
of Taching [oil field] and Tachai [model production brigade]; to be thor-
ough revolutionaries; to persist in the struggle against capitalism and

feudalism; and to be good workers and good members of the society of the Mao Tse-tung era.

The overseas Chinese were also exhorted to obey local laws and not smuggle currency or illegally remit foreign exchange, as well as to "educate and influence" their relatives and friends abroad.

As long as Nationalist China keeps its embassy in Tananarive, and as long as President Tsiranana's government or a similar one remains in power, the Chinese colony in the Malagasy Republic is not likely to be a threat to Africa. Meanwhile Peking watches and waits. Its European satellite, Albania, has shown special interest in the Malagasy Communists, both those in the AKFM and the clandestine Communist Party. President Tsiranana has allowed entry of a Soviet trade mission, but very little other East-bloc influence.

Réunion and Mauritius are French- and British-ruled islands respectively about 400 and 550 miles east of Madagascar in the Indian Ocean. Both have been mentioned in Western diplomatic reports as places where the small local Communist parties were developing a penchant for Chinese doctrines. Many Indians and a few Chinese work and trade on both islands. Mauritius obtained full internal self-government and a new constitution in 1964.

Mauritius was a French colony until 1810. It became a British Crown Colony in 1814. Its 700,000 people, living on 720 square miles, include about 440,000 Indians and 24,000 Chinese. The rest are Africans, Europeans and people of mixed origin. Its four principal political parties reflect ethnic divisions, as do the languages spoken on the island: English, French, Creole, Hindi, Telegu and Chinese.

Moscow Radio took notice of Mauritius on May 18, 1964. It reported that the first issue of *L'Etincelle* (The Spark), newspaper of the Young Communist League of Mauritius, had stated that sixteen committees of that League were represented at its first congress, at which the League's first revolutionary manifesto was adopted. By November 1964 the "Mauritius Lenin Youth Organization" was holding regular classes for children. In February 1965 it sent a delegation to the AAPSO economic seminar in Algiers. Soviet bloc attempts in the United Nations to demand that Mauritius be "given back to the natives" gave the British delegation a marvelous opportunity for introducing some light relief into the debates: the "original inhabitants" of Mauritius, they pointed out, were the famous dodo birds!

Réunion lies about 420 miles east of the Malagasy Republic.

About 400,000 people live on 969 square miles as citizens of an overseas department of France, governed by a Prefect. The French succeeded the Portuguese as colonizers in the seventeenth century, and came to rule a mixture of Africans, Malays, Annamese, Chinese and Malabar Indians.

Réunion enjoys a privileged status in Red China's African offensive. Jacques Verges, editor of the Chinese-line European magazine *Révolution,* stems from a family that launched Communist activity on the island. Jacques Verges was born in Siam in 1925 of a Vietnamese mother and a father from Réunion, Raymond Verges, who founded the Communist Party of Réunion in 1946, during the heyday of postwar Stalinist parties in the French Union. Regular contacts between the island's Communists and Peking seem to have begun in August 1961, when Paul Verges, Jacques' brother and First Secretary of the Réunion Communist Party, visited China with Gervaise Barret, a member of the party's politburo. Réunion's racial mix and conglomeration of Afro-Asian cultures must fascinate the Chinese planners who map Peking's expansion in the Indian Ocean.

The four Comoro Islands—Mayotte, Anjouan, Grande Comore and Mohéli—form an archipelago between the northern tip of Mozambique and the Malagasy Republic. They represent one of the farthest southern extensions of Arab influence in the Indian Ocean: Arabs are the dominant ethnic group. African, Malagasy, Indian and Chinese elements make up the rest of a total population of about 200,000. The archipelago is an autonomous overseas territory of France. There is an active "Comoro Islands Liberation Front," with main branches in Algiers and Cairo. One of its officials, Mrs. Zahara Ibrahim, visited China in July 1964 after stopping off at a women's congress in Moscow. Subsequently she criticized the congress and Soviet policy. Ali Mohammed Shami, who heads the Liberation Front, regularly visits China and attends AAPSO meetings of various kinds.

The Chinese also have an eye on the Seychelles Islands, because of their strategic location in the equatorial zone of the Indian Ocean, nearly 1,000 miles east of Mombasa, Kenya. They are ninety-nine granite and coral islands, with their capital at Port Victoria on the island of Mahé, which lies 1,750 miles south of Bombay.

A United States satellite and missile tracking station began operations in the Seychelles in July 1963, employing about ninety Seychellois. This extended electric power to the islands of La Misère and Grand'Anse, site of the transmitters. There is much unemployment and some economic distress, despite the gentle tropical climate. British administration contributes generously to alleviate it. Seychellois students are trained in Britain. Little political activity was reported up to 1964. One of the most influential people in Mahé was a Seychellois merchant named F. Ah-Mane, a nominated member of the Executive and Legislative Councils, who like some of the other 45,000 Seychellois is of partly Chinese extraction.

The Indian Ocean seems certain to become again, as in ages past, an important avenue between Africa and the Chinese mainland. In December 1964, British Royal Interocean Lines announced a new monthly service from East African ports and Beira, Mozambique, to Hsinkang and Shanghai. Anglo-American talks on a system of Indian Ocean communications and staging sites, which could support operations in Southeast Asia as well as watch the approaches to Africa, began in the spring of 1964. In January 1965, Washington passed on to London a list of preferred locations, based on a survey made by an American team aboard a British ship. Prime Minister Harold Wilson, answering a question in Parliament in April 1965, denied that any British or United States submarine bases were contemplated in the region. Robert Estabrook, London correspondent of the *Washington Post*, wrote that even if Indian Ocean facilities were small, their "presence would be potential reassurance to governments that might be intimidated by Chinese nuclear weapons."

The United States gave first priority to Diego Garcia, a dependency of Mauritius in the Chagos Archipelago, 1,000 miles southwest of Ceylon. The administration of the island would have to be transferred directly to London, since constitutional talks on self-rule and possibly independence for Mauritius were scheduled for the fall of 1965. Another site considered in Washington and London was the Aldabra Islands, dependency of the Seychelles 300 miles northwest of Madagascar: Britain wished to build an airfield there. Washington was also interested in the Agalega Islands, another Mauritius dependency 500 miles northeast of Madagascar, and the Cocos Islands, owned by Australia, 500 miles south of Sumatra. None of these Indian Ocean facilities, said United States officials, would be full-scale bases with garrisons: they would be staging points and service centers for conventional forces, as well as communications relays. They would also, of course, help monitor any Chinese air or naval activity along the eastern approaches to Africa.

CHAPTER TEN

Below the Color Line: South Africa
and the High Commission Territories

A COLOR LINE WINDS THROUGH THE SOUTHERN QUARTER OF AFRICA. It is the Zambezi River, boundary between Northern and Southern Rhodesia. Below it lies Southern Rhodesia, one of former British Africa's last bastions of white supremacy. Then there is a zone of intermediate dependent territories that have been under British controls but are strongly subject to the pressures of the other bastion, the Republic of South Africa. The entire region is a seething cauldron of black racial resentment against white economic strength. It seems to promise Africa's most terrible drama: an all-out racial war. Red China means to play a major role in sowing this whirlwind in the hope of reaping vast benefits from it.

The strategic stakes in South Africa are enormous. Much of the Western world's uranium, copper, gold, industrial diamonds and tin have come from its mines. Even more critical is its status as a focus of the world conflict between whites and non-whites. Its ruling philosophy of apartheid, racial separation, has become anathema to most of the world. It is very possibly the future cause of a major African or even world war.

South Africa is more than the only white-ruled independent state in Africa: except for Ethiopia and Liberia, it is the oldest independent African country. In 1965 it had perhaps five times as many European inhabitants as any other African country, with Morocco and the Portuguese territories of Angola and Mozambique probably second. The origins of this white aristocracy go back to the seventeenth-century Dutch settlers, who drew a line not between races but between Christians and barbarians. These Afrikaners, as they came to call themselves, set the style for the waves of other white immigrants that followed: French Huguenots, British (now the second largest European group) in the early nineteenth century, and Germans in the second half of the same century.

There is no space here to sketch the dramatic and often bloodstained history of this frontierland. Much of it can be read in the impassioned cries of novelists like Alan Paton, who demand elementary human justice and equality for South Africa's blacks. We must instead discover some hints of what Red China's attitudes have been, and what they are likely to be, in exploiting for its own ends this tragic twentieth-century drama.

Some statistics are necessary to give a frame of reference: The Republic's 472,359 square miles are bounded in the north by the Limpopo, Orange and Molopo Rivers, and extend south to the Cape of Good Hope; the official 1961 census figures showed a total population of 15,982,664. Of these 3,088,492 were white; 10,907,789 were African; 1,509,258 "colored" (of mixed race); and 477,125 Asians, nearly all Indians.

Communications, roads, power networks, industry and other elements of the infrastructure are the best-developed in Africa. The Union of South Africa left the Commonwealth and set up the Republic of South Africa on May 31, 1961. A referendum among white voters had decided in favor of this by only a 52.05 per cent majority. One of the principal reasons for the move was the mounting world pressure, both among the Afro-Asian nations and in the West, against the regime of apartheid. The cabinet of May 31,1961, was headed by the Afrikaner statesman Dr. Hendrik Verwoerd as Prime Minister. Verwoerd's name has become at once a symbol and a target round the world.

One country that has concentrated some of the bitterest attacks on Dr. Verwoerd, especially since it became actively interested in Africa at Bandung in 1955, has been Red China.

The South African Communist Party, though it was still Soviet-oriented in early 1965, had already become a logical target for penetration by Peking. This is because its founding in 1921—its antecedents go back to 1915 and 1916—makes it one of the earliest and strongest parties founded outside the Soviet Union, and as old as the

Chinese Communist Party itself. Its leaders, who have been recruited from all racial backgrounds, were active in the great mining strikes in the 1920s. It made one major tactical error in 1924: supporting a government formed by a pact between the Afrikaner Nationalist and the Labor Parties, which stood for white rule. Soon afterward it disavowed this support and began all-out efforts to attract more non-white members. South African Communists were instrumental in launching the first African trade unions in 1927, and in the 1930s, a time of declining influence, it tried to cooperate with the leading non-Communist African party, the African National Congress.

While it still legally existed, it had the classical Communist role of creating "effective mass organizations." It was the only party in South Africa admitting non-Europeans on a basis of *absolute equality* with Europeans, and this was a very strong drawing point among educated Africans. On its national executive in 1947, for example, there were ten European whites, three Indians, three Africans and one "colored" with an African general secretary, Moses Katane. Thus the Communists could assert that they had actually begun to realize the multi-racial society that others were only talking about. Both before and after the party was officially disbanded with legal suppression in 1950 it could use its old links with the Soviet and European parties, since its white members could circumvent the restrictions on travel, work and other vital activities imposed on Africans.

The strongest native African Red voice today is the South African Communist Party's Moscow-line organ, *The African Communist*, published in London since the fall of 1959. From London it is widely distributed in Africa. It was introduced as a "forum for Marxist-Leninists throughout our continent." It concentrates its fire on the problems of class struggle in African society, the "petty bourgeois-ism" of African nationalists and the self-styled "African socialists," like President Kwame Nkrumah of Ghana and Sékou Touré of Guinea.

Available evidence points to great efforts by Peking not only to swing the South African Party away from Moscow, but also to penetrate the two major nationalist rivals, the African National Congress (ANC) and the Pan-Africanist Congress (PAC). The end of the sensational political trial of Nelson Mandela, the ANC leader, who was sentenced to life imprisonment in Rivonia in June 1964, threw into sharp relief the future roles of both groups. South Africans admit that the growing split between them increased the vulnerability of all the African organizations to Dr. Verwoerd's police.

The ANC probably has the larger backing among the Africans of South Africa's cities. Originally it was hostile to violent action against apartheid. Its head, Nobel Prize-winner Chief Albert Luthuli, has often disavowed violence. But in December 1962 the party embraced the thesis, dramatically expounded by Mandela at his 1964 trial, that apartheid can be beaten only by a long struggle that must include sabotage and "direct action." Communist elements have succeeded in penetrating the ANC, especially at its external offices in London, Accra, Dar es-Salaam, New York (where it has contacts with Black Muslims and Black Nationalists), Cairo, Lusaka and Algiers, where both Soviet and Chinese-bloc diplomats, journalists and others are in almost constant contact with ANC leaders.

The Pan-Africanist Congress was originally a splinter group that left the ANC between 1957 and 1959. On the face of it, it appears far closer to Peking's racist propaganda line than the ANC. Whereas the ANC supports a "multi-racial society," like the Communists, the PAC says in its manifesto that it wants a society "original in conception, Africanist in creation, socialist in content, democratic in form and creative in purpose—a democracy in which man shall at long last find his true self, and in which human personality shall blossom to the full."

John Makatini of the ANC told me in Algiers in 1964 that the PAC is "intolerant" and teaches "black supremacy." It admits very few non-Africans. A confidential Western report described PAC in July 1964 as "an army without soldiers or officers." Some of its leaders, such as Robert Subokwe, were in prison. Most lived in exile, in London or in African capitals. It has suffered from many internal schisms as well as from its quarrel with the ANC.

Peking's tactics appeared to be to back both ANC and PAC, and to work for a common front between them. This was good "Pan-African" politics. It was chosen by the Organization of African Unity's "Committee of Nine" in Dar es-Salaam to assist the "liberation movements," but without notable success. The Committee of Nine, in fact, refused all military aid to the South Africans until ANC and PAC could unite. The South Africans, like the Africans in the Rhodesias, Angola and South-West Africa, became extremely disillusioned with the Committee of Nine.

Peking's violent attitude on South Africa is clear from the dispatches of the New China News Agency's African service. In May 1963, for example, New China stories from Rabat and Cairo quoted statements by ANC members that "armed struggle is the only means for the people to recover their lost rights and gain freedom" and that "assault and violence are the methods to be used in their political struggle for freedom."

Active training of Africans for terrorism and guerilla warfare in the Republic was well underway by 1963. In Algiers I learned that South Africans were training nearby with Angolans and Africans from Mozambique and Portuguese Guinea, under the direction of Algerian army officers. When Premier Chou En-lai visited Algiers in December 1963 he discussed with President Ben Bella the need to "step up the struggle" in South Africa, among many other African "revolutionary zones."

The South African Communist Party is multi-racial. It includes whites, who in 1965 were still predominant; Indians, Africans and Coloreds. Its orientation was pro-Soviet. But there existed among Cape Coloreds a radical pro-Chinese movement that was driven underground in 1964. It was named the Yu Chi Chan Club, a name taken from the title of Mao Tse-tung's writings on guerilla warfare. Its leaders were K. G. Abrahams, originally from South-West Africa, and Dr. Neville Alexander. Its membership was drawn from the youth section of the Non-European Unity Movement, of Trotskyite persuasion and composed mainly of Coloreds. Some were trained in guerilla warfare and subversion in China. In 1965 Alexander was in jail in South Africa. Abrahams, after being kidnapped by South African agents from Bechuanaland, where he had worked in the South-West African People's Organization, affiliated to the African National Congress, was permitted by the South African authorities to return to Bechuanaland after vigorous British government protests.

For its propaganda support Peking has relied heavily on the Chinese Afro-Asian Solidarity Council, which consistently demands a "total economic boycott" of South Africa. A Council statement issued by the New China Agency on April 20, 1964, implicated the United States in the South African persecution of Nelson Mandela. It added: "The United Nations, controlled by the United States, have not taken and never will take any measure of sanctions against the South African authorities."

In March 1964, Peking was instrumental in organizing in Accra a conference (the second such) of an "international trade union committee for solidarity with the South African workers and people." A short time later it sent Red Chinese delegates to a non-Communist International Conference on Sanctions against South Africa, in London.

Peking propaganda frequently equates South Africa with the American South. At the Accra meeting, Huang Min-wei, the chief of the All-China Trade Union Federation delegation, said that "the world's workers" would "develop and amplify actions" in time for a new "Day of Solidarity with South Africa" (which took place on February 7, 1965) and would also "support the American Negroes." Huang went on, according to the New China News Agency:

President Mao Tse-tung has expressed the desire of the 650,000,000 Chinese to firmly support the struggle of the American Negroes and the South African people. The Chinese will always stand at the side of the people of South Africa. . . . Just as Premier Chou En-lai indicated during his voyage in Africa, the perspectives of the revolution in Africa are excellent. The South Africans will win.

At the same time Peking constantly stresses that China helps only those who help themselves. Mao Tun, one of the Chinese delegates, told the Afro-Asian Solidarity Council meeting in Algiers in March 1964 that "the Chinese people are full of confidence in the liberation of the South African people. The oppressed nations should not count on anyone but themselves to win freedom. The aid that comes from the outside is important, but it can only be a secondary and auxiliary factor in the struggle conducted by the people themselves. It cannot replace this. We are sure that the South African people, thanks to their own strength and to the experience that they have accumulated during their long struggle, will certainly find a true pathway for their liberation."

This is simply a way of warning Africans that Peking's resources are too limited to be totally committed in one area, and that spreading them too thin too soon will do no good.

The Chinese must observe one important caveat in their propaganda beamed to South Africa. This concerns race. Asians, among many African communities, are equally as or even more unpopular than whites. Therefore "Afro-Asian Solidarity" is not a major theme of the Peking line on South Africa, despite the fact that the Afro-Asian Solidarity Council disseminates it.

Though Chinese residents of South Africa have generally been given better legal treatment than Indians and others of darker skin, there is a tradition of anti-Asian resentment. This extends to Chinese as well as to the Indian merchant class. The biggest Indian influx, between 1860 and 1911, was meant to provide field laborers for the sugar plantations of Natal. Immigration from India was prohibited in 1911. Chinese labor was imported in the late nineteenth century. Settlers who could not get enough indentured Zulu laborers sometimes used Chinese coolies. Many of the mines, especially subsidiaries of the fabulously profitable Rand mines, used coolies too. In 1905 the Chinese constituted 17 to 18 per cent of the labor force. Shortly afterward Chinese immigration was also banned. In the Group Areas Act of 1950 such "Areas" were set aside for Colored, European, African and Asian residents. In some areas there was a further subdivision of the Asians into Malay and Chinese. The African hate of the Asian residents has emerged in several terrible race riots in Durban, one of which began when an African was knocked over by an Indian trader.

Even more adverse in its effect on Peking's efforts in South Africa, and especially on its attempts to capture control of the world Communist movement, is the hypocritical demand of Peking for a boycott on Western trade with the Pretoria regime—while continuing its own trade with it.

Red China's trade has of course been only a part of that conducted by Communist-bloc nations. In March 1964, John Tettegah of Ghana, who was later elected president of the neutralist All-African Trade Union Federation, complained that despite commercial sanctions and arms embargoes he had seen reports proving that Eastern countries were continuing their trade. The Soviet Union, Red China, Czechoslovakia, Poland and East Germany have all been involved. By 1964 China's trade with South Africa had reached a level that had begun to embarrass Peking. According to the trade manager of the South African Maize Control Authority, South African exports to China rose to 3.7 million rand ($5.18 million) in the first quarter of 1963. The monthly extract of trade statistics published by the South African Customs Service shows that in eleven months from January through November 1963 South Africa imported merchandise worth 1,711,819 rand ($2,396,556.60) from Red China. The *East African Standard* reported on January 15, 1964, that China had more than tripled its trade with South Africa. South African exports have been mainly corn to alleviate Red China's endemic grain shortages. To circumvent the official boycotts, most of it has passed through various international trading organizations, such as the French firm of Louis Dreyfus.

The question arises whether any strategic materials such as uranium or industrial diamonds have also found their way to China through clandestine channels. In the never-ending conflict between political principle and economic self-interest, it would appear that the latter is stronger. In 1964 the Pretoria government maintained a permanent "Commissioner for Trade with the Chinese People's Republic" in Hong Kong. A Kenya report in January 1965, citing statistics from the International Monetary Fund, listed China as the country whose South African trade was up most. An African National Congress representative with whom I discussed this shrugged and told me: "China is a country friendly to us. But we are investigating these reports."

Red China has numerous opportunities for troublemaking in South-West Africa and the so-called High Commission Territories of Basutoland, the Bechuanaland Protectorate and Swaziland. All are peopled by African tribes as backward as any Bantu in South Africa. Peking has shown its interest in extremist leaders in all of them.

South-West Africa is a 318,099-square-mile territory with a complicated history of colonization, international mandates and strong influence from the Union (now the Republic) of South Africa. Ever since 1933, when it was still ruled under a League of Nations mandate, Pretoria has pressed for its total incorporation. In the United Nations since 1960 the independent African states have repeatedly accused the South African government of violating its international agreements on South-West Africa. In 1963 a United Nations Commission and the General Assembly declared themselves in favor of a United Nations presence in the territory. There has been a constant legal battle to prevent the extension of Pretoria's apartheid policy in its formal entirety to South-West Africa. This battle went before the International Court in The Hague in March 1965.

Among the African political organizations in the territory, and in exile outside it, Peking has shown interest chiefly in two. One is called the South-West African National Union. It was founded in 1959 and headed by Fanuel Jairetunda Kozonguizi, the son of a farm laborer of Windhoek Province, who received a good education and some administrative experience in South Africa. He has worked to form a united front with the African National Congress and other organizations in the Republic, a project that seems to have Peking's blessing. On March 21, 1964, Radio Peking quoted him in an orthodox Chinese-line call for violent revolution. "There is no prospect of a peaceful solution," it concluded.

The Chinese are also interested in the South-West African People's Organization, orginally founded in 1958 as the Ovamboland People's Congress by South-West African laborers in Capetown. Its most prominent leader has been Sam Nujoma, a petitioner for the party at the United Nations, who was based in Leopoldville in mid-1964. It aims at complete independence for South-West Africa, with United Nations trusteeship as an interim measure. Another leader mentioned in Peking propaganda media is Peter Nanyemba, representative in Dar es-Salaam.

Some of the New China News Agency's interviews with South-West Africans suffice to show the drift of Peking's thought, which is categorically opposed to United Nations intervention or action: "We are just like the Chinese people. We love peace"; but "There is no other way out of our plight but to take up arms" (September 18, 1963) or "The most important thing is to fight" (November 12, 1963).

Basutoland is an 11,716-square-mile enclave surrounded by the territory of the Republic of South Africa, ruled by a paramount chief with British supervision. It was moving toward self-government in 1964 and independence in 1965 or 1966. The Basuto people are more sophisticated than the Swazi, Bechuana and many other of the tribal communities, but their country, where according to a U. N. census in 1959 only 638,857 Africans and 1,926 Europeans lived, is beset by economic depression and mass emigration of workers to the Republic of South Africa, mainly the Rand mines.

Existence of a "Lesotho" (Basutoland) Communist Party was publicly disclosed for the first time in November 1961. Its founders were exiled members of the South African Communist Party. *The African Communist* (No. 8, 1962) reports that "Marxist study groups" worked in almost every village in Basutoland and that the way had been "thoroughly prepared for further Communist penetration." Early in 1962 the Party made an unsuccessful attempt to seize control of the principal non-Communist nationalist formation, the Basutoland Congress Party. On March 11, 1964, the Moscow-line Czechoslovak News Agency said: "Basutoland's youngest party, the Communist Party" was fighting for a "united front" of "progressive forces." East Germany, as elsewhere in Africa, also bolstered the Moscow line: late in 1963, 40,000 Red brochures printed in the German Democratic Republic were smuggled into Maseru, Basutoland.

Peking's policy in Basutoland was similar to that of Moscow. The Chinese sought to bring about a united front between the Communists and the Basutoland Congress Party. Whenever a Congress Party member demanded full independence or violent revolution, as did Bishop Mpeta in Accra in April 1964, the Peking news media gave him a big play.

Bechuanaland is another British-supervised protectorate, 275,000 square miles in size, bounded by South-West Africa, Rhodesia and the South African Republic, and rapidly heading toward full control of its own affairs. Its principal ruler is a moderately inclined traditional tribal chief, Seretse Kahama. His party won an overwhelming victory in the Bechuanaland elections of 1965, and he became Prime Minister.

The Bechuanaland People's Party, founded in December 1960 just as a new draft constitution was being published, was headed by a former teacher and composer of music. To greet the constitution of Bechuanaland and Swaziland when they emerged in final form in 1963, Peking broadcast statements attributed to Africans that "We shall fight to the last drop . . . we shall make the constitution unworkable" (June 4, 1963) and "The struggle between the colonialists and the colonial people is a life and death struggle. Only through a revolutionary struggle by the mass of the people can we achieve our aim— the independence and the liberation of Bechuanaland" (July 28, 1963). Peking backs a small, violent revolutionary group, the Bechuanaland Popular Party, headed by K. T. Motsete. There is also a Communist Party.

Swaziland is a small (6,704 square miles) territory bordered by the South African Republic on the west, north and south, and by Portuguese Mozambique on the east. The last census in 1959 showed 231,122 Africans and 5,919 Europeans. The Portuguese authorities in Mozambique, as well as the authorities in Pretoria, are naturally apprehensive about possible large-scale Communist or African nationalist infiltration because of Swaziland's location.

On July 3, 1964, elections in Swaziland supervised by the British brought an overwhelming majority in the governing council for twelve candidates favorable to the paramount chief of the Swazi nation, Ngwenyama Sobhuza II. He has visited Britain and attended a Royal Coronation. He is a traditional king who loves his tribal ritual and observes it meticulously. Sobhuza has given very little encouragement to reform of any kind, and maintains close contact with the white South

African authorities. There seems to be a strong possibility of a time of troubles in Swaziland, with a mounting African nationalist opposition —Peking has of course actively encouraged it—that will oust the Chief. Organized non-extremist nationalist groups, such as the Swaziland Progressive Party of J. J. Nquku, seek the democratic enfranchisement of the Swazi people and the building of a racially integrated society, free of apartheid. A Swaziland Communist Party was reportedly organized in 1963 by the South African Communist Party. Peking paid particularly close attention to it because the Soviet Communist organizations were slow to recognize it. It also backed the Progressive Party of Swaziland headed by O. M. Mabuza and the "National Liberatory Congress of Ngwane."

Red Chinese policy toward the Republic of South Africa and the High Commission Territories thus is multiform. Armed aid is given only on a limited and clandestine basis, where it can be done without much detection or where it will be immediately effective. Propaganda will continue to encourage the "armed struggle" (it holds up the bloody African peasant revolt of Pondoland in the Republic of South Africa in 1960 as an example). It contends, as did Mao Tun in his speech before the Algiers Afro-Asian Solidarity Council meeting, that "American imperialism, Public Enemy Number One of the world's peoples, has become the master of the Fascist government of Verwoerd." Peking will continue all-out efforts to infiltrate the Communist parties and all the African "mass organizations" that oppose white rule, whatever their ideologies or local politics.

China ignores U. N. actions on South Africa but does give constant and very active encouragement to African campaigns to exclude Pretoria representatives from all the major international bodies, such as the International Labor Office and the World Health Organization. Though demands for economic sanctions will continue, they seem to have little chance for major success, in view of the enormous Western capital investments in the South African economy. The United States did take one positive step when it halted arms shipments to the Republic at the end of 1963.

An armed confrontation between the Pretoria regime, allied with the Portuguese in Angola and Mozambique and the whites of Southern Rhodesia and the High Commission Territories, may still be years away. But when it does come Peking seems certain to be a principal beneficiary.

CHAPTER ELEVEN

Astride the Color Line:
Zambia, Rhodesia and Malawi

THE NEW STATE OF ZAMBIA, FORMERLY NORTHERN RHODESIA, WON independence on October 24, 1964. It is of considerable importance to Peking in mapping its future African strategy.

Zambia, 288,193 square miles in area, and containing about 2,370,000 Africans, 77,000 Europeans and 10,600 Asians and other residents (including a few Chinese merchants), is, through its copper and other minerals, one of the wealthiest of the independent African states. Its 1963 copper exports alone came to $330 million. Cobalt, which Peking eagerly seeks and has found elsewhere only in Morocco, is produced at Nkana and by the Copper Refinery in Ndola for the fabulously wealthy Chibulama Mines Production.

Zambia's internal situation perhaps lends itself less to subversion than that of many other African states. Even while it was still a part of the Central African Federation—dissolved in 1963—with Southern Rhodesia and Nyasaland (now Malawi), it had its own separate government under a British Protectorate. Within it, like a Chinese puzzle box, was the separate smaller Protectorate of Barotseland, which has a special agreement with Britain. The Northern Rhodesian government was competent for all questions not reserved to the federal authorities and was fairly stable and enlightened. There was considerable constitutional progress, and by December 1962 Northern Rhodesia had an elected African majority. In January 1964 Dr.

Kaunda's United National Independence Party won fifty-five seats in the Legislative assembly. This provided a fairly solid base for the independent state set up in October 1964.

Zambia's consitution is modeled on Western lines, combining characteristics of both the British and American systems. It has ample provision for protection of individual and property rights regardless of "race, place of origin, political opinions, color, creed or sex." Radio Peking in 1965 began to concentrate on the theme that this guaranteed the white community the same privileges it had before.

Lusaka, capital and seat of Dr. Kenneth Kaunda's rather pro-Western government, was scheduled to replace Dar es-Salaam as headquarters of the African "Committee of Nine" to aid liberation movements. Its choice by the United Nations as the seat of the southern region of the U. N. Economic Commission for Africa was another proof of its growing central role, a role Dr. Kaunda's government had some serious reservations about accepting.

This importance would be further enhanced if a projected railway link connecting Zambia and Tanzania were to be built. This would connect Zambia with the sea by a route other than the existing ones across white-ruled Southern Rhodesia and the Republic of South Africa. Five strategic lines would then connect it with Lobito, in Portuguese-ruled Angola; Capetown in South Africa; Beira in Mozambique; the Congo (Leopoldville); and finally, with Tanzania.

Lusaka is geographically a natural choice as a capital for the subversion of white rule in southern Africa. Zambia touches all the African countries dominated by whites: Angola, Mozambique, Rhodesia, South-West Africa and Bechuanaland, which in turn is a steppingstone to the Republic of South Africa and the other High Commission Territories. Though Dr. Kaunda has declared that his new country's policy will be one of non-alignment, it has proven difficult to stay uninvolved in the problems of his neighbors. Like President Nyerere of Tanzania, he was aware that in granting asylum to their would-be "liberators," both African and foreign, he would risk the security of his own potentially prosperous state. In December 1964 the government restricted liberation movements to one office apiece. They had to be in Lusaka, and campaigning for funds without permission outside Lusaka was forbidden.

The Angolan nationalists were especially interested in making their major base in Lusaka instead of Leopoldville, since Tshombe failed to keep his promises to aid them. The frontier that Zambia and

Rhodesia (formerly Southern Rhodesia) share with Mozambique suggests to some nationalists that the assault against the Portuguese can be better planned and led if the nationalist movements of Angola and Mozambique work from a common headquarters, pooling their resources. Peking, from 1963 on, showed increasing interest in such coordination. Chou En-lai placed great stress on this when he conferred with President Ben Bella and the other Algerian leaders in Algiers in December 1963.

Before June 1964 there were few important direct contacts between Zambian leaders and Peking, except for the usual delegations of exiles received in the Red Chinese capital.

Red China made its first diplomatic pitch just as Duncan Sandys, British Minister for the Commonwealth, was completing work with the Zambian leaders on arrangements for independence. The diplomat it chose to make it was Ho Ying, whom we have already met as Ambassador in Dar es-Salaam, and who was accredited to Zambia after independence. The first Peking chargé d'affaires was Li Chen-ho: he arrived in November 1964.

Ho Ying had cultivated two of the Zambian cabinet ministers who had looked most kindly on ties with Peking: Finance Minister Arthur Wina and his brother, Minister of Public Health Sikoto Wina. Ho Ying also saw a great deal of the Minister of Labor and Mines, J. H. Chimba, probably about purchasing strategic ores.

Only one-third the size of Zambia, but from Peking's viewpoint far richer in trouble-making possibilities, is Rhodesia—formerly Southern Rhodesia—with 150,333 square miles, and in 1960 some 2,870,000 Africans, 225,000 Europeans and 60,700 Asians and others. Africans call it Zimbabwe, the name of the most ancient and highly cultured pre-colonial African kingdom.

Ruled by last-ditch white-supremacy advocates, Rhodesia rapidly became the chief headache of its northern neighbor, Zambia. Ever since the epoch of white colonization by the followers of Cecil Rhodes in the 1890s, Rhodesia's history has been a story of whites trying to break away and form their own independent, white-supremacy state, if possible free of all control by London, and if need be, of all Empire and Commonwealth ties.

Southern Rhodesia consequently is one of Africa's most explosive centers of racial discord. The United Nations General Assembly has gone on record as opposing independence as long as a government has not been elected by universal suffrage, which would bring into power an overwhelming African majority. While British policy has vacillated between trying to please the settlers and attempting to comply with the U. N.'s wishes, Peking has been consistently in favor of one thing: violent revolution. At the same time South Africa has made it clear that it favors an independent, white-ruled Southern Rhodesia, provided Britain grants independence legally and the white settlers do not take matters into their own hands.

There are two main nationalist parties in Southern Rhodesia, the Zimbabwe African People's Union (ZAPU) under Joshua Nkomo, and the dissident Zimbabwe African National Union (ZANU), under the Reverend Ndabaninge Sithole. Dr. Kaunda in Zambia has bent every effort to reconcile them. He notified the Southern Rhodesian government in Salisbury that if it declared independence unilaterally he would break all ties between Lusaka and Salisbury. He would then place his territory at the disposal of the British troops who would— he hoped—arrive with United Nations orders to reduce the rebellion of the white "ultras," as the U.N. had earlier reduced the Congo "ultras" allied with Moise Tshombe in Katanga.

Nkomo told me at the Addis Ababa Conference in May 1963 that he would "take aid from the devil himself." In the spring of 1964 he announced that he would set up a Zimbabwe government-in-exile in Zambia. Radio Peking loudly applauded this announcement in its African service programs during April 1964.

In 1963 a ZANU emissary returned from Algiers and an interview with Ben Bella to report that Southern Rhodesian fighters would be trained at the Beni Messous guerila warfare camp, near Algiers. Ben Bella, the ZANU man said, asked that volunteers be routed through Dar es-Salaam, where the Chinese Embassy would arrange for the onward journey. According to the Lusaka press, Peking in September 1964 promised aid to two ZAPU officials, George Nyandoro and Jasan Moyo, if they formed a government-in-exile: Nkomo, by this time, was undergoing one of his periodic periods of detention at a remote Rhodesian settlement.

Another name for ZAPU was the "People's Caretaker Council." Its key figure, who in early days was one of Nkomo's most important lieutenants, was James Robert Chikerema, who was jailed in February 1959 and was held in prison without trial for many months, then disappeared from view. Chikerema is unpopular among Africans and is considered uncompromising. He was likely to emerge as the leader of violent revolt in Rhodesia if the ruling whites, under the Governor, Sir Ian Smith, went ahead with plans to set up an independent government on their own. On February 21, 1964, the *Central African Mail* of Lusaka quoted Chikerema as announcing that he had just returned from Peking and Moscow. He was reported to have boasted that the Chinese had given him £7,000 ($19,700) for the "People's Caretaker Council."

Peking announced a "Zimbabwe Solidarity Day" on March 17, 1964. The Chinese Afro-Asian Solidarity Council promised its backing against "British colonialists," who, it said, "are trying to create an 'independent' colonial government composed of a handful of whites, with the intention of continuing their criminal domination of Zimbabwe." Radio Peking added on March 16 that "American neocolonialism seeks to pillage the riches of Zimbabwe and to replace British colonialism."

This is the stuff of which race wars are made, and Peking knows it well.

Nyasaland, called Malawi, or "flaming water" (after the sunrise on Lake Nyasa), since it became independent on July 6, 1964, is a lovely little country of 36,700 square miles settled largely by Scotsmen. It was the site of an early and signal Chinese failure. It is ruled mainly by Africans whose educational and cultural traditions have been largely acquired in Britain and the United States. Foremost among these is Dr. Hastings Banda, the first Prime Minister, born in 1906. By working in the South African gold mines, he earned his fare to the United States, and graduated from Wilberforce College, Ohio, the University of Chicago, and Medical College in Nashville, Tennessee, where he won an M.D. Dr. Banda not only went on to win diplomas in Glasgow and Edinburgh, but also became an Elder in the Church of Scotland. He lived in London and knew such Africans as Kwame Nkrumah and George Padmore from 1945 to 1953, but remained singularly unimpressed and uninfluenced by Marxist interpretations of pan-Africanism.

Banda's Western and religious turn of mind did not prevent him from returning to his native country to battle against the British-created Central African Federation of the Rhodesias and Nyasaland, which he, like other Africans, considered an artificial creation designed to perpetuate white rule. He campaigned for maintenance of his country as a British Protectorate as it had been since 1904. With

Harry Nkumbula, president of the Northern Rhodesian African National Congress, he shared foreign exile, and spent thirteen months in prison in 1959 and 1960.

Neither Banda nor any of his important associates were ever much attracted by the blandishments of Moscow or Peking. One of Malawi's bright young men is Henry Chipembere, Treasurer of the ruling Malawi Congress Party, who in 1964 and 1965 led a dissident faction against Banda's authority.

Dr. Banda's distrust of Peking and his desire to keep entirely out of the China question actually had the opposite effect: Malawi became a diplomatic battleground in Red China's African offensive. It came about this way:

On June 13, 1964, three weeks before independence, Dr. Banda talked in his capital, Zomba, with Ho Ying. It was Ho Ying's second visit—on both occasions he was accredited Ambassador in Tanzania —having already seen Dr. Banda in March. Nationalist China and Peking were both preparing to send ambassadors to Malawi, which favored the "two Chinas" concept. Banda finally refused to recognize either China.

Dr. Banda invited both Peking and Taipeh to send emissaries to the independence celebrations in July, despite his intention to recognize neither of them. Peking refused. It accused Dr. Banda of collusion in a "plot to create two Chinas at the expense of the age-old friendship between the Chinese and Malawi peoples."

Ho Ying pressed for recognition. He offered Malawi a loan, reported by British newsmen to be about $18 million, but possibly less than this, if Dr. Banda would agree. "You Chinese are a people with an ancient civilization and famous for your patience," Dr. Banda told him publicly, according to British newspaper reports. "Just be patient." When the Foreign Minister, Kanyama Chiume, tried to undercut Banda by reporting on the Chinese aid offer to parliament, Banda told the body: "The language of dangling bribes before my face and eyes is not easily understandable to an Elder of the Church of Scotland." He was said to have added that while the West had relinquished control of the body of Africa, the Chinese were scrambling for its soul.

In September 1964 Dr. Banda accused Chiume of plotting to murder him in cold blood. He dismissed him and several other cabinet ministers, including Henry Chipembere, who was then Minister of Education, because he said they were plotting with Ho Ying against

him. Ho Ying was said to have increased the original loan offer, if
Malawi would open its gates to a Chinese mission. Chinese propaganda now began to whisper loudly that Dr. Banda's policy was
pro-imperialist because of his reluctance to antagonize the Portuguese
in Mozambique, the white government of Ian Smith in Rhodesia, or
Dr. Verwoerd in South Africa—things that many "militant" Africans
were already saying.

The remainder of Dr. Banda's cabinet resigned, and Henry
Chipembere escaped from restriction and took to the Chilipa Hills on
the Mozambique side of Lake Malawi to form a guerilla "army." In
early 1965 this was harassing Dr. Banda's small army, built around
one battalion inherited from the forces of the old Central African
Federation, and a police force of about 4,000. The other five ministers who resigned or were dismissed found sympathy and support in
Zambia and Tanzania.

Chiume and former Housing Minister Augustine Bwanausi gave
interviews to East bloc journalists in Dar es-Salaam. They said Banda
was in the pocket of the Portuguese, the white Rhodesians and the
South Africans, and was opposed to social change in Malawi. Chiume
accused the honorary consul of Malawi in Lourenço Marques, the
capital of Mozambique, of being an agent of the PIDE (the Portuguese political police) and of the son-in-law of Dr. Salazar. He also
accused him of concluding a deal with Ian Smith to do everything
possible to prevent Joshua Nkomo, in a detention camp in Rhodesia
in March 1965, from ever becoming Southern Rhodesian Prime Minister.

The Chinese news media, of course, gave these charges full play.
Banda was high on the list of Peking's priority targets. For the moment Malawi's need for its trade and transport links with Rhodesia
and Mozambique precluded major policy changes, short of those
brought about by a revolutionary upheaval in the entire area.

CHAPTER TWELVE

The Cameroon Revolt

RED CHINA'S MOST AMBITIOUS AFRICAN VENTURE HAS BEEN ITS support of full-scale guerilla warfare to expel Western influence from the Congo. This had an important early rehearsal that drew much less world attention: the previous revolt that Peking backed in the Federal Republic of Cameroon.

Like so many "new" African states, the Cameroon Republic is an artificial creation. It was constituted as an independent state in 1961 out of two utterly disparate elements. One was the tropical, humid French-ruled southern rain forests, peopled by Bantus who had proven somewhat receptive to French educational and development efforts. The other was the arid, northern desert, populated largely by conservative Moslems living under a system of feudal fiefs and feudal chiefs.

The new government in Yaoundé seemingly had two and a half strikes against it before it could even begin to function: a full-scale guerilla revolt, drawing upon tribal elements for its troops, with the active backing of the world Communist movement. Here was a situation tailor-made for Peking, which entered the scene only after the Africans themselves had already started the drama.

The Union des Populations du Cameroun (UPC) was one of the oldest and at the same time most completely Communist-dominated of all African nationalist movements. It was founded in French Cameroun (then a United Nations Trust Territory) about 1947. Originally it

had links with the French African Community's regional Rassemblement Démocratique Africain (RDA). It severed these links when the
RDA refused in 1951 to break with the French Communist Party.
Under the capable leadership of its first leader, Rubem Um Nyobe,
the UPC developed tough youth, labor and women's "mass organizations." Nyobe tried long and unsuccessfully to secure United Nations
supervision for the creation of a sovereign and independent state. The
UPC claimed that in the French repression which followed its nationalist manifesto of April 1955, 20,000 Africans were killed. The UPC
and its affiliates were banned.

On July 12, 1956, the UPC launched full-scale guerilla war against
the French. It called for national unity and reunification of French
Cameroun and the British Cameroons in a single state with democratic institutions. This guerilla war continued after independence and
reunification, with sporadic ups and downs, into 1964, but was limited to the southern region. At times the UPC's guerilla army, organized along classic Chinese Red Army lines, gained considerable control over the Bamileke and the Sanaga-Maritime regions of the Republic.

The exiled UPC leaders, from Cairo, Conakry, Algiers, New York,
Moscow and Peking, conducted an international campaign for the
withdrawal of French troops and the overthrow of the moderate pro-
Western regime of Premier Ahmadou Ahidjo, a shrewd and capable
politician of Northern Region Moslem stock.

When Ruben Um Nyobe died in 1958, UPC guerilla operations fell
under the command of the UPC President, Dr. Felix-Roland Moumié.
He had studied in the Soviet Union and Czechoslovakia. At this
time, much as in Algeria, there is evidence that the Soviets were
quietly advising the Cameroun nationalists to negotiate with the
French, while the Chinese were urging them to fight.

Moumié settled in Conakry in early 1959, after the rupture between France and the Republic of Guinea. The French Cameroun
became independent on January 1, 1960, but French troops were
permitted by the independence agreement to stay on. The UPC rebellion undoubtedly was important in Ahidjo's decision to keep them in
the country. One of the UPC leaders, Mayi Matip, accepted Ahidjo's
offer of an amnesty and left the rebellion. Moumié, however, said the
UPC would not lay down its arms unless all foreign troops left the
country and unless it could take part in a coalition to supervise
elections. Moumié made his first trip to Peking just about the time the

Soviets recognized the new independent government and apparently promised to urge the UPC to negotiate. Communist Czechoslovakia was the UPC's principal supplier of arms at this time.

Then, after a second visit to Peking, Moumié returned to his Conakry headquarters in April 1960. He was firmly committed to the Chinese line by the time he was poisoned in Geneva, allegedly by a French secret service agent.

After his death, the Red Chinese Embassy in Conakry took charge of aiding the UPC, as the influence of the Russians and Czechs, discredited through their blunders in Guinea, steadily declined. Mme. Moumié, Dr. Moumié's widow, took over the liaison work with Peking. Her continued activity was confirmed when she appeared with the Cameroon delegation at the Afro-Asian Solidarity Council meeting in Algiers in March 1964.

Western officials released details of the experiences of six Africans who underwent a ten-week course for Cameroon terrorists in China in 1960 and who were later arrested by the Ahidjo government. These were substantially the same courses that have been taken by cadres later chosen for the operations in the Congo, Portuguese Guinea and elsewhere. Upon arrival in Peking in March 1961—they had left the Cameroon without travel documents—they were enrolled in classes that included both classroom work and a battle course. They learned how to make and use explosives to blow up bridges, houses, rails, tanks and trucks; how to sabotage airfields and telecommunications; and how to destroy power plants and radio and television broadcasting facilities. They were taught about ambushes and how to fortify villages, what to do about sentries and unsympathetic villagers.

Moving up the ladder a rung to the "political" level, the six Cameroon recruits were then told about killing off puppet agents and traitors, and how to maintain the climate of psychological warfare that must accompany all successful terrorist ventures. They learned about infiltration of those firms and organizations of key importance in a national economy. Then they returned to the Cameroon Republic, carrying detailed instructions for the UPC's politico-military program, and binoculars, cameras and transistor radio sets.

The Cameroon United Nations delegate in December 1961 indicted Red China in an exposé that should have received far more attention in the West and in Africa, since it accurately reflected China's projects elsewhere. "Guerilla weapons and many propaganda pamphlets that have been seized and are still being seized enable us, beyond a shadow of a doubt," he said, "to establish the responsibility in the leading and the equipping of localized underground groups in the Cameroons . . . Many young Camerounais, inveigled and led into China under false pretexts, receive there psychological and military preparations for the ultimate goal of being sent to our national territory, there to engage in subversive activities and to serve as the instructors and personnel in an effective general rebellion."

In November 1961, only weeks before the U.N. debate, Radio Peking quoted Mao Tse-tung's solemn assurance that "China has for a long time supported the fight of the UPC. The Chinese people will continue to assist this movement in its fight to the bitter end."

On several occasions since then, President Ahidjo has been equally solemn in declaring that his government can neither recognize Red China nor support its admission to the United Nations, because "China fosters the Cameroon rebellion . . . [and therefore] does not fulfill the fundamental conditions prescribed by the Charter." But Peking continued its support to the UPC. Once again, on February 8, 1964, Yaoundé Radio quoted President Ahidjo as saying that if Cameroon did not follow the example of France and other African countries in recognizing the Peking regime, it is "because we have observed that it interfered in our internal affairs." By early 1965, there were indications that Peking might allow the guerilla movement to die in return for recognition.

The UPC had one principal base in Accra, where it published a Chinese-line newspaper, *La Voix du Kamerun*. In its issue of March 1964 it reported that on April 25, 1963, the anniversary of the Bandung Conference, the UPC held a "People's Assembly" somewhere in the *maquis*. This gathering was said to have heaped praises on "the militant action of the advance guard of the Cuban, Chinese, Algerian and Ghanaian peoples at the side of the revolutionaries of Latin America, Asia and Africa." The thinking disclosed here is highly interesting: Ghana and Algeria seem to be earmarked to play the same revolutionary role in Africa as Red China in Asia, and Cuba in Latin America.

The same newspaper reported the public execution by President Ahidjo's government of eleven UPC partisans. It published articles in praise of African revolutions, particularly the one in Zanzibar. It demanded that the African Unity Organization send an investigating commission to the Cameroon Republic to check on the status of

French forces and French and NATO bases at Kouden, Koutaba and Douala. It listed UPC goals as immediate liberation of all political prisoners and evacuation of all French troops and bases; "democratic liberties" for the people; abolition of the "Fascist" single-party system; work for the unemployed and land for the peasants.

The UPC has continued its work among Cameroon political refugees. These have turned up in Ghana, Guinea, Togo, Dahomey, Chad, the Central African Republic, Congo (Brazzaville), Congo (Leopoldville), Gabon, Senegal and the Ivory Coast. Though in some of these places Chinese Communist influence was formerly absent or minimal, it can be assumed that it was spread through UPC activities.

The guerilla methods and the political indoctrination tactics of the UPC, with more or less discreet Chinese backing, were essentially the same methods and tactics that came to be applied in the Congo when that vast territory was rent by leftist revolt beginning in 1963. Dr. Moumié and some of the lesser leaders and advisors of the UPC, between 1960 and 1963, had passed on their philosophy and their tactics to Patrice Lumumba and his followers through such intermediaries as Anicet Kashamura. But neither the Soviet Union nor Communist China can be said to have played any active, prominent role in the Congo events that drew world attention immediately after the Belgians granted independence in July 1960.

The former Belgian Congo was one of Africa's largest (over 900,000 square miles), and at the same time most sparsely populated (perhaps 16 million people) territories. It was scarcely a nation in the modern sense of the term.

There was no Congolese Communist Party. At the Afro-Asian Conference of 1958 in Conakry, both Russians and Chinese had agreed to back Patrice Lumumba's Mouvement National Congolais and Antoine Gizenga's Parti Solidaire Africain. Lumumba and Gizenga, after independence, became Premier and Vice-Premier respectively. They had been assisted by Dr. Moumié before his death, and by some French Communist advisors who went to the Congo from Conakry, and later others from Paris and Rabat.

When the para-military Force Publique mutinied and the Belgian Army intervened, Peking echoed Soviet charges of a Western "conspiracy" backed by NATO. But while Moscow concentrated on getting Security Council action, then later turned against Secretary-General

Hammarskjold, the Chinese characteristically largely ignored the the United States and, of course, the U.N. as a "tool of American imperialism."

By August 25, 1960, when the Chinese Ambassador in Cairo, Chan Hiang-kang, arrived in Leopoldville on a visit, Lumumba and his supporters had already begun an active correspondence with Peking. On September 8, Gizenga, as deputy premier, formally asked the Chinese for volunteers, arms and materials of various sorts, including fighter planes. Chang replied that it would be "difficult" to send volunteers. But by this time Lumumba's political decline, which ended in his strange and tragic death, had begun. Peking paid over $2.8 million in cash, but withheld the rest. Later, the Republic of the Sudan refused permission for the arms aid to cross its territory.

By October 1960, when the Vice-President of the Chinese People's Institute for Foreign Affairs gave a grandiose banquet for a Congolese delegation in Peking, including Information Minister Anicet Kashamura, no less than eighty-four Congolese delegations had visited Peking. One eyewitness of this banquet told of how an acting correspondent of the New China News Agency "harangued" the visitors with "anti-white diatribes." Kashamura, with whom I spoke at considerable length in Rabat in 1962, was probably one of the few Congolese who understood what Communism was really about. He was anxious then to represent himself as a true neutral. He wanted to exclude both Eastern and Western meddling from the Congo. In 1963 he accepted Adoula's offer of an amnesty for ex-Lumumba supporters and returned to the Congo. Within a few months he was reported leading pro-Chinese rebels in Kivu province.

From late 1960 on, the Russian and Chinese lines on the Congo diverged increasingly. Moscow concentrated on getting the U.N. out of the Congo, while Peking ignored the U.N. and leveled its fire at the United States. The Soviets managed to send their ambassador to the rump regime of Gizenga in Stanleyville in July 1961 before the Chinese did. Then, a month later, when pro-Western Cyril Adoula formed a new parliamentary coalition regime in August 1961, with Gizenga as deputy premier, Moscow sent its blessings. Peking, however, branded Adoula a "Western stooge" and attacked him for maintaining relations with Nationalist China. Though it finally withdrew the Red Chinese Ambassador from Stanleyville, Peking continued to call the former Gizenga regime "the only legal government of the Congo." It has consistently opposed Adoula, and welcomed his fall from power when Tshombe returned from exile to form a new government in July 1964.

Peking always presented the various actions of U.N. forces to reduce the secession of Moise Tshombe's Katanga province as basically a move by American business interests to expel Belgian and British business interests, using the United Nations as a tool. The great Union Minière combine that has always kept Katanga going produces 7 per cent of the world's copper and *nearly 70 per cent of all its cobalt.* Uranium from Katanga made the atomic bomb that fell on Hiroshima. There is also much tin, zinc, radium, germanium, cadmium and silver.

When Gizenga fell from favor with Adoula and was arrested, the Moscow and Peking lines once again briefly converged, to protest Gizenga's confinement. Peking, however, used warmer language about Gizenga than Moscow, always describing him as a "true Congolese patriot." This despite Gizenga's statements of his neutralism, such as in an interview he had given *Le Monde* on March 25, 1961, in which he said: "Because we are an African country and underdeveloped, we need to keep out of the Cold War and not ally ourselves with either of the two blocs."

During 1962 and 1963, when the Congo occasionally slipped out of the world limelight because the United Nations, with the help of massive American and Belgian aid, seemed to be stabilizing the situation, Peking was busy behind the scenes. By 1962, it had invited fully 140 Congolese students to Peking and a few trade union people as well.

By October 1963 the followers of Gizenga, especially a certain Pierre Mulele, were organizing for a guerilla revolt against the government of Cyril Adoula in Kwilu province. In a news conference on October 23 the Central Defense Minister for Leopoldville province referred to "copies of Mao Tse-tung on Guerilla Warfare," which he said Congolese security forces had found in the abandoned hideouts of Gizengists. Few observers in the West paid any attention.

CHAPTER THIRTEEN

The Congos

BY THE SUMMER OF 1964 THE WITCH DOCTORS IN THE CONGOLESE bush and the Red Chinese diplomats encouraging them from Bujumbura, Brazzaville and Peking seemed to be having things their own way.

The waves of tribal revolt were spreading in the western province of Kwilu, and in the eastern provinces of Kivu and North Katanga. Propaganda had made the rebels believe that fetishes and "anti-bullet pills" gave them protection. The rebels had occupied and terrorized vast tracts of land. South of Kwilu, along the Angola border, the fighting had dipped into Kwangu province. Exclaimed the English-language edition of the Peking *People's Daily* gleefully on June 24:

An excellent revolutionary situation is emerging on the vast expanse of the Congo. . . . Like the Chinese people, the Congolese people have also been compelled to take up swords and embark on the road of armed struggle after suffering defeat in their revolution and after investigation and study. . . . The Congolese people will surely continue to grow stronger, extend their war gains and win still greater victories. An independent, free Congo is bound to emerge like a phoenix from the flames of struggle. . . . In the Congo, the U. S. imperialists will face the same doom they are facing in South Vietnam.

The departure of the last of the U. N. troops, who had left 236 dead behind them during their four years in the Congo, had just written finis to the period when the West still hoped it could bring peace and order out of the vast, surrealistic chaos that is the Congo.

They left behind only 600 Nigerian policemen. A million Congolese and Europeans had died in fighting or of hunger in four years of the Congo's "independence."

What had put thousands of Congolese up to daubing their bodies with red paint, discarding their European clothes for animal skins, and taking up spear, knife, machete or "poo-poo" gun (primitive muskets) to go out and kill white men and their legally appointed government officials?

The answers are not easy to discover in the mass of sensational, contradictory news that flows out of the Congo. But some can be traced through the thickening skein of Red Chinese involvement, or spotted in the stories of some of the men whom Peking has used to ignite the flames of war.

In every account of the Chinese-backed Congo revolts one name persistently recurs. It is that of Pierre Mulele. He was once a model pupil of Belgian Catholic missionaries who left the Catholic Church at the age of fifteen because he refused to believe in the virgin birth of Christ. He became a hard-bitten, determined doctrinaire, evidently incorruptible, ready to use the darkest weapons of tribalism, arson, looting and all the atavisms of the Congolese bush in his determination that absolute Communist power should triumph over relative, Western-style order.

Mulele proved to be an ideal instrument for Peking. A United Press International correspondent in Leopoldville reported that Mulele had first come under Communist influence after World War II, when he met some Greek Communists who had fled to the Congo from the Greek civil war. After some time spent in Conakry and Cairo, Mulele went to Peking and took five months of the same sort of guerilla training that Dr. Moumié's Cameroun partisans had had.

By 1960 Mulele had returned to the Congo to serve in the first Lumumba cabinets. When Lumumba's star fell, he served the separatist Gizenga regime in Stanleyville, and in December 1960 was appointed permanent liaison officer of Gizenga in Cairo. By this time the first clashes had occurred in Kivu province between the local population and outsiders of the Bakongo people, President Joseph Kasavubu's tribe. A gendarmerie mutiny in Kikwit, the Kwilu capital, was broken only by the arrival of Colonel Joseph Mobutu's paracommandos—the same Mobutu who, as the general commanding the Congolese army, was to see his heavily armed regular troops fleeing before spear-equipped, Chinese-advised rebels in 1964.

On January 2, 1961, Mulele officially opened the Gizenga government's offices in Cairo. Patrice Lumumba, a prisoner of the central government now, was transferred to Elizabethville on January 17 and apparently murdered on the same evening. On February 14, a day after his death was officially confirmed, Mulele published a proclamation in Cairo blaming it on "Belgian colonialists, their Congolese hatchet men" and Dag Hammarskjold, as "the political instrument of the American administration."

Gizenga and his Parti Solidaire Africain (PSA) set up a new rump government in Stanleyville, Oriental province. Gizenga told *Le Monde* in an interview March 24 that "my party's social program is inspired by African traditional structures. Our people have never known a capitalist regime." Tribal life, he went on, was founded upon a community system under which land and property were owned collectively. Two weeks later Pierre Mulele published a "decree" of the Gizenga regime announcing President Kasavubu's "overthrow." By December 1961, he was back in Cairo issuing inflammatory statements against the new Adoula government from there.

Signs of the coming drama in Kwilu multiplied throughout 1962 and 1963. According to a confidential report from a Roman Catholic missionary in the diocese of Idiofa, the "youth" (*Jeunesse*), a name already applied to tribalist rebels in 1960, began to train for violent revolution, beginning in July 1963, and possibly before then. Acts of sabotage against bridges, roads and administrative buildings began in December 1963.

By January 19, 1964, the "Mulelists," as they were already being called, had begun to attack, pillage and burn missions and to kill missionaries. The missionaries noted a marked difference between the extremist *Jeunesse* who had been trained outside the province and were ready to commit any outrage, and the local people of Kwilu, who were far more moderate and even protected Europeans against the others.

President Kasavubu declared a state of emergency on January 21. Mulele's faction, claimed the *Hindustan Times* of New Delhi on December 29, 1963, had received from Communist China 200 airplane tickets "obviously to and from Peking" for the training of military cadres from the Congo, under the direct supervision of the Chinese War Academy.

By January 31 the Bishop of Idiofa was reporting to his superiors: "The catastrophe is considerable and has already surpassed the most pessimistic predictions: we mourn . . . three first-class missionaries . . . twenty-four missions out of twenty-eight have been evacuated; some of these set afire . . . all are delivered up to looters."

The President of the Kwilu provincial assembly noted in an official report that Gizenga's PSA had been working in close league with Mulele's tribal terrorists to stir up the region. "Since October 1963," he said, their "purpose was to boycott all the legally established institutions, from the Chief of State to the provincial governments."

Mulele did not act alone. He had a highly mobile field headquarters. Behind him was the "Committee of National Liberation" (CNL) in Brazzaville, a motley grouping of Lumumbists and malcontents led by Christophe Gbenye that sent him arms and money. Third was a group in Leopoldville itself, headed by Bernardin Diaka, who had long been Gizenga's representative in Peking. Another pro-Chinese agent in Leopoldville was Thomas Mukwidi, who returned from Peking just before a plot to assassinate President Kasavubu, Premier Adoula, Justice Minister Justin Bomboko and General Mobutu was smashed in March 1964. Mukwidi escaped and joined the CNL in Brazzaville.

Even as the war spread in Kwilu, Moise Tshombe was preparing one of the most sensational political comebacks of modern times. The economic position of the increasingly discredited Adoula regime was fast deteriorating, despite the hundreds of millions of dollars poured in by the United States, the United Nations and Belgium. The central government had little authority outside Leopoldville, let alone in the twenty-two other provinces. Disease and hunger were rampant.

After some discreet dickering with the Adoula government from his Madrid headquarters, Tshombe published his own version of Lumumba's death. This implicated Adoula and thus advanced Tshombe a step closer to collaboration with the CNL in Brazzaville, where recognition of Peking in February and the later arrival of a Red Chinese ambassador, Chou Chiu-yeh, made the CNL's liaison with Peking much simpler. On July 15, Tshombe announced the release of the imprisoned Gizenga as the first step toward the "national reconciliation" he sought.

Meanwhile, another Chinese-supported revolt was underway in eastern Kivu province, bordering Burundi, where Peking's logistical base was the Chinese mission in Bujumbura.

To understand the importance of Burundi to the Chinese effort in the Congo, we must return to the wars between the Watusi and the

Bahutu of Rwanda and Burundi, which we looked at briefly in connection with the refugee situation in Uganda. Both Rwanda and Burundi had won their independence in July 1962. Burundi then became a focus of Chinese Communist attention. Rwanda was its deadliest rival.

The young Watusi Mwami, or King, Kigeri V, began a comfortable exile in Belgium, then moved to Kenya. About this time, the Communist bloc began to show sympathy for the Watusis on the grounds that "Belgian imperialism" backed their former serfs. To forestall United Nations intervention the Belgians set up a Rwanda government of Bahutus. An anti-Communist clause was inserted in the Rwanda constitution. In the meantime the "Royalist" Watusi were becoming firmly anti-Belgian, anti-Catholic and anti-American. Mwami Kigeri V began to collect a regular pension from Peking after settling in Kenya. The New China News Agency sent Kao Liang, one of its correspondents, to spread the good word among the 21,000 Watusi refugees in Tanganyika that the time was coming when they would return in triumph to their rightful homeland, Rwanda. Liaison was set up with the "Inyenzi" (Cockroach) movement of the Watusi terrorist vindicatory organization.

In November 1963, 3,000 Watusi armed with 2,500 spears and 20 rifles set out to invade Rwanda. Some got to within twelve miles of Kigali, the Rwanda capital. The republican Rwanda government got Belgian help against the wave of eleven further raids that followed, and it launched vicious reprisals. United States diplomatic sources estimated that about 2,500 Watusi were killed (not 15,000 or 25,000, as some press reports said) and that some 180,000 refugees in all fled, most to the Congo.

Up to the time of the first Watusi raid the Rwanda regime had been one of the most stable and hard-working in Central Africa. The raids shook it badly, particularly after the Chinese role was revealed. A Chinese attaché assigned to Peking's embassy in Kampala was in an automobile accident. The tracts and other documents found in his car proved Peking's involvement with the Watusi. The principal Chinese headquarters in the area was Room 21 in the Paguidas Hotel in Bujumbura, the capital of Burundi. Chinese money had been handed over for the Watusi operation in dollars. It was used to buy arms from U.N. soldiers, Congolese army men and others.

The *Guardian* of London reported on February 12 and 15, 1964, that Peking had paid Watusi terrorists several thousand pounds at irregular intervals. The Rwanda chargé d'affaires in Bonn told a news conference that three Communist Chinese and a Czech helped to train Watusi tribesmen raiding in Rwanda. Modern Chinese and Czech mortars and machine guns had been captured from the Watusi. The real head of the pro-Chinese Communist movement in Rwanda was the ex-king, Kigeri V, *Le Progrès* of Leopoldville reported on January 30.

Rwanda's Catholic Premier, Gregoire Kayaibanda, did not move to stop the reprisals against the Watusi. Burundi protested to the United Nations, which effected nothing either. Burundi recognized Peking on the very day of the Watusi raid, and an anti-Western wave seemed to roll through the parliament and government. Rwanda broke diplomatic, customs and financial ties with Burundi. Overnight Bujumbura became one of the principal Chinese Communist bases in Central Africa.

Burundi politics, under the intelligent but feudally advised king, Mwambutsa IV, were mostly absorbed by clan warfare. The Chinese in the country employed bribery—slipping banknotes into envelopes with documents given to ministers was the most common method—flattery and all manner of intrigue to gain the favor of Burundi's chief ministers. One Burundi official complained that nearly every night at dinnertime a Chinese embassy car would arrive before his home in Bujumbura. A Chinese attaché would alight from the car, come to the front door, and ostentatiously embrace him on the doorstep of his own home: this identified him publicly with the Chinese and was highly embarrassing.

Meanwhile the Chinese installed a training camp at the town of Murore for 10,000 Watusi refugees from Rwanda. Six Peking-schooled Watusi taught the refugees military tactics. Arms were unloaded from the freighter *Ho-Ping* and other ships at Dar es-Salaam and shipped overland to Kigoma in Tanzania and various points in Uganda and Burundi. (Later, in the winter of 1964-65, they were supplemented by Soviet arms flown from Algeria and Egypt to the Sudan.) The arms were then divided between the Congo rebels and the Watusi refugees.

In early 1964 the Burundi Premier was Pierre Ngendamdumwe, who seems to have had only the interests of his country at heart. When he went into retirement he was replaced by Alban Niamoya, more inclined toward Peking. The affairs of Chinese Ambassador Liu Yu-feng prospered, despite the defection of one of his young attachés,

Tung Chi-ping, to the American embassy on June 1, from which he was whisked away to the United States in August, carrying a seventy-two-page report on Chinese activities in Africa. The Niamoya government signed a trade and payments agreement on October 22: China was to deliver cotton textiles, rice, pharmaceutical products, steel and machines in exchange for Burundi's cotton, coffee, hides, peanuts and other raw products. In November, Niamoya aligned Burundi in a public statement with Peking's position on the need for a world-wide conference to ban nuclear weapons. André Muyumbu, director of the Ministry of Foreign Affairs and Foreign Trade, went to Peking in December and conferred with Chou En-lai.

But King Mwambutsa had a change of heart. On December 19 the Burundi parliament passed a censure motion against Niamoya. The reasons given were Burundi interference in the Congo, which the Tshombe government had bitterly protested, and "severity in tribal disputes." On January 7, 1965, the King dismissed him and replaced him with Ngendamdumwe. On January 15 a Burundian accountant who happened to work for the American embassy, Gonzalve Muyenzi, shot and killed Premier Ngendamdumwe. The King declared marital law, threw a cordon of troops around the Chinese embassy, and ordered Ambassador Liu and his staff to leave for meddling in Burundi affairs.

The embarrassment in Peking was visible: this was its first major diplomatic setback in Africa. The Chinese Foreign Ministry ascribed it to "pressure of U. S. and Belgian imperialists." By March 1965 the Burundi government had absolved both the U. S. and China from any responsibility in the shooting of Ngendamdumwe. Foreign Minister March Manirakiza said ties with China would be restored as soon as the situation in Burundi "returned to normal."

Meanwhile the CNL in Brazzaville, Bujumbura and elsewhere appeared to have assumed main control of the Congo rebellion. Communist influence, Chinese and otherwise, seems to have been limited during this period to propaganda, discreet advice and encouragement, and a few arms. The CNL found a temporary ally in an unexpected quarter: a force of former Katanga gendarmes, operating as a dissident group from bases in Angola. Their presence on the frontier, or near it, immobilized units of the already hard-pressed Congolese National Army. Tshombe moved to repatriate these gendarmes after he became Premier in July 1964. The Sino-Soviet quarrel showed through in the early rivalry between the two main figures in the CNL.

Christophe Gbenye, who at first leaned toward Moscow, was close to being eclipsed by André Lubaya, who shared Mulele's affinities for Peking. Later Gbenye became the leading figure.

The CNL seemed to have some serious supporters in Leopoldville itself. In addition to politicians like Kiwewa, and others of the old Gizenga clan, there were numerous young students who had studied in China and other Eastern countries and returned: Peking's solicitude for Congolese students in the first months of independence was already paying off. A group of CNL emissaries arrested at Coquilhatville carried money, propaganda material and Chinese guerilla instruction manuals printed in French. The new thing about these instructions was that they mentioned how to incite units of the regular Congolese Army to mutiny.

Tshombe included André Lubaya as Minister of Health in his new government. Evidently he hoped that Lubaya would be able to help arrange a truce with the CNL, and perhaps with their Chinese mentors. Peking, however, let out all the stops against Tshombe, calling his return to power "an American imperialist plot." The Chinese-oriented faction of the Belgian Communist Party, whose leader Jacques Grippa had just been visiting Peking, chimed in.

The role of Grippa and his party, both before and after he switched allegiance from Moscow to Peking, had to be discreet. White European Communists have never been popular in the Congo, where they are commonly referred to as *les sales blancs rouges* (the dirty red whites). This is one more reason why Peking, like Moscow, searches eagerly and constantly for Africans willing to follow the orthodox Communist line, without reservations and without reference to "African socialists" like Nkrumah, Sékou Touré or Ahmed ben Bella of Algeria.

By January 1964, some Soviet arms were arriving in Brazzaville. Premier Adoula showed newsmen in Leopoldville some revolvers shaped like cigarette lighters and rifles with telescopic sights, seized on the Congo river ferry from nearby Brazzaville.

In late April a Red Chinese freighter arrived at Pointe Noire to deliver a 75-watt radio transmitter destined for the CNL, which was installed near Brazzaville, the better to coordinate the various revolts in different regions of the Congo. Before finding permanent quarters the CNL had been lodged in the police station of Brazzaville by the chief of police of Premier Pascal Lissouba's government. The CNL sent emissaries abroad to collect funds. Its biggest training camp in the Congo (Leopoldville) was at Brabanta in Kasai province, and it operated another at Gambona, in the Congo (Brazzaville).

Averell Harriman noted the threat, though he seemed to underestimate it, in a news conference in Washington on April 3, 1964, as the United States stepped up its military aid to the Adoula regime. After a week's fact-finding tour in the Congo for President Johnson, Harriman listed the Communist-backed action and "difficulties . . . coming from Angola and assisted by the Portuguese," by which he meant the remnants of Moise Tshombe's gendarmerie, as the two main dangers the Congo faced.

For Peking, the Congo (Brazzaville) as a base of operations had both advantages and drawbacks. The former French Congo (129,000 square miles, about 8 million people) was chosen by General de Gaulle in 1944 as the scene of an important African conference where constitutional rule in the French African territories was advanced. It had kept its close ties and good relations with France after voting in 1958 to become a self-governing member of the French African Community. These ties, were, in the main, an asset to Peking. The Abbé Fulbert Youlou, a defrocked priest who had ignored the Communist world and ruled in collusion with right-wing French interests, had been overthrown by a popular revolution on August 15, 1963. French troops in Brazzaville evidently received orders from Paris not to interfere, after at first resisting the rioters. But Peking at first did not have clear sailing. Soviet-bloc activities were increasing in Brazzaville. The Catholic labor unions played at least as important a part in Youlou's overthrow as those under French Communist influence.

Such influence, however, was not lacking in the new government. Alphonse Massemba-Debat, who had been assistant to the Education Minister in the first African government, and then President of the National Assembly, became President. He had been a member of Youlou's *Union Démocratique,* but had often been openly critical of Youlou and his policies, though he had never had close ties with the Communists.

Annette, the wife of Premier Pascal Lissouba, was another story. She was reported to be an influential member of the French Communist Party. She contributed each week to the Communist weekly *Dipanda,* printed on the official Brazzaville government press. *Dipanda* was edited by two Congolese students, Ndalla and Lounda, who had recently returned from Moscow. *Dipanda* supported the Mulelist rebellion in Kwilu.

The Lissouba government was the first African regime in the former French Community to recognize Peking after the de Gaulle government gave recognition on January 27, 1964. But French influence declined rapidly.

Red China's usual advance guard in a new zone of interest, the New China News Agency, arrived first. Premier Lissouba and Justice Minister Pascal Okiemba conferred with correspondents Tsien Se-kieh and Cheng Liang-ping on March 23. In the meantime they had received the usual greetings from the Chinese-African Friendship Association and the Chinese Afro-Asian People's Solidarity Council. Pierre Boukambou, general secretary of the African General Confederation of Labor, who had been instrumental in overthrowing Youlou, received an invitation to Peking from the All-China Trade Unions. Another official, Paul Banthoud, spent a month in China.

For a very brief spell, Brazzaville toyed with the idea of recognizing "two Chinas." A Nationalist Chinese Embassy was already there. This was a test case for other African countries. On April 10 the first Red Chinese chargé d'affaires, Kan Mai, arrived in Brazzaville with a five-man team to open the first embassy. Foreign Minister Charles Ganao was quoted by *West Africa* of May 2, 1964, as commenting: "If we can keep diplomatic relations with Taipeh at the same time as we make links with Peking, and thus bring the two sides to co-exist in the Congo, we shall have pulled off an exploit here that no one up to now has managed." The Lissouba government did not manage either: Nationalist Chinese Ambassador Sampson Shen soon left.

Only one day before Kan Mai arrived, Foreign Minister Ganao summoned the American chargé d'affaires, Hendrick van Oss, to scold him for Harriman's statements about Brazzaville support for the revolts in the former Belgian Congo, the New China News Agency reported. So sensitive was Brazzaville about publicity for the CNL that on June 9 Ganao also summoned the British chargé d'affaires to protest an article in the *Sunday Telegraph* describing the arrival of the radio transmitter and also mentioning the return to the Gambona training camp of partisans schooled in the Peking guerilla operations center since 1961.

Ambassador Chu, when he arrived in June, was well alerted to the possibilities of internal strife that existed within the former French Congo. Maurice Thomas, a correspondent of *Le Figaro,* reported on June 18, 1964, that the government was riddled with a "spy complex" and fear of a possible counter-revolution, as well as apprehension that many Europeans who left "on vacation" would not return.

The Catholic labor federation, despite its contribution to overthrowing Youlou, was resisting integration into the general "revolutionary" program. Even Abbé Youlou, who was interned, still had supporters left: they were largely in his own Laris tribe. But despite what was at least toleration of the CNL, the Lissouba regime seemed determined to follow a "non-aligned" foreign policy. It needed good relations with both France and the United States, which it hoped would finance a dam on the Kwilu River.

By early 1965 Ambassador Chu and his staff had firmly established in Brazzaville Peking's most important bridgehead—and probably its most solid one—in West Africa. Lissouba's one-party National Revolutionary Movement had come to reflect Chinese foreign policy and the principles of "scientific socialism." Fifty more Chinese diplomats swarmed over Brazzaville and the surrounding countryside. Chinese military advisors appeared at the CNL's camps in Impfondo and elsewhere.

Dipanda and Radio Brazzaville were being actively advised by members of the New China News Agency staff. Chinese aid came to match that of France. The radicals in the National Revolutionary Movement pushed aside the Catholic groups and formed Chinese-line labor unions and women's movements and made use of the paramilitary organization of young people called the *Jeunesse* (not the same as the Congo rebels' organization) to terrorize and sometimes to eliminate their opponents. They almost certainly murdered the President of the Supreme Court, Chief Justice Joseph Puabou; the Attorney General, Lazare Matsokota; and Anselme Massouemi, director of the Congolese Information Agency. All had been moderates, as well as partisans of Abbé Youlou.

Though in October 1964 Massemba-Debat had highly praised General de Gaulle and his policies, Paris watched the Congo situation with mounting alarm. Some 1,200 French troops, the last remnants of the garrison, were due to leave under French redeployment schedules before the end of 1965. Their departure, and the resulting drop in French spending, coupled with an influx of refugees from the Leopoldville side of the river, were certain to bring further complications for what looked like the first recognized "People's Republic" along quasi-Chinese lines in West Africa.

In Burundi, the CNL representative had been another Congolese without any known background of Chinese training, Gaston-Emile Soumialot. He was, in fact, with Martin Kassongo, the co-founder of the Bujumbura branch of the CNL in 1963. Newsmen in Bujumbura frequently encountered him just before or after his visits to the Chinese Embassy in the Paguidas Hotel, where he even occupied a suite next to the embassy once for a time. Soumialot dressed in leopard skins and liked to carry an ivory-tipped swagger stick: these picturesque accoutrements fitted in with his frequent invocations of tribal magic. In August 1964, Soumialot led the rebel forces that captured Stanleyville. Christophe Gbenye named him "defense minister" in the Stanleyville regime that Gbenye headed, before the rebel camp broke apart in quarreling factions in 1965. Then his chief assignment became liaison trips to Cairo to discuss military aid with the Egyptians and Algerians.

Western newsmen in 1964 were occasionally able to penetrate those camps of the partisans of Soumialot and other rebel leaders that were inside the Congo (Leopoldville). In June 1964 a Belgian and two Americans visited Soumialot at his headquarters in the Ruzizi Plain. One of Soumialot's associates, "Colonel" Louis Bidalira, standing amid a threatening crowd of rebel "simbas," told the newsmen that Belgians were welcome but Americans were not, because "The Americans are attacking us." This referred to air strikes by light T-28 aircraft of the Congolese National Army, which the New China News Agency claimed over initial American denials were being flown by American pilots who had contracted directly with the Congolese government. Ruefully the State Department had to confirm the story after Western media picked it up, and applied pressure to stop it. Anti-Castro Cubans and others were being hired to pilot the planes in an operation to interdict rebel supplies that appeared to be managed by the Central Intelligence Agency, possibly in conflict with State Department policy.

The next development in the rapidly decaying Congo situation was a mutiny of Congolese army troops, this time at Albertville, in North Katanga province, on May 27. Albertville, a city of 150,000 on the western shore of Lake Tanganyika, is a vital port on the lake, and, as the New China News Agency pointedly commented, "a large center of communications for the Eastern Congo." Government troops were reported to have retaken Albertville. The leader of the revolt was arrested and taken to Elizabethville for trial, after more than 100 lives had been lost in North Katanga. Said Radio Peking on June 2: "The struggle of the patriotic forces at Albertville will go on."

A referendum held in nearly all provinces beginning June 20 gave widespread approval to a new draft constitution, the essential feature of which was to strengthen the powers of the President, still Joseph Kasavubu, and to make him chief of the central government. The Chinese propaganda media pooh-poohed the referendum. Terrorists made grenade attacks in the Leopoldville area in attempts to disrupt the voting, killing and injuring a number of people. The referendum was followed, as planned, by the resignation of the Adoula government. Moise Tshombe, after secret negotiations that had taken him from Madrid to Bamako and Brussels, announced he was returning to the Congo to bring about "a general and sincere reconciliation."

The initial Chinese reaction to Tshombe's return was hostile, though not so hostile as that of the Soviets, who called for U.N. action against Tshombe. When Tshombe formed his coalition government, giving himself the top posts of Prime Minister and Foreign Minister and also the portfolios of Information and Foreign Trade, Radio Peking expressed satisfaction with his decision temporarily to suspend anti-rebel operations, and to free all of the Congo's several hundred political prisoners. The fact that immediately after Tshombe's prior secret talks with President Modibo Keita of Mali in Bamako, Keita's top aide, Economics Minister Jean-Marie Koné, left hurriedly for a long visit to China was probably coincidental. It was certain, however, that Koné would inform Peking of Tshombe's intentions as fully as he possibly could.

Tshombe's first cabinet, formed July 10, included only two figures from past regimes. One was Godefroid Munongo, Interior Minister, who as Tshombe's own iron-willed Interior Minister in Katanga had successfully defied the United Nations in the old days, and who had been instrumental in his return. The other was the picturesque and ruthless "King" Albert Kalondji of Kasai, who was given the Agriculture portfolio. The Adoula men were out of the cabinet, and there were no prominent Lumumbists.

Tshombe's efforts to negotiate met with no success. By August 12, 1964, it was admitted that the rebels controlled one-fifth of the national territory. On August 5 the rebels took Stanleyville. By September 7, Christophe Gbenye had proclaimed "The People's Republic of the Congo," with Stanleyville as its "capital." Soumialot was appointed "Defense Minister." The U.S. appeared committed to full support of Tshombe, despite a rising tide of African hostility against him. President Johnson said he would "attempt to see that the people of the Congo have as good government as possible." After the fall of

Stanleyville, Washington and Brussels conferred and decided to maintain their technical assistance to Tshombe and the Congolese National Army, but not to send troops as Tshombe wished.

G. Mennen Williams, U.S. Assistant Secretary of State for African Affairs, indicated on August 18 that the U.S. would be willing to contribute costs of maintaining African troops in the Congo, if the Organization of African Unity was willing to send them. He said the rebellion was being fomented by "external" Chinese Communist forces (chiefly the staff group working under Colonel Kan Mai, the military attaché in Brazzaville). But the OAU, whose "militant" members, especially Algeria, the U.A.R. and Ghana, were determined to topple Tshombe if they could, refused to send troops. Tshombe, for his part, continued to use his hated white mercenaries from South Africa, Rhodesia and elsewhere as the spearhead of his otherwise ineffectual army.

Tension rose throughout Central Africa. On November 5, 1964, Gbenye announced on Stanleyville Radio that due to bombing raids by U.S. planes "all Americans and Belgians in liberated areas are considered to be prisoners of war, and this measure may also be extended to their allies." Gbenye agreed to delegate one of the rebels' ablest diplomats, British-educated Thomas Kanza, to negotiate with the Americans, and offered to allow President Jomo Kenyatta of Kenya, chairman of the OAU's *ad hoc* Congo commission, to visit Stanleyville. By mid-November missionary circles reported that "liquidation lists" were being drawn up.

In the November 13-14 edition of the rebel newspaper *Le Martyr* Gbenye wrote: "We will make our fetishes out of the hearts of Americans and Belgians, and we will clothe ourselves in the skins of Americans and Belgians." After careful deliberation at the highest levels U.S. transport planes ferried Belgian paratroops to a staging area on Britain's Ascension Island, then dropped them on Stanleyville on November 23, the morning after Gbenye broadcast another message telling the rebels to "grill the hostages alive." None of the appeals for release of the hostages, including those of Kenyatta and the U.N. Secretary-General, U Thant, had been of any avail. Arrival of the paratroops coincided with the recapture of Stanleyville by the Congolese National Army. Peking and Moscow took the lead in a great world chorus of protest; Nigeria was the only significant exception in all Africa. Many African countries believed Gbenye's claim, broadcast by the Voice of Kenya, that not a drop of blood had been shed before the paratroops arrived. But they ignored the fact—in reporting the undoubtedly real Congolese Army atrocities against the population—that rebel action had accounted for the murder of at least 20,000 Congolese. (President Joseph Kasavubu insisted the figure was far higher.)

In the U.N. Security Council, Belgian Foreign Minister Paul-Henri Spaak revealed that he had had secret talks with Gbenye, to no avail. U.S. libraries and information centers in close to a dozen countries were attacked or burned. Never before had Peking's tone been so jubilant.

After a vituperative Security Council debate had introduced what U.S. delegate Adlai Stevenson termed "the ugly spectre of racialism," the Council managed to agree on a resolution asking all states "to refrain or desist from interfering in the domestic affairs" of the Congo. Algeria, the U.A.R., Uganda, the Sudan and some other African states, however, continued; and Moscow, anxious not to be overtaken by Peking, freely underwrote their efforts.

Despite dissension in his own ranks, Gbenye strengthened his ties with Peking. He gained strength, too, from a meeting on January 14, 1965, at Mbale, Uganda, with Presidents Kenyatta and Nyerere and Prime Minister Obote, with the consequences we have already seen. The OAU took a few hesitant, positive steps. They sent a subcommittee to Leopoldville, Brazzaville and Bujumbura, and dropped their earlier condition that Tshombe withdraw the mercenaries before they would consider his complaints about outside African and Communist interference. The entire issue of Chinese subversion in West and Central Africa was considered at a meeting of thirteen French-speaking states at Nouakchott, Mauritania, in February: they set up a new "Common Organization" and agreed to meet in January 1966 at Tananarive, Malagasy.

After delays and postponements, Tshombe's government held national elections during April 1965. Tshombe received official support in areas where tribal allegiances were in his favor and in some others as well. His supporters took heart at signs that the rebel leadership was disintegrating. Tshombe himself claimed total victory at a news conference on May 7. Optimistic reports of rebel successes formerly carried by Communist and other news media favorable to the rebels, especially China, Algeria and the U.A.R., had nearly disappeared by the summer of 1965.

In March and April 1965, the Congolese National Army's white mercenaries had sealed off rebel supply routes from the north and northeast. Government forces controlled the principal towns and roads. They captured large amounts of abandoned weapons and ammunition, which the Leopoldville regime said were mainly of Russian and Chinese origin, flown in during the winter airlifts from North Africa. At this point the U.A.R. suspended its arms deliveries, realizing that they were only going to swell the Tshombe government's stockpiles.

On April 26, 1965, rebels in Cairo announced the formation of a "Supreme Council for the Revolution" with Gaston Soumialot as president. This did not supersede Gbenye's rebel "People's Government." Confusion and dissension mounted in rebel ranks. Though Gbenye and his two main rivals, Pierre Mulele and R. Bocheley-Davidson, were elected members of the council, they took no part in the meetings that set it up.

Moscow Radio described the split between the rebel factions with just a bit of relish, probably because many of the rebel leaders involved had been identified with the Chinese. The CNL in Brazzaville —the faction now in closest contact with Chinese diplomats—was now led by Bocheley-Davidson, who had little personal following. Pierre Mulele led the *Jeunesse* movement in Kwilu province of the Congo (Leopoldville). Finally, there was Gbenye's more recent "revolutionary committee" of the *Mouvement National Congolais-Lumumba* (MNC-L), based in the Eastern Congo. Gbenye had previously seized control of this from another group, consisting of Laurent Kabila, Moise Marandura and Gregoire Amisi. Gbenye and Bocheley-Davidson, as Moscow Radio correctly reported, were engaged in a personal vendetta. Soumialot had also quarreled with Gbenye.

Antoine Gizenga, in African eyes the most legitimate "heir" of Lumumba, re-interned by Tshombe after their brief reconciliation in July 1964, had never firmly and publicly backed the insurgents. "Foreign Minister" Thomas Kanza, after his diplomatic role in the Stanleyville affair, was living in Nairobi and playing no visible part in Congolese politics. More, Gregoire Mwamba-Mukanya, one of the very few rebel leaders with international standing—gained through winning the Moscow-directed World Peace Council's Gregoris Lambrakis prize in 1964—was one of the rebel leaders to accept Tshombe's offer of an amnesty and to return to Leopoldville. Mwamba-Mukanya publicly denounced the lack of democracy in the

Congolese "People's Republic." He attacked the "massive extermina-
tion of the civilian population," the "destruction of economic and
social structures" and the embezzlement of funds by Gbenye, Soumialot and "General" Victor Olenga, the rebel commander at Stanleyville. All three had taken huge quantities of gold and cash when they
fled the stricken city.

If the Chinese had expected the complete disintegration of the
Leopoldville regime, or success by rebels favorable to themselves, the
events of 1964 and 1965 disillusioned them. But their position of
strength in Brazzaville and their growing network of listening posts in
bordering states made it certain that they would seek their own profit
in the new Congolese turmoil that probably lay ahead.

CHAPTER FOURTEEN

Peking and Portuguese Africa

PEKING HAS HELPED TO UNDERMINE PORTUGAL'S AFRICAN EMPIRE, which the authoritarian regime of Dr. Antonio de Oliveira Salazar considers part and parcel of an almost mystic "Portuguese Community." At the same time it has found the "revolutionary situation" in the Portuguese overseas empire to be less promising than in the Congo.

Yet in early 1965 Portugal was seriously considering opening diplomatic relations with Communist China, despite Peking's repeated declarations of support for the rebels in Portuguese Angola, Mozambique and Guinea. Portuguese Foreign Minister Franco Nogueira told one Western journalist: "There are no serious reasons for not recognizing Peking, and many reasons for doing so."

Two of Portugal's main reasons for not antagonizing Peking are in Asia, not Africa. They are Portuguese-ruled Timor, in Indonesia, and Macao, on the China coast. Timor is subject to pressure from the Jakarta government and therefore indirectly from Red China. Macao is a small peninsula and two islands opposite Hong Kong. Lisbon attaches both sentimental and commercial value to Macao, which it has ruled for over four centuries. Macao and the Red Chinese mainland authorities are on excellent terms.

Both Peking and Lisbon benefit from this state of affairs. Profitable East-West trade of all sorts passes in both directions through Macao. Lisbon, which has maintained diplomatic relations with the Chinese Nationalists, seems to have toyed with the idea of trying out the "two

Chinas" policy of recognizing Peking while keeping up relations with Formosa. Portuguese newspapers and public opinion sided with Red China in the Sino-Indian border conflict. This was because India had seized Goa and the other Portuguese enclaves in India in December 1961.

Portugal's holdings in Africa include Angola (488,000 square miles, 4,145,266 people), Mozambique (297,657 square miles, 5,732,317 people), Portuguese Guinea (14,000 square miles, about 700,000 people), the Cape Verde Islands (1,516 square miles, about 150,000 people) and the islands of São Tome and Principe (372 square miles and about 60,000 people). All are considered integral parts of metropolitan Portugal and are called Overseas Provinces. They represent a considerable remnant of the vast, world-wide empire that Portugal began to build when she was the world's leading colonial power in the fifteenth century, before being eclipsed by Spain.

This long colonial past deeply influences not only the official policy of all Portuguese governments but also public opinion in Portugal. The Portuguese are proud of what is officially said to be the lack of racial discrimination in their African territories. In Peking's propaganda beamed to Portuguese Africa it is interesting to note the relative lack of racist themes used elsewhere. Concentration is rather on classical anti-colonialist themes, and of course on the United States as senior NATO ally of Portugal, and on American investment in the Portuguese African territories. Peking does, however, stress "African" ethnic and tribal themes as opposed to Portugal's ruling philosophy that in imparting its civilization to Africans it must also give them its language, customs and religion, in order for them to become what used to be called officially *assimilados,* or persons fully "assimilated" into the Portuguese way of life.

Lisbon has made considerable efforts in health, education, social welfare and even administrative reform since the revolt in Angola broke out in 1961. This was partly because of widespread criticism in the outside world of forced and "contract" labor, which was widespread until officially eliminated in 1963. Lisbon watches over the territories, as it watches over metropolitan Portugal, through one of the most efficient, effective and ruthless political police forces in the Western world, the PIDE, or *Policia Internacional e Por la Defesa del Estado.*

One by one various nationalist groups have arisen in the territories, or, more often, have attempted to bore into them from their places of exile abroad, especially Ghana, the Republic of Guinea, the two Congos, Tanganyika and Uganda. Training camps, propaganda centers, newspapers or bureaus of liaison and logistics also exist in such places as Algiers, Cairo, Addis Ababa, New York and London. During the embryo years of revolt in Portuguese Africa, 1960–63, Peking's active role in fostering these movements was evidently far behind that of Moscow. Beginning in 1963, however, there were signs of vastly increased Chinese Communist interest in Portuguese Africa.

One of the first Soviet-encouraged African organizations was FRAIN, or Front Revolutionaire pour l'Independence Nationale des Colonies Portugaises. This was set up in Conakry in 1959 and 1960 with the blessings of the Soviet Ambassador to Guinea, Daniel Solod, a veteran African specialist who failed in his attempts to encourage pro-Soviet subversion in Guinea. Even at that time, Peking showed that it was interested in the revolutionary potentialities of Portuguese Africa. On December 7, 1960, for example, the *People's Daily* reported that the Communist summit conference in Moscow had discussed the "next phase in the liberation of Africa." Angola was to be dealt with first, then Portuguese Guinea.

The first revolt took place in Angola three months later, with a rising led by the leftist MPLA (Movement for the Liberation of Angola) in Luanda, the capital. This followed shortly after the seizure of the liner *Santa Maria* in January 1961, by Captain Henrique Galvao, acting under orders from General Humberto Delgado, leader of non-Communist resistance to the Salazar regime in European Portugal. General Delgado told me that it had been planned that way, and that there had been "some coordination" between his "Iberian Revolutionary Directorate" and the MPLA. Delgado and his Brazilian secretary were murdered while on a clandestine mission to contact Delgado's followers in Portugal from Badajoz, Spain, on the frontier, in February 1965. The Spanish government announced on May 8, 1965, that it had confirmed that the bodies were indeed those of Delgado and his secretary. The General's supporters generally agreed that the PIDE was responsible, though the tone of press dispatches from Lisbon indicated that Portuguese officialdom desired to blame the murder on Delgado's Communist rivals in the opposition movement.

General Delgado told me in 1962, just before an unsuccessful attempt to provoke a military uprising at Beja, Portugal, on New

Year's Day, 1963, that he had planned to sail the *Santa Maria,*
rechristened for the moment the *Santa Liberdade,* to Spanish Guinea
and establish an African beachhead there. This would have made it
possible for his partisans in Angola, mainly anti-Salazar Europeans,
to extend the movement of revolt into the main body of Portuguese
Africa. The *Santa Maria* got no further than Recife, Brazil. After a
series of adventuresome but unsuccessful attempts to stir revolt in
Portugal itself, and to conclude coalitions with the various African
nationalist groups, General Delgado traveled in 1963-64 to Prague,
and then to a new base in Algiers, where he led an anti-Salazar
"National Liberation Front" that included the Portuguese Communist Party. After Delgado's murder, his Communist rivals sought
full control of the movement.

Red China was the first Communist power to initiate Portuguese-
language broadcasts, beamed both to European Portugal and to
Africa, in September 1960. But Peking appeared to be definitely
committed neither to the MPLA nor to its more pro-Western rival,
the Union of Angola Populations (UPA) of Holden Roberto,
founded clandestinely in 1954. The UPA draws its supporters largely
from the Bakongo peasants in northern Angola and the southern
Congo. Partly for this reason, the Congolese authorities in Leopoldville, its main rear base for the guerilla war it launched in March
1961, favored it over the MPLA. Congo President Joseph Kasavubu
is himself a Bakongo.

The MPLA corresponds far more to old-fashioned Soviet Communist ideas of a revolutionary party. Its main leader has been Mario
Pinto de Andrade, born in Angola in 1928. He was an accomplished
poet and a graduate of universities in Lisbon, Paris and Frankfort.
He worked in the underground Portuguese Communist movement,
had close French Communist Party contacts and went to Warsaw and
Moscow in 1955. French police questioned him after his return to
Paris from an Afro-Asian Writers Conference in Tashkent in 1950
because they found documents on him indicating contacts with Peking. In several articles for *Pravda,* Andrade revealed the Marxist
ideological bases of the MPLA. At a Conference of the Nationalist
Organizations of the Portuguese Colonies in Casablanca in April
1961, both Russian and Chinese "observers" sought to strengthen
their ties with Andrade.

The MPLA was founded underground in 1957. It had some European members. Its most distinguished African founder, apart from

Andrade, was Dr. Agosthino Neto, who "escaped" from house arrest in Portugal, possibly with Portuguese complicity, in 1962 and since then has evidently played only a limited role. He does not give the impression of a forceful personality. The MPLA, unlike the UPA, has a long and detailed program for redistribution of land and elaborate political and social reforms.

None of the many attempts by the MPLA and the UPA to form a common front were successful. An African Unity Organization commission that investigated both in the summer of 1963 found that the UPA had the only effective guerilla force. Its troops have been reported by various sources to number anywhere from 5,000 to 15,000. They operate from advance bases in the frontier zone between the Congo (Leopoldville) and Angola. At various times they have controlled more or less large portions of northern Angolan territory adjacent to the Congo but probably never more than 5 per cent of Angola even after the terrible massacres of the spring of 1961, when the revolt was at its height, and Lisbon was rushing in troop reinforcements. By January 1965 the revolt had lost most of its momentum. The MPLA claimed control of some guerilla units inside Angola, but its main strength seemed to be concentrated at cafe tables and coffee bars in Algiers, Rabat, Accra, Cairo, Moscow and London.

The MPLA, the Communist bloc and the Portuguese government all accused Roberto of being "pro-American" or a "tool of the Central Intelligence Agency." They based this, apparently, mainly on Roberto's contacts with the American Committee for Africa in the United States, and his background of education by American Protestant missionaries. His leadership was challenged by Jonas Savimbi, the twenty-five-year-old Foreign Minister in Roberto's "Provisional Government of Angola," who resigned in July 1964. Roberto suffered a gradual eclipse due to delay in deliveries of arms and financial aid and in guerilla training, difficulties that were aired in the African Summit Conference at Cairo in July 1964 and various other later meetings. The Congolese authorities were reluctant about letting weapons pass through Congo territory. They were slow to release funds made available by the African Unity Organization.

Roberto met Marshal Chen Yi and other Chinese officials at the Kenya independence ceremonies in Nairobi in December 1963 and afterward announced that a UPA delegation would visit Peking to discuss arms aid. But whether Roberto actually received much real aid from Red China is doubtful. The Portuguese were skillfully exploiting the differences between Roberto and his followers, and between Roberto's group as a whole and the MPLA.

In 1963 the MPLA split into one faction headed by Dr. Neto and another under Viriato da Cruz. The first, after measures taken against it by the Leopoldville government, crossed the river and set up its headquarters in Brazzaville. The second, in April 1964, associated itself with Holden Roberto's "Revolutionary Government of Angola in Exile" (GRAE). Viriato da Cruz, based mainly in Algiers, and his followers in Leopoldville, are strongly influenced by the Peking line. Neto's faction is more sympathetic to Moscow. Some of its leaders, such as Lucio Lara, are said to be former or present members of the Portuguese Communist Party. Neto himself has no Communist background. In 1965 the MPLA in Brazzaville was an army of officers with very few troops: intellectuals with no mass base. Until it became clear just who was to lead the Angolan national movement, if anyone, it seemed probable that Peking, true to its pragmatic policy throughout Africa, would avoid a definite or lasting commitment to any of the groups concerned.

The Chinese did continue to diffuse communiqués of Roberto's "Army of National Liberation" under an Algiers dateline. They reported, for example, on May 26, 1964, that the Army had "liquidated" several score of Portuguese soldiers and captured a large quantity of war material during the period May 3-16. They claimed partisan attacks not only in northern Angola but at Piedras Negras and Dangi Ia Manha, about 80 miles southeast of Luanda, and at Mussende, in central Angola, about 120 miles south of Luanda. They also reported partisan attacks to the north in the little Portuguese enclave of Cabinda, separated from the main part of Angola by the mouth of the Congo River. In Cabinda the CNL in Brazzaville would have an easier time channeling Chinese or other arms to the partisans. MPLA elements were active in Cabinda.

If all the Angolan movements finally transferred their main base from Leopoldville to Lusaka, Zambia, Peking could tighten its liaison with all of them through its first-rank diplomats working in East Africa, such as Ho Ying. At the same time Algiers, with both UPA and MPLA offices, would continue to be an important rear base. Official Algerian sources told me that Chou En-lai, during his visit in December 1963, promised that China would make a solid contribution toward continuing a guerilla training school near Algiers. This school's alumni, believed to number 1,500 in 1963, were being sent all over Portuguese Africa, as well as to staging areas north of South Africa.

Almost unnoticed by the West in the welter of African news was a classic guerilla war of the Indochinese type fought between the Portuguese and their African opponents in the jungles, swamps and bushlands of Portuguese Guinea. This war began in earnest on January 24, 1963. By the summer of 1964 the rebels and the Red Chinese were echoing claims to control 40 to 60 per cent of the mosquito-ridden tropical territory, whose main crops are rice and peanuts.

Portuguese Guinea was first settled in 1470. Lisbon trained many African administrators, proportionately more than in the much vaster territories of Angola and Mozambique. African rebellion began to smolder during World War I, erupting into uprisings that were ruthlessly suppressed in 1917, 1928 and again in 1936. Since 1955 it has been governed like the other African territories as a full-fledged Portuguese province.

Among 750,000 African inhabitants, more than 99 per cent are illiterate, and so had no voting or civic rights. Life expectancy for the Africans is about thirty years. There are probably close to 30,000 lepers.

The most active and by far the most important of several nationalist groups is the African Independence Party of Guinea and the Cape Verde Islands (PAIGC), founded in 1956. Its chief is Amilcar Lopes Cabral, a cultivated, soft-spoken Cape Verde Islander who is an agronomist by profession and a revolutionary by vocation. He was educated in Portugal and has a knowledge of the political salons of Paris and London. When I met him at the Addis Ababa African summit conference in May 1963, he impressed me as the epitome of the educated African leader, determined to impart some sort of national existence to "the other Guinea" or "Bissau Guinea," as the nationalists call it after the name of the coastal town that is its capital.

Cabral himself has compared the guerilla war in Portuguese Guinea with that in Vietnam. Otto Hapsburg, the pretender to the Austrian throne, and a sympathizer with white rule in Africa, made the same comparison in his book *Européens et Africains, L'Entente Nécéssaire* (Paris: Hachette, 1963). When he visited Portuguese Guinea in the summer of 1963, Hapsburg found that Commandante Vasco Antonio Rodrigues, the air force officer who took command of the Portuguese troops at the outbreak of the rebellion, had, like

Cabral, carefully read Mao Tse-tung on guerilla warfare, and so was applying "counter-insurgency" tactics of his own. Dr. Hapsburg says that a group of Cabral's cadremen first went to Peking in July-November 1960 and that the first regular training courses in Communist China were given to them in September-December 1961. He adds that more guerillas were trained for Portuguese Guinea in Czechoslovakia and that in the summer of 1963 a new group of twenty Africans, after basic training in Ghana, went to Peking for more training before returning to the Republic of Guinea. Another non-Portuguese Western source reported that some of Cabral's men had completed a six-month course in guerilla training in Peking by August 1963.

Cabral politely declined to answer my own questions about outside aid and training of his revolt. He admitted to a Tunisian reporter that some "military men" had "studied in Algeria, Morocco, Ghana and Guinea" but never outside Africa. Only "delegations" had visited Russia and China. "We count mainly on ourselves," he said.

Nighttime guerilla operations began in 1962. The Republic of Guinea was PAIGC's main base, despite some difficulties with President Sékou Touré's government. Cabral's men, using the Viet Cong tactics of fighting by night and hiding by day, while gradually winning the villagers and peasants to their side, managed to gain control of a broad triangle of territory adjacent to the border on the southwest side. By night they struck at isolated Portuguese garrisons—which had to be supplied by air—communications lines and the farms and villages of those white Portuguese settlers and their African friends who had not been "regrouped" for safety in one of the better-defended coastal towns, fenced off by barbed wire, such as that around Bissau. Isolated and sporadic attacks gave way to steady pressure after the attack in force that penetrated the region of Fulacunda in January 1963.

Another guerilla front was opened in the north from the Republic of Senegal, where President Senghor's government allowed truck convoys to cross the border from the Casamance region of Senegal into Portuguese Guinea with arms and supplies. Retaliatory Portuguese air strikes and the Portuguese use of napalm to burn "hostile" villages often led to tension between Lisbon, Conakry and Senegal. Neither of the latter maintained diplomatic relations with Portugal by 1963.

The PAIGC held its first congress on the soil of Portuguese Guinea in "liberated" territory on the Geba River, February 13-17, 1964, according to Cabral. It created regional sections of five to seven members, who chose local committees to look after public health, primary education and maintenance of civil records.

Most of PAIGC's first leaders were townsmen of Bissau, or educated mulattoes from the Cape Verde Islands. Many were involved in a disastrous dock strike in 1959 in which fifty Africans were killed. By the time guerilla operations had begun, the PAIGC was concentrating on building up a following among the peasants. Its troops are mainly Africans who live from subsistence agriculture. Their lives have always been miserable, and most probably they felt they had nothing to lose and perhaps everything to gain by fighting the Portuguese. This makes the Portuguese Guinea revolt an ideal situation for Red China.

Whatever the real degree of concrete Chinese aid—and even for Portuguese intelligence, this is one of the most difficult places to assess this in all Africa—the Peking information media call them "the people's fighters of Guinea." Peking disseminates their communiqués issued in Conakry and Algiers, and glorifies their successes to the maximum. The Chinese Afro-Asian Solidarity Council regularly announces collections of funds for the PAIGC.

In Casablanca I monitored a typical Red Chinese report on the fighting on June 6, 1964. The French-language African service of Radio Peking, in a dispatch supposedly filed by a correspondent on the spot, said that the guerillas had been fighting heroically "in the tropical forests against modern arms . . . furnished by the clique of imperialists with the United States at their head." Cabral, Peking reported, had just returned to Conakry after a trip to the battle zone, and had visited war wounded.

In 1962, said Radio Peking, the rebels "used all manner of weapons, such as arrows, spears, swords, shotguns, pistols against the modern-equipped Portuguese forces." They learned to camouflage their camps and hideouts with brush and palm leaves. After training, and "through their own efforts," they learned to use better arms. With bases in the "liberated regions" now secure, a regular flow of food and supplies was assured to the guerillas. For this reason, Africans were fleeing to these "liberated" zones.

There was a hint of action in the Cape Verde Islands in the statement that "the relationship of forces in Guinea and Cape Verde has greatly changed. The situation is favorable to the people and unfavor-

· able to the enemy." The broadcast distinguished between "the People's Revolutionary Army, the popular militia and the actual guerilla units," though it did not specify the difference between these three types of formations, the nomenclature of which was familiar from Chinese Communist usage during the Chinese revolution.

Lisbon seemed determined to hang on, fearful lest the loss of Guinea should create a bad example for its administration elsewhere or lower morale in the Portuguese armed forces. A new administration under a new governor was appointed in 1964. He was a tough military man of German extraction named Schulz. Cabral hesitated to form an "exile government" as Holden Roberto had done in 1962 for Angola. On numerous occasions he expressed regret that Roberto, as he claimed, had refused all contact with PAIGC. Instead PAIGC maintained close relations with the MPLA of Mario de Andrade, especially through its offices in Conakry, Rabat and Algiers.

It appears likely that the Portuguese will, in fact, be obliged to give up Guinea. Despite the presence of 20,000 troops, with strong air and naval support, and the expenditure of vast amounts of escudos from the overworked defense budget, Lisbon seemed to have scored no spectacular gains against the rebels by 1965.

Once some sort of independent state has been established in Bissau, there is likely to be a scramble to divide it between Sékou Touré's militantly neutralist Republic of Guinea and Léopold Senghor's cautious, pro-French government of Senegal, the two neighbors that have served as bases for the rebellion.

Apart from some of the usual exchanges of delegations, Peking made no real progress in Senegal until the fall of 1964. Senghor's decision to recognize Peking seems to have been dictated partly by the indiscretions of Chen Hou-jou, the Nationalist Chinese Ambassador. On September 7 the Senegal Foreign Ministry announced severance of relations with Taipeh and Chen's expulsion. He was accused of "corrupting Senegalese officials" and especially of violating the rules of diplomatic usage by inviting Babacar Diac, a press officer of the Foreign Ministry, on a private visit to Taiwan despite the Senegalese government's opposition. Relations were opened with Peking a short time later.

If Peking wished to pursue a double-faced policy in Senegal, its new diplomatic emissaries in Dakar could support the Parti Africain de l'Independence, which had some affinities with the PAIGC of Guinea. Senghor had prohibited the party, which had already caused him trouble during election riots in December 1963. However, it seemed more likely that the Chinese would bide their time and content themselves with building up their new listening post in the strategic Atlantic coastal port of Dakar.

Mozambique, until the autumn of 1964, had remained an East African haven of peace and, for the white Portuguese settlers, of relative prosperity. From Red China's viewpoint, the "revolutionary situation" was none too good. Race relations were not disturbed. In the 1950 census there had been nearly 60,000 Asian residents, mainly Goans and Indians, as well as a few Chinese. Most of the Goans and Indians were repatriated to India after Nehru seized Goa in December 1961. Like Angola, Mozambique exports its products mainly to Portugal. These include sugar, cotton, tea, copra, cashew nuts, sisal and vegetable oils. South Africa and the Rhodesias are important customers too. The Portuguese Foreign Ministry has acknowledged that there is some Mozambique trade with Red China.

The two most important African movements that have set their sights on Mozambique are the older and smaller Democratic National Union of Mozambique (UDENAMO), founded secretly in 1960 inside Mozambique, and the Mozambique Liberation Front (FRELIMO) of Dr. Eduardo Mondlane. FRELIMO was the result of the merger of several smaller groups in 1962, and Mondlane unsuccessfully tried to incorporate UDENAMO into it. Dr. Mondlane is a former United Nations official and professor at Syracuse University. FRELIMO's base is in Dar es-Salaam. Peking has shown considerable interest in both UDENAMO and FRELIMO. After Dr. Mondlane visited Peking in November 1963, serious moves to unite all of the Mozambique movements began. They had achieved no notable success by mid-1965.

Mondlane, in an exclusive interview that reached me from Lagos in the spring of 1964, predicted a "well-coordinated" revolutionary action throughout Mozambique by November 1964.

Forays by terrorist groups based in Tanzania, and sponsored both by UDENAMO and FRELIMO, did, in fact, begin in October 1964. The Portuguese had expected them and were ready. About 25,000 troops were deployed to meet the poorly and sporadically trained "freedom fighters" from the Tanzanian camps. About 8,000 refugees streamed across the flat marshes and bushland separating Mozambique from Tanzania. The Russian-trained Tanzanian Army unit was moved from Zanzibar to the border, but it misbehaved so badly that

President Nyerere had to move it back again. The raids into Mozambique looked to many observers like rather frantic attempts by the OAU's Committee of Nine to prove that it was serious about "liberation" of Mozambique. The Chinese gave their usual propaganda support to the operations, but otherwise seemed to be holding their hand for the time being.

After Moscow Radio quoted Mondlane, during a visit to the U.S.S.R., as thanking the Soviets for their "aid," the Portuguese authorities in Lourenço Marques showed some signs of nervousness. General Carrasco, Commander-in-Chief of the army, declared flatly that Tanganyika "is in danger of becoming the major base for subversion in Central and East Africa." He said Soviet and Chinese ships had been sighted off the Mozambique coast, but outside territorial waters.

Lisbon is commonly believed to have an unpublished understanding with the governments of South Africa and Southern Rhodesia about military assistance in time of need. South Africa's main stake in Mozambique, apart from African contract labor that it hires from there for its mines, is in keeping open the rail and road links across the mining area between Johannesburg and Lourenço Marques and Beira, farther north. This would probably continue after an African government took over in Southern Rhodesia. Northern Rhodesia, now Zambia, needs both the railroad westward to Benguela in Angola and eastward to the Mozambique ports.

Malawi is also hardly a promising base for revolution in Mozambique because, as we have seen, it needs its outlets to Beira and Nacala, another Mozambique port. There is a Portuguese military plan to strike swiftly at Malawi, across Lake Nyasa, separating the two countries, cutting Malawi in half inside of a few hours in case of any rebel invasion from its territory. Dr. Hastings Banda, Malawi's first Premier, has long had an agreement with the Portuguese that there would be none.

Peking began a vigorous propaganda campaign on Mozambique in May 1964. It opened with a New China News Agency dispatch from Dar es-Salaam on May 23, quoting FRELIMO's organ, *Mozambique Revolution,* in an appeal to the Mozambique people "to prepare for the armed struggle for liberty." Comparisons were drawn between the coming struggle for Mozambique and those in Cuba, Vietnam and Algeria. "We must develop an anti-colonialist culture," *Mozambique Revolution* said. The struggle would be not only against Portugal "but also against other imperialist countries that are pillaging the country, such as the United States."

The *Peking Review* in June 1964 quoted Leo Milas, a former Mexican Army officer with a California background who had been supervising liaison and training of Mozambique partisans in Algeria, as declaring that "we are left with no alternative but to win independence through armed revolution." It added a quote from Paul Jose Gumane of UDENAMO: "Armed force . . . is the only language that Salazar and his ministers can understand."

On May 25, New China reported "panic" among Portuguese settlers, the parachuting of 2,500 troop reinforcements into the region, and "massive arrests and persecutions." But the attacks that did get underway in the autumn of 1964 began slowly and inauspiciously. Mozambique, in fact, looked like one of the toughest nuts in the Portuguese empire for Peking or anyone else to crack, though if all-out racial war began in southern Africa, Mozambique might blaze up with the rest.

CHAPTER FIFTEEN

Socialism in West Africa

IN THE INDEPENDENT AND MILITANTLY NEUTRALIST WEST AFRICAN states of Ghana, Guinea and Mali, Peking has attempted to profit from the errors of the Soviets and the Soviet satellites. Cautiously, it has avoided asking for political support in return for the aid it has provided these countries since 1959. Evidently the Chinese consider that the entire area, especially Guinea and Mali, are assets to its African policy because they are established and authentic centers of "African revolution," even though their socialism has leaned far more toward the home-grown African variety than toward the "scientific socialisms" of either Moscow or Peking.

Ghana, because of its natural wealth and the visionary pan-Africanist doctrines of its President, Dr. Kwame Nkrumah, must have certainly appeared interesting to the Chinese when they began their African adventures at Bandung in 1955. As a leader to cultivate, Nkrumah had the asset of having led his country ever since 1952, when he became Prime Minister, five years before the British-ruled Gold Coast, as Ghana was called then, won independence.

Nkrumah has shown an increasing penchant for personal power. He has created virtually a one-party state ruled by his Convention People's Party. Despite this and his considerable aid to African revolutionary movements, and his frustrated dreams of a single government for all of Africa with himself at its head, Ghana was not a zone of significant early Chinese success.

One of the reasons for this was Ghana's continued strong attachment to the Commonwealth. Dr. Nkrumah showed this again at the Commonwealth Prime Ministers' Conference in London in July 1964, where he came forward with some interesting suggestions for strengthening the Commonwealth.

Another reason is Nkrumah's unmistakable mistrust of Communism in practice, however warm his welcome for Communist support of his own anti-colonialist vision of Africa and the world. This mistrust was strongly shown on numerous international occasions. One was the All-African People's Conference at Accra in December 1958 and January 1959. Nkrumah warned that "colonialism and imperialism" may "come in a different guise—not necessarily from Europe." Despite keynote speeches by Paul Robeson and the late American Negro Communist prophet of pan-Africanism, Dr. W. E. B. Dubois, the East bloc lost in their attempts to win control of that meeting.

Nkrumah has also confided to various African diplomats and statesmen, including the late King Mohammed V of Morocco, his dislike of the Afro-Asian solidarity organizations. He had already proven this by inviting only the Egyptian section of the Solidarity Council, and none of its Communist ones, to the Accra Conference already mentioned. Nkrumah's frequently heard appeal of "Africa for the Africans" looked like a clean break with Bandung and Afro-Asian "solidarity." As such, it was just as discouraging to Chinese ears as to Russian ones.

The year 1961 was vitally important for Ghana's relations with the Communist world, and for Nkrumah personally. In that summer he toured Eastern Europe, the Soviet Union and Communist China. The trip began in Moscow July 10 and ended in Peking on August 20. During it, Nkrumah made it clear that he would not take sides in the developing Sino-Soviet split. This remained true into 1964. After the Russian portion of his tour, the Soviet-Ghanaian communiqué supported the "immediate restoration of the legitimate rights of the Chinese People's Republic in the United Nations."

During his seven-day visit to China, which began August 13, Nkrumah said at a state banquet given by Chairman Liu that China's admission to the U. N., which Ghana has always supported, "raises the fundamental question of the structure of the General Assembly itself." He advocated complete revision of the U.N. organization to "represent the present balance of forces."

During this same Chinese tour, Nkrumah further showed his independence by implicitly backing the Soviet and American theses on the overwhelming need to ban the "catastrophe of nuclear war." After conferring with Chou En-lai he went to Hangchow as the guest of Mao Tse-tung. Here, before a mass rally of 100,000 on August 18, he uttered what must have been, to Chinese ears, the supreme heresy for a visiting African guest: "Today we hear . . . of Afro-Asia, which does not make sense. Africa is Africa."

Nevertheless the visit ended with the signing of a Ghana-Chinese friendship treaty and agreements on economic and cultural cooperation and trade and payments. Ghana was promised an interest-free Chinese loan of about $20 million—less than Guinea had received a year earlier from Peking. In return, Nkrumah backed China against India in the Sino-Indian border dispute.

Since then Ghana has reportedly opened the port of Takoradi to Chinese Communist arms bound for partisans in Angola and elsewhere in southern Africa. Nkrumah has inaugurated several Chinese trade exhibitions. Whereas in 1960 Ghana sent only six delegations to Red China, and received none in return, in 1963 thirteen Ghanaian delegations visited Peking, which sent four of its own to Ghana.

In one respect, Ghana has leaned more toward Peking than to Moscow. In the continuing debate among Africans on how to deal with colonialism and "neo-colonialism," it has generally favored violent revolution. Nkrumah's editors and propagandists have stiffened their line against the British upon such occasions as the British intervention in the East African army mutinies. They have shown their outspoken hostility to the idea of an East African Federation, and toward President Nyerere of Tanganyika and Zanzibar. But they mitigated their anti-American campaigns in the spring of 1964, when Washington made it clear that this might have serious consequences on the large American aid program for Ghana, notably support for the Volta Dam scheme, which for Ghana is nearly as important as the Aswan Dam is for Egypt.

Nkrumah's theatrical escapes from numerous attempts on his life by domestic opponents have always brought effusive congratulations from the Chinese, as from the rest of the Communist world. When Chou En-lai, Chen Yi and the Red Chinese delegation visited Ghana during their African tour on January 11-16, 1964, Chou delivered a personal message from Chairman Mao accusing "imperialists and reactionaries" of attempts on his life. This was well timed to coincide with explanations of the episode in the controlled Ghanaian press.

The joint communiqué after Chou's visit was in general if not complete agreement with Chinese policies. It declared that the new Afro-Asian Conference of June 1965, desired by Peking, was "necessary" and that active steps should be taken to convene it, whereas a sort of super-conference of "Afro-Asian-Latin American peoples" was "desirable."

Among the results of the visit were a second $20 million credit accord in technical assistance and money, signed on July 15, and an offer to send Peking's rice experts to Ghana to help diversify an agricultural production that has depended on cocoa as its main export crop. This would end imports of rice, a food becoming popular in Ghana. In 1965 Peking agreed to buy more cocoa, industrial diamonds, manganese ore and timber from Ghana, and sell the country more meat products, oil products, chemicals, textiles, sewing machines and hardware, all on the usual barter or compensation basis. Peking promised to take part in the big Accra Trade Fair in 1965.

Negative aspects of Chou's visit were highlighted in a release by Tanjug, the news agency of Yugoslavia, a socialist country that is highly popular in Africa and that actively opposes Red Chinese policy. A Tanjug commentary on January 22, 1964, said that Ghana was dissatisfied with Chou's visit. Aid promised in 1961 had turned out badly, or not materialized at all in some lines. In his statements on Ghana, Chou never mentioned the ruling Convention People's Party. Chinese support for Nkrumah, said the Yugoslavs, was lukewarm because Peking's policy was actually "to wait for fresh forces more revolutionary-minded than the present ones, which emerged from the anti-colonial struggle."

Certainly Commonwealth, United States and even Soviet aid to Ghana had so far outstripped that of China that Peking's assistance seems almost microscopic by comparison. Moscow buys 60,000 tons of Ghana's cocoa or more each year. It has sent considerable heavy machinery not available from China. It has built industrial plants of various sorts, and operates Ghana Airways with its Illyushin jets.

Peking has discussed with Accra possible Chinese participation in the Volta Dam project. To step up its already considerable distribution of English-language propaganda, Peking through the Chinese Embassy in Accra regularly supplies the Nkrumah Ideological Institute in Winneba with books and brochures.

Ghana was certain to become the focus of new efforts by Peking to penetrate the African labor movements. In May 1964 the neutralist All-African Trade Union Federation moved its secretariat from Casablanca to Accra. John Tettegah, the vehemently anti-colonialist and rather anti-Western boss of the Ghana Trades Union Congress, became general secretary. Originally created in May 1961 by Mahjoub ben Seddik of Morocco's Union Marocaine du Travail (UMT), who remained president, AATUF's secretariat had included representatives of Morocco, Algeria, Guinea, Ghana, Mali and the United Arab Republic.

Now, after its second congress in Bamako in May 1964, the secretariat was expanded to include unionists from Tanganyika (including the Labor Minister), Senegal, Gambia and about fifteen other countries. It was committed to rivalry with the pro-Western African Trade Union Confederation (ATUC), based in Dakar. It was determined to end all affiliation of African unions with either Communist- or Western-controlled labor internationals. Since very few unions in Africa were still connected with the Moscow-directed World Federation of Trade Unions (WFTU) in Prague, this meant that AATUF would turn its guns, now aimed from Accra, principally on the anti-Communist International Confederation of Free Trade Unions (ICFTU) in Brussels, with affiliates in twenty-four African countries. For this reason, Peking showed pleasure at the new development. Western labor experts expected a major increase in activity by the Chinese labor attaché and his staff in Accra as a result. The Ambassador, Huang Hua, one of Red China's most capable English-speaking diplomats, had already been quietly strengthening his staff for months.

Nkrumah's particular brand of "African socialism," as outlined in his book *Consciencism* (London: Heinemann, 1964), looks like a challenge to Communism in Africa in all its forms, especially the Chinese. He calls the thesis of "consciencism" a new "philosophy and ideology for decolonization and development with particular reference to the African Revolution." He retouches Marxist theory and tries to adapt it to African conditions. Nkrumah denies that class struggle is essential to achieve an "African socialist" society, and does not insist on violence as the only means to achieving a "people's" government.

The Spark, Accra organ of the Ghana Institute of African Affairs, became the principal journalistic organ of "Consciencism." It advocated not only a continent-wide African government but also one mass political party for all of Africa. It would have three components: a few governments and ruling parties that are openly "socialist" and aspire to be more so; mass organizations that exist under governments considered "neo-colonialist"; and the revolutionary organizations set up to liberate the remaining colonial territories.

None of this is very promising grist for the Chinese mill. At least until such time as power in Ghana passes into other hands, Peking's direct influence seems most likely to be exerted mainly through whatever aid it can send to "revolutionary" movements through Accra.

Of all the states of the former French-speaking African Community, Guinea was the only one (130,000 square miles, 2 million people) to vote "no" to retaining its French economic and cultural links in the French referendum of 1958. The French left indignantly, taking anything with them that had made the economy operate. This and the deserved reputation of its President Sékou Touré for militant anti-colonialism, which brought a flow of political exiles from all over Africa to Conakry, made it look to the East bloc like an especially promising target.

Guinea had been brought forcibly under French rule between 1883 and 1911, not without a great deal of resistance and bloodshed. Sékou Touré, the son of poor peasants who claims descent from Almany Samory, a Guinean national hero who fought the French bitterly in the 1880s, rose through the ranks of trade unionism to build his Parti Démocratique du Guinée into a "mass party." His contacts with world labor leaders, both Communist and otherwise, and his term in the French National Assembly beginning in 1956, gave him a valuable background in practical politics at home and abroad. Touré founded Black Africa's first independent trade union movement, the Union Générale des Travailleurs de l'Afrique Noire (UGTAN). The Communist WFTU immediately tried to penetrate it.

Despite these circumstances and its one-party system, Guinea has what many Communist purists would call a "national bourgeois government." Sékou Touré has warned that "Communism is not the way for Africa." Like Nkrumah he is a leading exponent of "African socialism," which tries to adapt and change Marxist theory to suit African conditions of underdevelopment.

Since Guinea voted itself out of the French Community in 1958, the Chinese have been working in competition rather than in cooperation with the Soviets. Pei Yen, the Red Chinese Ambassador to Morocco, visited Guinea in April 1959, and brought 5,000 tons of rice with him as a gift. In October, China and Guinea signed a cultural agreement and agreed to establish diplomatic relations. During the same year Guinean diplomats like Abdoulaye Diallo, the Guinean envoy in Ghana, were making contact with the Communist bloc governments and with the world-wide Communist front organizations, then largely dominated by the Soviets and their satellites. Antoine Gizenga, the leftist Congo leader, and Dr. Felix Moumié, the Cameroon rebel chief, visited Guinea. In the same year, Soviet aid, much of it inept and ineffectual, began to pour into the country. By 1964 the Soviets, who had suffered many bitter experiences in Guinea after a clumsy attempt to subvert President Touré's regime in 1961, seemed to be reducing their commitments while the Chinese were increasing theirs.

Sékou Touré visited Peking in September 1960. The Chinese went out of their way to demonstrate to him that their policy in Africa was in fact separate from that of the Soviets, and that they were signing the first big "treaty of friendship" with an African country. An initial interest-free loan of $25 million was granted. This was supplemented by a new and unpublicized protocol signed in Peking in May 1963. This provided a smaller quantity of newer aid, which may have been military in nature, possibly destined in part for Amilcar Cabral's guerilla fighters in adjoining Portuguese Guinea.

Apart from the experiments in rice culture, which have been reportedly quite successful, Chinese economic aid to Guinea through 1964 concentrated on building a tobacco and a match factory and several roads. Two large shipments of heavy Chinese goods arrived in Guinea in 1963, including a big caterpillar crane, trucks and the Red Flag automobiles already seen in the country in 1961 and 1962. Guinean teachers and students went to China by the hundreds, though few have stayed there long. China needs and imports Guinea's raw rubber, coffee, industrial diamonds and other raw materials, just like any capitalist country. In return it has bartered its construction materials, medicines, textiles and, of course, books and periodicals. Some of these were brought by the first Red Chinese freighter to visit West Africa in January 1963.

How Chinese economic aid compares in quantity with that of the rest of the East bloc shows up in figures on aid to Guinea's three-year development plan published November 7, 1963, by the Conakry newspaper *Horoya* (Liberty): the Soviet Union, $75 million (the most given by Russia to any African country except the United Arab Republic and Algeria); Red China, $25 million; Czechoslovakia, $12 million; Poland, $4.2 million; Hungary, $2.52 million; East Germany, $2.52 million; and Bulgaria, $1.96 million.

An inquiry into the quality of Chinese aid and its reception in Guinea usually leads to such remarks as these, coming from a Western diplomat stationed in the country and in a position to watch Guinean reactions: "Few of the personnel of the Communist-bloc embassies or missions, except the Chinese, have attempted to employ local labor, or have made much of an effort to learn local languages.

"The Chinese have an entirely different approach. They stress manual labor and do not hesitate to perform the humblest tasks, as in road-building, along with the Guineans. Their rice experts and their engineers live like the Guineans, in native villages, without PX or commissary privileges, earning no more and eating no better than the Guineans they work with. They create an impression of frugality and austerity. As a result, they are far more popular than the Western missions and their air-conditioned offices, big cars, and the rest."

Jon Randall, West Africa correspondent of *Time* magazine, described for me the activities of a Chinese construction gang, imported to work side by side with the Guinean laborers.

In the past the Soviets and Czechs had made the mistake of sending their own foremen, who knew no French or African languages, and who were, of course, white men. This did not work at all. The Chinese sent laborers and foremen who, instead of trying to supervise the Guineans, said: "Let us have socialist competition. You work on that part of the road and we'll work on this. We'll see who finishes the best job first." The result, Randall observed, was always the same: the Guineans came out ahead. It was, he said, "rather like playing golf with the boss."

One Western official source reported that Chinese diplomats stationed in Guinea "seem to have been chosen for their intelligence and courtesy." Peking takes pains to see that under no account do they resemble the popular African image of a burly, sweating white man who issues orders—the way in which the Chinese propaganda now depicts the Russians, as well as the Americans.

A Western-backed project in Guinea that Peking watches with jealous eyes is the Compagnie Fria. This treats the country's vast bauxite deposits to produce over 400,000 tons of alumina each year, the largest production in the world. President Touré has given Fria, a consortium of the Olin-Mathieson Chemical Corporation of the

United States, France's Pechiney-Ugine, the British Aluminium Co., Ltd., and West German and Swiss firms, iron-clad guarantees against nationalization. The firm employs about 900 Guineans and 400 Europeans. Other Western ventures that the Guineans look with favor on have been the return of some of the French teachers who left in 1958, a large and active United States Peace Corps contingent, a modest but appreciated United States Food for Peace Program running under $20 million annually since 1962, and a good United States Information Agency program. This was unfortunately curtailed in 1963 when President Touré ordered foreign libraries and information centers closed.

During their African tours Chou En-lai, Marshal Chen Yi and the delegation from Peking spent January 21-27, 1964, in Guinea. On the eve of their visit Conakry Radio reported establishment of direct radiotelephone and telegraph communications between Conakry and Peking. The final communiqué found that both countries believed "conditions exist" for calling a second Afro-Asian Conference and that preparations should be made for it. Sékou Touré was far more noncommittal after again listening to China's side of the Sino-Indian border dispute: the Guineans said they "heard with interest" China's explanations of its "efforts to reduce tension" along the Sino-Indian border.

During a mass meeting on January 23, Chou En-lai criticized the Soviet doctrine of peaceful coexistence. His speech was well covered in the Guinean press. Guineans, reported the Tunis newspaper *Jeune Afrique* on March 23, 1964, were "extraordinarily impressed" by the fact that the Chou mission was the only foreign delegation that had visited Guinea since independence without having passed out advice, asked for anything, or insisted on anything from its hosts.

Among the Guineans Peking has singled out for special favor are Barry Arbaba, a journalist active in the Chinese-sponsored Afro-Asian journalists' activities, trade unionists and leaders of women's organizations of the ruling *Parti Démocratique du Guinée* (PDG). In May 1964, Yang Sieu-feng, Red China's Minister of Education, visited Guinea during a larger African tour and promised Peking's aid to Guinea's education, probably in the form of additional grants for study in China. Peking and Conakry signed a new cultural agreement on this occasion, which was later supplemented by one signed with North Korea. Chinese technicians were assigned to work on the Kinkon hydroelectric dam.

Despite continued disillusion with the Soviets over non-fulfillment of their aid projects—the only major one on schedule was extension of the runway at Conakry airport, which the Russians needed to operate flights to Cuba—the Soviet Communist Party was managing to keep abreast or even ahead of the Chinese in tightening links with the PDG. In May 1964, Guinean emissaries attended the French Communist Party Congress as "fraternal delegates." There were increases in exchanges of party and other delegations between the Soviet Union and Guinea. Alexei Voronin was appointed new Soviet Ambassador, doubtless with instructions to avoid the mistakes of the unfortunate Daniel Solod.

In November 1964 there was a reorganization of the PDG that appeared to be not unconnected with Soviet influence. Instead of the "mass party" that had been an article of faith since Sékou Touré rejected the idea of a ruling "elite" in 1959, membership was now restricted to "activists who have proved themselves." Senior officials who had not been sufficiently active would be dismissed. Private traders could not belong.

The cabinet reshuffle announced by President Touré on November 8 reflected a strong swing leftward by the PDG. More "activists" were included in a sweeping party reorganization that also involved dismissal of the Minister of Commerce and creation of six new secretaries of state. Stringent moves against rampant currency smuggling and speculation accompanied a drastic move back toward increased state control of trading and nationalization in a reversal of liberal measures announced in September 1963.

In the same November actions, the number of private traders was cut from 25,000 to 5,000. Renewed stress was placed on the formation of farm cooperatives to counter the growing drain on the rural labor market caused by the industrial and infrastructure needs of the Seven-Year Plan.

Annette Stiefbold, a political scientist at Columbia University, has pointed to interesting similarities between the structures and functions of the Chinese Communist Party and the PDG—similarities that are certainly not lost on the Chinese. In both countries there has been a gradual abolition of the competition between the party and the civil service, to the benefit of the party. The units in the PDG rise from the Unités du Travail, at the lowest echelon, up through village and neighborhood committees to the sections, which correspond to Guinea's larger administrative divisions. In China there is a similar progression from the party group up through the branch, the general branch, to the commune committee. (No attempt has been made to introduce communes into Guinea.)

Both the PDG and the Chinese Communist Party are modeled on a non-Western agrarian society. Each used Marxism-Leninism for its guidelines, and Guinean references to the Chinese experiment have included a statement of Touré's to the effect that the two movements grew up in "identical historical circumstances, working for the same objectives." Each has adopted as its three guiding principles the slogans of "popular dictatorship, democratic centralism and the mass line." The latter principle, which requires a continuous mystique, depends on a highly disciplined and coordinated party structure.

If the Chinese exploit these similarities and continue to improve their position in Guinea, and are not caught trying to subvert President Touré's government, as were some of the Russians and Czechs, it may provide them with an excellent base for future West African operations. Conakry might, for example, provide a platform for the subversion of Spanish Guinea, which Madrid wishes to hold with the looser rein of internal autonomy. It has already proved useful, as we saw, as a staging area for Amilcar Cabral's guerillas in Portuguese Guinea. But Sékou Touré's insistence (which he reaffirmed to me in conversations I had with him in Rabat in 1958 and Addis Ababa in 1963) on his disdain for doctrinaire "scientific" socialism would tend to keep Guinea, like Ghana, out of the zone of strong Chinese pressure as exerted in East and Central Africa.

The Mali Republic (582,000 square miles, about 4 million people) is another former French African territory with a tradition of political radicalism. The French conquered a territory roughly equivalent to present-day Mali from bases in Senegal, but the boundaries of the so-called French Sudan, of which it was a part, were often changed. Most of Mali, unlike tropical Guinea, is desert or semi-desert, but some parts include extremely rich agricultural land.

Mali's ruling party, which has produced such leaders as President Modibo Keita, is the *Union Soudanaise,* originally a territorial branch of the *Rassemblement Démocratique Africain* (RDA). It was founded at Bamako in 1946. The French Sudan and Senegal, both then still under French rule, formed the Federation of Mali. This was named after the great Mali Empire, which had attained a high degree of civilization in the Africa of the thirteenth and fourteenth centuries.

The Federation won independence within the French Community in June 1960 but broke up less than three months later, basically because Sudanese ideas of "African socialism" were more radical and Marxist and far less favorable to close dependence on France than were those of the Senegalese rulers. The Sudanese part of the Federation took the name of the Republic of Mali.

Mali is a full-fledged socialist state, ruled by one authoritarian party. The government carries out decisions made by the party's nineteen-man politburo, which is dominated by President Keita. The official foreign policy of the country is non-alignment. Mali's socialism is strongly "African" in tone. Hard work and pragmatism are valued virtues at all levels of its new society. The Communist countries have probably committed fewer blunders, political and economic, in Mali than in Guinea. But apart from individuals there is probably no sentiment in the country that the East bloc in general or Red China in particular holds the answer to Africa's well-being, or even Mali's.

Various visitors have reported nervousness about the continued presence of a large French colony. Occasionally President Keita has warned French residents that they must not interfere in domestic affairs. The Chinese too, however, have been quietly warned, notably on the occasion of a door-to-door campaign in favor of the Chinese trade exhibition held in Bamako during December 1963-January 1964.

Modibo Keita is a six-foot-four-inch, husky African born in 1915 of a wealthy and powerful family of the Bambara tribe. Like Sékou Touré he has sat in the French parliament, and showed an early interest in neutralism and personal independence of East and West. In 1961, following the neutralist Belgrade Conference, he visited President Kennedy in the United States and afterward said that the world's problems could be solved if Khrushchev showed the same spirit of good will as Kennedy.

Peking's activities in Mali began in full force in February 1961, with the visit of a trade mission headed by the Chinese Vice Minister of Commerce. The Mali Foreign Minister commented after his first visit to Peking that China was "advancing at a dizzy pace" and in its economic reconstruction was demonstrating a "most remarkable test of the capacity for development of underdeveloped countries." The exchange of delegations skyrocketed from two Mali delegations to China and one Chinese delegation to Mali in 1960, to seven each way in 1963.

Several new Red Chinese projects in Mali were timed to coincide with the general period of the visit of Chou En-lai, January 16-21, 1964. An agreement on cooperation between Mali and Chinese broadcasting services was signed November 30, 1964. A one-month Chinese "exhibition of economic construction" opened in a pavilion on the banks of the Niger River in Bamako on December 29, just next door to American and Russian exhibitions. On December 31, Bamako Radio announced that China was to assist Mali in building factories making cigarettes, watches, sugar, vegetable oils and a cotton mill. The amount of financial aid was not disclosed. Peking's agricultural specialists, who had been working for Mali for some time, were revealed to include experts in tea, construction, rice, sugar cane and water conservation. They were receiving salaries not exceeding $80 monthly, as opposed to three times this level paid to experts from other Eastern bloc states. Chinese aid was to be governed by the "eight points" that are supposed to guide all of Peking's assistance to underdeveloped countries (see Appendix B). In Chou's public remarks to Modibo Keita he again stressed that the Chinese technicians were to have the same standard of living as "the experts of the recipient countries and no special amenities. . . . Doubtless we are a great country, but an underdeveloped one. In our country we have the same worries you have."

Modibo Keita told Chou, according to Bamako Radio: "You have understood that we are in a hurry, and you have avoided the error of people who are attempting the conquest of space before completing the liberation of man on earth," a slap at both Russia and the West. In the final communiqué Mali said that like China it was not interested in the "new Belgrade" meeting of non-aligned powers (held in Cairo in September 1964) but was very eager to back a "new Bandung" Afro-Asian Conference.

After a fifty-two-day tour of ten countries in the Far and Middle East in 1964, President Keita returned wearing Chinese costume. He delivered a speech in Bamako November 28 in which socialism, especially the Chinese variety, came in for some of the warmest praise ever voiced by Africans. Socialism was neither naturally repugnant to good Moslems and Christians, nor, he added, really a doctrine that sacrificed the individual:

That is a falsehood which we should no longer believe. A man can develop all of his aptitudes only in countries where there is people's democracy. . . . In capitalist countries . . . we see the places where men are robots. We are robots too because we have not yet been fully decolonized: this is the heritage of the capitalist regime. . . . In the countries I visited, people have long been satisfied with a single meal a day. Despite this, they never hesitate to accept new restrictions in order to be able to help a country like our own.

President Keita was also highly impressed, he said, by the methods of work, the anti-racist education and the care given to old people in China, North Korea and North Vietnam.

The care with which Peking selects the projects for its modest programs of technical assistance is shown by one example in Mali. Schistosomiasis is a disease that persistently ravages Mali. In April 1964, at the same time that a Mali Afro-Asian Solidarity Council delegation was being entertained in rousing anti-colonial fashion, the director of hygiene services of Mali's Public Health Ministry and the chief physician of the Mali central biology laboratory were invited to Peking. They were given a tour of southern China especially to study the prevention and treatment of schistosomiasis.

As in Guinea, Peking pays special attention in Mali to youth and women's movements, and above all to penetrating its information media, with some rather rewarding results in the latter case. Chosen for special attention in Peking have been a Mali journalist named Papa Abdoul Sy, chief news editor of the state broadcasting service, and Fabala Diallo and Amadou Moctar Dia, both correspondents of the governmental Mali News Agency. The Chinese-backed Paris magazine *Révolution* had a permanent correspondent in Bamako, Demba Diallo.

In May 1961 the Soviet-backed and Czech-sponsored International Journalists' Organization (IOJ) held its first conference in Bamako. But by May 1963 the Chinese had succeeded in setting up the rival Afro-Asian Journalists' Organization (AAJO) in Jakarta. Mamadou Gologo, the Mali Information Minister, has been in China several times and appears to be Peking's most convinced and influential friend in Mali: he was made AAJO's general secretary. He helped establish the affiliated, Chinese-line Pan-African Journalists' Union and reported to the AAJO secretariat's second meeting in November-December 1963 on the Union's Conference a short time earlier in Accra. The New China News Agency reported plans for a news center, a periodical for the association, and an "Afro-Asian Academy of Journalism." Other members of the secretariat were from Algeria, Tanganyika, the South African National Congress—and Red China.

In February 1964, Gologo launched a new monthly called *Mali Magazine*. The New China News Agency reported that it had devoted "many pages" to Chou En-lai's visit. Gologo contributed an article on China. Gologo is editor of the weekly newspaper *L'Essor* (Growth), which follows a line almost identical with Peking's on most issues. On March 12, 1964, for example, under the headline "The Capitalist World Declares War on the Under-Developed World," it published a vicious attack on the United States Peace Corps and the American Food for Peace Program. It said that while all the talk about "peace" was continuing "people are being exterminated because of their color, because they do not wish to have strategic bases on their soil or because they do not wish interference in their affairs."

Gologo contributed to *Révolution* (No. 9, 1964) a remarkably unreserved defense of Red Chinese policy in Africa, Asia and Latin America, entitled "The Great Conspiracy Against China." According to Gologo, the Chinese are the very best friends of the Africans. The "myth" of the "yellow peril" and that the Chinese are "bellicose, expansionist, animated with the desire to dominate the world" are fabrications of the "imperialists and their lackeys," Gologo said. He repeated his earlier warnings against the United States Peace Corps and attacked "English and American imperialists" for all their global doings. He did not once mention France, which by then was well launched on its new relations with Peking—a near-immunity from criticism duplicated all over French-speaking Africa. ". . . The Chinese People's Republic started at zero," Gologo wrote. "The successes of the Chinese people are the fruits of its realism, its ingenuity, its will, its patience, its moral and physical courage."

The Mali reaction to the first Chinese nuclear test in October 1964 was one of the most enthusiastic in all Africa. Gologo called it a "peaceful" atom bomb, and ranked it along with China's communes as a contribution to world progress. In his New Year's message for 1965, President Keita said that "the atom bomb of socialist China . . . was also the bomb of the peoples of Asia, Africa and Latin America and other parts of the world."

Gologo's writings have undoubtedly contributed to an African and world image of Mali as a country thoroughly infiltrated by Red China. This was undoubtedly a false image in 1965. Mali is an authentic African neutral. But there can be no doubt that Peking has had considerable success in Mali. An American who returned from the most recent of a series of visits to Bamako in June 1964 told me that the Chinese were by far the most popular of all foreign diplomats in the country. Anti-Americanism was running high in the capital. The Russians, who were reported to have seventy "technicians" in the little town of Gao alone, and their satellites were looked upon as white men and largely discredited, just as the Chinese intended.

Mali's major problem is that it is landlocked. If Red China or any other power seriously helped to supplement its only route to the sea, the Dakar-Niger railway, with new highways or air links, they would be much appreciated. When Chou En-lai and Chen Yi, during their visit to Algiers in December 1963, hinted that China would support construction of a new trans-Saharan road, they doubtless had at least one eye cocked at Mali, which needs new land routes to transport its farm products up to North Africa.

The Federation of Nigeria is certainly one of Red China's long-term targets. In demographic terms this is the giant of the continent, with about 55 million people living on 373,250 square miles. Its federal form of government, unique in Africa, survived a stormy parliamentary election in December 1964, after the non-Moslem regions had threatened to break all ties with the predominantly Moslem Northern Region.

Economically strong and stable by comparison with other African states, Nigeria is an ancient, vast and complex land, rent by regional and tribal disputes, but with a strong and intelligently led labor movement and urban intellectual class. Its Prime Minister, Sir Alhadji Abubakr Tafawa Balewa, is one of Africa's most distinguished statesmen. He values his ties with the Commonwealth and the other Western countries. Though Nigeria had diplomatic relations with Moscow, by 1965 it had refused to recognize either Peking or Taipeh. The Red Chinese ambassador in Ghana, Huan Hua, did visit Lagos, the Nigerian capital, in early 1964, in an unsuccessful attempt to persuade the government to open negotiations for recognition. Nationalist China put in its own bid for recognition, steadfastly opposed by one of the powerful, strongly nationalistic political groups, the Nigerian Youth Congress, headed by Tunji Otegbye.

The Nigerian People's Party was the first admittedly Marxist group in any former British territory. There has been Soviet support through the WFTU for the Nigerian Trade Union Congress. The Nigerian Communist Party was nominally pro-Soviet, though its constitution was modeled on that of the Chinese Communist Party. Moscow paid little attention to it, and it was not represented at the Twenty-second Congress of the Communist Party of the Soviet Union in 1961. Several hundred Nigerians are studying in Communist countries, including China. By 1964 there was an active Nigeria-China Friendship Association, working chiefly in the Moslem Northern Region, largest of the three Regions.

Inevitably there are anti-Western forces at work in the complex fabric of Nigerian society. The *Nigerian Morning Post* of Lagos, for example, wrote on March 6, 1964, that some of the members of the United States Peace Corps were "spies" who "are pursuing the cold war politics of the U. S. government." Radio Peking eagerly picked up the story.

But the Nigerians are wary of the Chinese. On June 30, 1964, the authoritative Nigerian newspaper *West African Pilot* warned its own countrymen and others that "in tending the hand of friendship to the Communist Chinese, Africans may find they are putting themselves in the clutches of an octopus."

In sum, Peking has scored some impressive gains in Ghana, Guinea and Mali, especially Guinea and Mali, considering the modest means it has employed. If it has not made the spectacular progress it seeks in West Africa, this is partly because French influence remains strong if not predominant in the economies of Guinea and Mali, as well as in their cultural life. The friendly ties with London that Ghana's Commonwealth membership helps preserve have served as a counter-balancing influence, as have memories of past Communist bloc blunders. But continued Red Chinese progress in West Africa seems highly probable, even inevitable.

CHAPTER SIXTEEN

The Maghreb: Algeria

ALMOST SINCE IT BEGAN IN NOVEMBER 1954, THE NATIONALIST AND the ensuing socialist revolution in Algeria have been held up as models by Peking. Like the Cameroon Republic, the Congo and the Egypt of the Suez war in 1956, Algeria was considered one of the great African "battlefields" of the war against Western colonial domination. It was also a center of a revolutionary ferment that could spread to the rest of "bourgeois" or "feudal" North Africa; i.e., Morocco, Tunisia and Libya.

Algeria therefore attracted Communist China's enthusiastic military, moral and diplomatic support. It received all three in generous quantities. As early as 1949, Chairman Mao sent greetings to the Algerian Communist Party. General Ho Lung, one of Red China's highest military leaders, in October 1960 called the "heroism" of the Algerian people in throwing off the rule of Frenchmen who had dominated them for 130 years ". . . a brilliant example for the other African peoples in their fight for national independence."

The story of Red China's interest in Algeria goes back to the Bandung Conference of April-May 1955. The Algerian National Liberation Front (FLN), the revolutionary party, had begun its guerilla war against France only a few months earlier. The tiny Algerian Communist Party, inspired and guided by French Communists, had committed the terrible tactical blunder of failing to support the war at first, calling it a "bourgeois uprising."

Now, at Bandung, Chou En-lai confronted two FLN emissaries

who were to play fateful roles in their country's future. One was M'hammed Yazid, later the ubiquitous Information Minister in the wartime provisional Algerian government (GPRA), and President ben Bella's unofficial but indispensable envoy on countless delicate missions—including attempts to mediate the Sino-Soviet conflicts in the Afro-Asian Solidarity Organization—after Algeria won independence in 1962.

The second Algerian emissary who met the Chinese at Bandung was Hocine Ait Ahmed, a close friend of Ben Bella. Like Ben Bella, he had been one of the first to advocate an armed uprising as the only way to shake off France's iron economic and political control. By 1965 he had become Ben Bella's most determined adversary and had been captured while heading a new guerilla campaign, this time directed against Ben Bella, in his native Kabylia mountains.

There is no record of exactly what passed between the two Algerians and the Chinese Premier. But more than eight years later, when Chou visited Algiers as Ben Bella's official guest in December 1963, a Western journalist who had first met Chou at Bandung spoke with him again.

"Whom are you going to talk with on this trip?" she asked Chou, with a touch of teasing. "The same Algerians you saw at Bandung?"

With a flicker of a smile, Chou replied, "I am here as the guest of the President of the Republic. And that is all I am going to tell you!" In June 1965, Chou was the first world statesman to endorse Ben Bella's overthrow by his rival, Army Commander-in-Chief Houari Boumedienne.

During the years since Bandung, much history has been written in Algeria. In eight and a half years of terrorism and guerilla fighting an Algerian nation that had scarcely existed since 1830 was reborn. It won the admiration of all the world, including many Frenchmen, for its courage, its persistence and its patriotism. Algeria now had its freedom. It was a freedom heavily shadowed by a legacy of economic distress, poverty, unemployment, administrative chaos and hunger. All but a few of the 1.2 million Europeans who had kept the economy and the administration running smoothly had left by 1964.

The Soviets, the Chinese and the Eastern European bloc are vying with one another to replace the French economic aid and influence, which are still strong. After Ben Bella's trip to the Soviet Union in May 1964 the Soviets seemed to be gaining on their Chinese rivals. European Marxists and Soviet-line Communists, as well as a few stray Trotskyites and old-line Socialists, were advising Ben Bella, writing his propaganda and press releases, controlling his newspapers and broadcasting services. The admiration of Americans, Britons and others in the West for the stubborn patriotism that had brought freedom to Algeria was now tempered by fears that Ben Bella, Colonel Boumedienne and their successors might, after all, not be able to remain non-aligned in view of the mounting pressure from the East.

To some extent the role of Red China in North Africa, which Arabs call the Maghreb, or "Farthest West" of the Arab world, has been linked with relations between Paris and Peking. The focus of Sino-French tensions in the early fifties, like Sino-American tensions in the mid-1960s, was Indochina. After the victory of the Chinese-backed Viet Minh forces against the French at Dienbienphu, and the French withdrawal from Indochina, the focus of Sino-French relations shifted to Algeria. At Bandung, Peking fully supported the Algerian resolution, despite the fact that French Premier Edgar Faure, only weeks earlier, had let it be known that while he did not favor recognition of Communist China just yet, he did feel that China was no longer usefully represented in the United Nations by Chiang Kai-shek's government.

As soon as the first Provisional Algerian Government, or GPRA, headed by Ferhat Abbas, was proclaimed in September 1958, Communist China and its Asian satellites immediately recognized it, though the Soviet Union and the East European Communist countries did not. In November 1958 a large GPRA delegation visited Red China for nearly a month, at which time it was offered arms and training facilities. Active support for the FLN, as for the UPC guerillas in the Cameroon Republic, now became the heart of Red China's African policy.

The other Communist bloc states, including the U.S.S.R., also backed the FLN. But China had more freedom to act openly, since it then had no diplomatic relations with France. Khrushchev, on the other hand, was anxious not to ruffle De Gaulle for reasons of European policy. By the time De Gaulle made his famous offer of Algerian "self-determination" on September 16, 1959, selected Algerians were already reported to be receiving military training in China. Tension between Nasser and Khrushchev had then reduced the value of Egypt to the Eastern bloc as a base of operations for Algeria. This was probably a principal reason why Peking had been quick to open diplomatic relations with Morocco in early 1959, as soon as Morocco made the necessary overtures.

Just as Moscow and Peking diverged over the issue of negotiation or armed struggle in the Cameroon Republic, so they differed in their reaction to De Gaulle's offer. After some hesitation and visits to Peking by GPRA Premier Benyoussef ben Khedda and Khrushchev (on his way home from his talks with President Kennedy), a New China News Agency release on October 7, 1958, termed the offer a "sugar-coated poison pill." Khrushchev, however, indicated his support. He did not become more militant on the Algerian question until after May 1960, when the Paris summit conference had failed and he saw nothing more to lose in annoying De Gaulle by advocating Algerian independence.

At this point the French Communist Party and most of the other world Communist parties, including the Algerian—its leader, Larbi Bouhali, also visited Peking in 1959—switched to support for negotiation. China and its satellites, however, remained intransigent. In 1960 Peking offered airplanes and Chinese volunteers, neither of which the Algerians accepted, though they tried to make the West think they would if peace talks were not seriously attempted.

Sometime in 1960 Mao is supposed to have told Ferhat Abbas: "The objective of war is the people. To win over the people, you must convince them: this imperative should take priority over all others . . . You can count only on your own strength. The stronger you are, the more support you will have. Chinese aid is granted you unconditionally."

The FLN was never in a hurry to accept too much of the Chinese heavy military equipment, much of which—with the notable exception of 90mm. Chinese mortars—they found ill-suited to the hit-and-run, highly mobile guerilla war they had to fight against the French. But artillery, small arms, ammunition, uniforms and many other items were transshipped through Morocco, Tunisia, Albania and other places.

Peking's propaganda eagerly took up the Algerian cause. A New China News Agency correspondent reported from the front along the Tunisian border on November 8, 1960, that there was much talk in Algerian ranks about "the Chinese war of liberation and China's experience in struggles." He said he found on the bed of an officer at staff headquarters a book entitled *War of an Uprising and Revolutionary War* with "one whole chapter devoted to the military thinking of Chairman Mao and the experiences of Chinese revolutionary wars."

The officer expressed eagerness to read more by Mao. The Algerians, found the New China journalist, were waging "tunnel warfare" against the French, just as the Chinese had against the Japanese. When I visited the field headquarters of Wilaya (Military District) IV in the mountains south of Algiers a month before independence, I saw French translations of the writings of Mao and some of the guerilla warfare handbooks. A Wilaya IV officer told me they had been smuggled across the barbed-wire French frontier barriers from Tunisia and Morocco.

Peking's particular interest in the Algerian army, as distinct from other aspects of the Algerian revolution, continued to be strong long after independence. This was true even after large deliveries of Soviet tanks and other heavy equipment began in 1963. Several large Chinese military missions visited Africa, beginning in 1962. On April 8, 1963, Algiers radio reported that seventy-five Algerian army officers had just left for Cairo "for further military training." Later published reports stated that they continued on to Peking. Six days earlier Algiers announced that fourteen trainee Algerian pilots had left for a two-year training course in China. Colonel Hu Pin-fu, the Chinese military attaché, had become one of the most active, if discreet, figures on the Algerian diplomatic scene by early 1964.

In November 1963, a few weeks after the border dispute between Morocco and Algeria had erupted into open warfare, official Western sources reported that a team of Chinese experts resident in Algeria was training Algerian army personnel in the use of weapons made in other Communist countries.

Moroccan officials went a step further. They assured me that Moroccan rebels eager to overthrow King Hassan's regime had been trained by Chinese officers. Some of these guerillas crossed the border in early June of 1964, and were intercepted and captured by Moroccan security forces. The Moroccans did not make public the charges about the Chinese officers having trained them. For the record, the Moroccan Interior Minister said simply that they were trained at Sidi Khaled, a former French gendarmerie barracks near Oran. My Moroccan sources told me privately that the Chinese officers were active at another camp near Ain Sefra, much farther south in the Sahara.

During his talk with FLN cadremen in Algiers in December 1963, Chou En-lai, according to the French-language *Pékin Informations* of January 6, 1964, told them:

A just revolutionary leadership, a large unified front and a revolutionary army: these are the elements that are important not only for the victory of the national and democratic revolution, but also for the continued development of the revolution. . . . Large masses of Algerian cadremen . . . have led a modest and simple life, maintaining close ties with the popular masses. Such an army of cadremen constitutes the real wealth of the Algerian revolutionary cause.

To Peking, the "revolutionary army" led by Ben Bella's enigmatic successor, silent Colonel Houari Boumedienne, might prove the best card to bet on in an Algeria where political instability is endemic, and economic chaos often seems just around the corner.

The Chinese have also shown especially strong interest in helping the Algerians to build up the "People's Militia" created by the FLN in 1964. One special mission led by General Yang Yung evidently discussed this during an inspection tour of Algeria in November 1964. In December 1964 and January 1965 an Algerian militia delegation headed by People's Militia superintendent Mahmoud Guenez returned the visit, and while in China listened to a speech by General Peng Shao-hui, deputy chief of the Chinese General Staff, on the importance of a sound national militia as well as a strong "People's Army." On February 10, 1965, the Algerian government signed an accord with Peking that, according to Guenez, covered "the supplying of some materials" to the militia. They had already seen service in fighting mountain guerillas, like those of Ait Ahmed, and bandits. Colonel Hu, the military attaché, said the accord was a contribution to the "common struggle." By supporting the militia the Chinese avoided the appearance of partisan support for Boumedienne's regular army, which might some day be a rival of the FLN's militia. At the same time they were aiding another Chinese revolutionary institution, a well-armed and well-trained peasant force.

After independence Peking quickly sent a diplomatic mission. It was converted into an embassy by the time Ben Bella had seized and consolidated his power under the new constitution in September 1962. There were some early contacts between the embassy and military men opposing Ben Bella, who sought out the Chinese. They led to nothing. The first Red Chinese economic aid was in the form of food, mainly grain, steel and medicines. Various commercial, technical and cultural accords were signed. Algeria showed its appreciation by recognizing Peking in 1962 and voting for its admission to the United Nations at the General Assembly session that same autumn, just after Algeria itself was admitted.

Shortly before Chou En-lai's visit of December 1963 the ambassador, Tseng Tao, negotiated a $50 million interest-free loan. Publication of the offer came just a few days after announcement of a Soviet loan worth $100 million but accorded under somewhat less favorable terms.

During this same eventful month of October, when Ben Bella's regime met the double test of Ait Ahmed's guerilla revolt in the Kabylia mountains and desert fighting with Morocco over the disputed Saharan regions, China donated the entire contents of its September trade exposition to Algeria. The principal item was a cigarette factory. A Chinese economic mission studied soil conditions around the eastern port city of Annaba (formerly Bône) for a proposed porcelain plant.

The Chinese Communist Party sent a large delegation to a congress of Algerian peasants, October 25-27. Ben Bella and other Algerian leaders explained the program of nationalizing French-owned farmland, now virtually complete, and its takeover by peasant *Comités de gestion*. But the first speaker was the leader of the Chinese delegation, who attributed miraculous powers to the "people."

The Sino-Soviet conflict had already begun to show its effects in Algeria. Moscow Radio broadcasts praised the Algerian Communists for supporting the Moscow-Washington nuclear test ban treaty against Peking's attacks. The Communists in Algeria had been banned as an organized party, as had all others, since November 1962, and had been asked both by Ben Bella and by Moscow to enter the FLN as individuals. Algeria signed the Moscow-Washington treaty. Other Moscow broadcasts quoted Algerian Communists as denouncing a small anti-Ben Bella resistance movement headed by Abderrazak Abdelkader, a writer and former officer in the French Army, as the head of a group of "French Trotskyites." Chinese leaders, said Moscow, had a "close alliance" with this group.

Signs of Soviet-Chinese rivalry increased as the time for Chou's visit approached. A long statement by Khrushchev on the national liberation movements was reported in Algerian newspapers, including the FLN's official Arabic and French-language organ, *The People,* as having been given in an interview with Algerian and Ghanaian journalists. It read like many of Khrushchev's other attacks on Chinese policy. He warned against attempts to isolate the national liberation movements from the people of the Soviet Union and the other socialist countries, or to replace the anti-imperialist line of the movements by "geopolitical" [i.e., Afro-Asian] or even racist ideas. Other main points were that the "national bourgeoisie" could play a role in a country liberated from colonialism, and that armed struggle was not always necessary to liberate a country from a colonial regime. The workers, rather than the peasants, it went on, are the revolutionary "advance guard." Finally, a young state cannot move directly to socialism without passing through the phase of "national democracy" (as Czechoslovakia had done before the Communists took it over in 1948). The Algerian Marxist theorists, especially Mohammed Harbi, tended to disagree with all these points.

The Soviet statement was printed December 20, the very eve of Chou's arrival in Algiers. It was evidently drafted in the Soviet Embassy in Algiers and passed on to *Alger-Républicain* (the Communist organ, "integrated" into the FLN in April 1964) and *The People* by the Soviet press attaché. His efforts to get the FLN weekly, *Révolution Africaine,* then edited by Harbi, to publish it were unsuccessful. Harbi said no such interview had ever been given. Algerian newspapers gave much simultaneous attention to the Moscow visit of Hadj ben Alla, one of Ben Bella's most faithful supporters in the FLN's Political Bureau.

Throughout Chou's visit (December 21-27), Ben Bella showed the same determination to avoid taking sides between Russia and China that has characterized Algerian policy since the Sino-Soviet dispute began. When he met the Chinese delegation at Algiers airport, Ben Bella pointed out in his prepared speech that peaceful coexistence should have its "full meaning," including China taking its seat in the United Nations. The Algerian greeting seemed otherwise rather improvised. Ben Bella shook hands with Chou, rather than embracing him as with most other visitors. Streamers and posters with misspelled Chinese characters were hastily fastened in place by a truck that preceded the motorcade into town. When Chou was in Algiers he was made an honorary citizen of the city, an honor previously accorded only to René Mathieu, the director of UNESCO, and a few weeks after Chou's visit, to U.N. Secretary-General U Thant.

During his stay Chou was the perfect diplomat, as he had been in Egypt, the first country he visited on his African tour. In public he never alluded to the conflict with the Soviets, nor did he even attack American "imperialism" as such. He was doubtless well aware that United States Ambassador William J. Porter had established excellent working relationships with the Algerians. With Algerian Agriculture Minister Ali Mahsas, Chou visited a nationalized farm at L'Arba, east of Algiers, then the Algerian trade union cooperative farm and marketing community at Boufarik, where he tasted the grapefruits and oranges and was given a gazelle as a gift. Later he saw the nationalized Tamzali vegetable oil plant, and the assembly line of the French automotive firm of Berliet, which was already turning out trucks for Communist China. He and Chen Yi hinted China might help to finance a new trans-Saharan road then being studied by African governments and U.N. agencies. Chou received by far the biggest applause in the poorest quarters of Algiers, such as outlying Hussein Dey, Maison Carré and the shantytown districts. Crowds in the center were indifferent.

In Oran province Chou and his technical advisors carefully looked over the Arzew petrochemical complex, which was to liquefy Saharan natural gas and send it to France and Britain by tanker. The Chinese also showed interest in Saharan oil, though they evidently made no concrete offers to purchase it.

In four long, secret political conversations with Chou and Chen Yi, details of which can be reconstructed fairly well from accounts of Algerians who attended them, Ben Bella and his advisors ranged over nearly the entire field of African and world politics with the Chinese.

Ben Bella and Chou agreed that France's impending recognition of Peking would greatly alter the world power balance in favor of Afro-Asia. They were in accord that the fight against colonialism in the Portuguese territories, as in South Africa in particular, should be intensified. Ways had to be found to convince various African governments to do more, a theme backed by Ben Bella and the Algerian delegation at various African conferences. Without trying to browbeat Ben Bella and his aides, and without playing up the race angle—since, after all, he was talking to white men—Chou explained the Chinese repugnance for Soviet and Yugoslav "revisionism." It was agreed that China should have a key role at the 1965 Afro-Asian Conference, though Ben Bella refused to commit himself to oppose Russia's participation.

Chou listened carefully to Algerian questions about why Peking did not rigidly insist on immediate cession of Formosa and Hong Kong, and gave complete answers. When asked why Red China continued its trade with South Africa, Macao and Mozambique, he said curtly: "We are not prepared to discuss this question." He gently chided the Soviets for cutting off their aid to China, calling this "not good Leninist internationalism."

Ben Bella later told a friend that he had come away with the impression that "we had been talking as equals, that our relations were not those that a great power usually has with a smaller one. We had the same problems, the same preoccupations." Another Algerian was impressed by Chou's careful avoidance of a "hard sell" of Chinese doctrines. Chou had said, in effect: "The Chinese experiment can only be a point of reference for you. Your own experiences are the most valuable. They can bear fruit only if adapted to your own national realities." Even Western aid, said Chou, in a display of his flexibility and diplomatic finesse, could be a good thing if used properly and to "help broaden the revolutionary program," as Algeria was doing with the massive aid it was still receiving from France (about half a billion dollars scheduled from 1963 through 1965).

In a final meeting with the FLN party leadership, Chou, if we are to accept the official Chinese text as carried in the French-language *Pékin Informations* on January 6, was more doctrinaire:

> Just as the banner of the Cuban revolution floats above Latin America, that of the Algerian revolution has been planted on the African continent. . . . The African people will make the revolution; they will make themselves the masters of Africa and will finish off imperialism, colonialism and neo-colonialism: Africa will become, most certainly, a free and independent Africa: this is a great historical current that no reactionary force can stem. . . . Countries where the revolution has already triumphed have the sacred duty of supporting and aiding the brother peoples who heroically struggle for independence and liberation. . . . American imperialism, armed to the teeth, has not been able to prevent the Vietnam population from marching forward in its struggle, nor the Cuban people from making progress in their revolution. . . .

Algerians told me that Chou discussed the difficulty of furnishing arms to Holden Roberto's Angolan "Liberation Army" and Mondlane's "Mozambique Liberation Front," since they were both "American tools." No definite decision seems to have been made on this or on aiding the South Africans, so long as the latter are divided into two rival groups. Chou did, however, promise Ben Bella support for the guerilla training center in Algeria, which had already been functioning for some months, as we have already seen.

In the economic field the Chinese reconnaissance of Algeria's oil and gas resources was followed up by a more thoroughgoing study group. This was a Chinese oil and gas mission that, after spending several weeks in France shopping for oil refinery equipment and steel piping, arrived in Algiers on February 12. At its head was Tang Ke, director of the Chinese Corporation for the Prospecting and Exploitation of Petroleum and Natural Gas. Ben Bella had suggested to Chou that Chinese technical assistance might be useful, especially in Saharan extraction operations and in speeding up the training of qualified Algerian personnel to replace French technicians. The Chinese indicated they might also supply certain types of machinery.

Like the American, Dutch, British and Italian oilmen then visiting Algeria, the Chinese were invited on a study tour of Saharan centers. Peking was strongly sympathetic to the Ben Bella government's desire for a greater share of oil royalties from the Western companies. But there was no indication that the Chinese would participate, at least for the time being, in Algeria's new National Research and Development Company, in which the Algerian government held 51 per cent of the stock and Western companies 49 per cent.

Only since the Afro-Asian Solidarity Council meeting in Algiers in March 1964, which we discussed in Chapter Three, have the Algerians seemed fully to realize that whether they like it or not they are squarely in the forefront of a new cold war, this time between Moscow and Peking. On every possible occasion the Algerian leaders indicated they were not interested in this, but rather in questions like disarmament (including ending French nuclear tests in the Sahara), frontier disputes (in view of the major one with Morocco, which was under arbitration by the African Unity Organization) and the falling world prices of raw materials, a major concern of all the African countries.

Ben Bella aspired to be the arbiter of conflicts among the "non-aligned" countries. This had already been shown by Algerian diplomatic overtures during the Cuban and Sino-Indian disputes. At various times he has also tried to end the warfare between Indonesia and Malaysia, that between the Cameroon guerillas and the Cameroon government, and the rivalry among the various Angolan, Mozambique and South African movements. At the second conference of African heads of state in Cairo in July 1964 Ben Bella made a concerted effort to generate Africa-wide pressure to oust Moise Tshombe from his new post as Premier of the Congo (Leopoldville). Then, with Soviet backing and blessing, he intervened to send military aid to the Congolese rebels. His overextended support to African "liberation" movements seems to have been one cause of his overthrow by Colonel Boumedienne in June 1965.

The Chinese seemed to view all this Algerian activity with mixed feelings. Both they and the Russians, for example, had to give public evidence that they approved Ben Bella's initiatives to bring Latin America into the Afro-Asian solidarity organizations. At the same time, they were highly apprehensive lest either Castro or Ben Bella should finally choose the Soviet line over the Chinese one at a huge conference of African, Asian and Latin American "liberation movements" that Castro wished to hold in Havana in 1965 or 1966.

Even more annoying for Peking was the result of Ben Bella's long-awaited trip to the U.S.S.R., Bulgaria and Czechoslovakia in May 1964. He brought back with him firm assurances from Khrushchev, soon to be borne out during Khrushchev's visit to Egypt for the Aswan High Dam ceremonies, that Moscow would now concentrate its economic aid in Algiers and Cairo. He also brought back promises of $128.8 million in new Soviet economic aid, over and above the $100 million already promised in October 1963.

The new Soviet credit was mainly to cover the cost of a steel complex with an annual capacity of about 350,000 tons of rolled metal that they planned to build near Annaba (Bône). This was an old French project that had never passed much beyond the planning stage, because French private investors backed out.

The Russians also gave Algeria an oil institute and a technical college capable of training a total of 2,000 students at once. It opened classes in 1964. The cost of other technical institutes, including one for textiles, was to be covered by the 1963 loan. This would also pay for agricultural machinery, two Ilyushin aircraft, additional Russian doctors (a few were already working in Algeria, and a team of Chinese physicians, specialists in acupuncture, was at work in Saida, in southwestern Algeria) and experts to start up factories left idle since their French owners abandoned or sold them. It would also cover the cost of a 19,000-ton oil tanker. It appeared, as *The Economist* remarked on May 16, 1964, that Chinese taunts of Soviet selfishness might drive the Russians to increase their future generosity further.

The Chinese impact on Algeria, apart from its considerable influence on the army, had so far not been great. Few Algerians went beyond showing the same sort of polite curiosity about China that that thirteenth-century North African traveler, Ibn Batuta, had once shown. Their interest in China was increased by Peking's central role in organization work for the Afro-Asian Conference scheduled for June 1965, just after Ben Bella's overthrow by Boumedienne.

The Red Chinese, like the Russians, and the Algerian leaders themselves, doubtless regard Algeria as the center from which to spread revolutionary ferment to Algeria's neighbors as well as to the Portuguese territories and to other areas whose nationalists are being trained in Algeria. Their appeal to the Algerians themselves, however, seems likely to remain limited. It is certain to continue stressing the peasant and agrarian aspects of revolution, as well as the military ones. China's attraction could increase in the case of serious Russian or Western errors. Meanwhile the Chinese are bound to work from their Algerian bases behind the scenes, and at an increasing pace, to exclude Western influence from Casablanca all the way east to Tripoli and Cairo.

CHAPTER SEVENTEEN

The Maghreb: Morocco, Tunisia and Libya

IN CONTRAST TO "SOCIALIST" ALGERIA, WHERE NOTHING IN POLITICS, society or economics was settled after independence, Morocco is a solid, semi-autocratic monarchy, established for over a thousand years. The hero of Morocco's own successful drive to throw off two generations of French and Spanish rule in 1953 was the late King Mohammed V, a statesman ranking with the world's finest. He had a basic mistrust of Communism. When his son Hassan II came to the throne in 1961, there fell to him the task of converting a feudal Islamic society into a modern, constitutional monarchy that would remain loyal to its ancient traditions, and yet become a political force in the modern world.

Morocco was one of the first African states to win its independence. The French protectorate, and the much smaller Spanish one, ended within a few weeks of one another, in March and April of 1956. Given its strategic position at Africa's northwestern corner, with coastlines on the Straits of Gibraltar, the Atlantic and the Mediterranean, Morocco looked to Peking like a good diplomatic base to complement the one already won in Egypt.

Morocco's internal situation must have looked interesting too. Since 1958 the kingdom had had a mildly socialistic government. The Premier was Abdallah Ibrahim, a journalist and leader of the Moroccan Labor Federation (UMT). Ibrahim, with Mehdi ben Barka, UMT secretary-general Mahjoub ben Seddik and several other like-minded politicians, had been instrumental in splitting the Istiqlal

Party, which had led the national movement from 1944 to 1956, into a leftist and a traditionalist wing. The leftist one became the National Union of Popular Forces (UNFP), led by Ben Barka. Ibrahim's government inclined toward the UNFP and had a forward-looking economic policy. It aimed at a five-year plan of intensive economic development built around heavy industry.

Red China's first appearance in Morocco was in the form of a commercial delegation and an exhibition at the Casablanca Trade Fair in 1957. Under the pro-Western cabinet of Ahmed Balafrej, Morocco became the second African state to recognize Peking, after the United Arab Republic, in 1958. By early 1959, Ambassador Pei Yen was hard at work in Rabat, and touring West Africa as well.

Pei Yen and his staff prudently avoided open commitments to any Moroccan political party, including the UNFP. They took special pains to avoid any appearance of favoring the Communists, just as the Chinese had done in Algeria. Peking was discreetly silent when several court decisions were handed down, between 1959 and 1964, that in effect banned the small Moroccan Communist Party. In 1965 this party was still pro-Soviet, and did not visibly lean toward Peking.

Clandestine trade between Morocco and Red China had long been conducted through the intermediaries of banks and exchange agents in the free economic zone of Tangier. A regular commercial agreement was concluded between Rabat and Peking for the first time in 1958. It has been renewed and expanded each year since then. The arrangement is the usual compensation or barter accord, and the value reached about $16 million in each direction in 1964. Morocco sells China its phosphate rock, cobalt ore (which caused a minor crisis with the U.S. State Department in 1964, as we shall see), canned sardines, Berliet trucks assembled in Casablanca, cork, cotton, grains, insecticides and artisan goods. In 1963 China sold to Morocco the major portion of Moroccan green tea and silk imports. Cotton and rayon textiles, machinery, chemical products, household goods, light metallurgical equipment and a few other items were included in the Moroccan purchases.

The Chinese made their biggest commercial effort at the Casablanca Fairs of 1961 and 1964. Each year their displays have been more tasteful and colorful and better adapted to local interests. The large Chinese show in April-May 1964, which was to become a permanent exhibition, featured everything from jade to bicycles and teapots. Its most popular feature was a retail store where Moroccans could buy tea, clothing, rattan mats and other popular items at absurdly low prices: the imports had been subsidized. There was a cinema for the children. The pavilion had far more impact than a nearby American show, arranged by the USIS, demonstrating the role automation can play in education.

The amount of printed Chinese Communist propaganda material available in Moroccan cities is enormous. The main distributor of newspapers, books and periodicals, Sochepresse, seems to have a subsidy arrangement, since the materials are sold below cost after coming by boat or air from Peking.

In 1961 Liu Shao-chi invited King Hassan to China, transmitting the invitation through the Vice-Minister of Commerce, Lu Chu-chang. Hassan accepted on principle, but did not go. Moroccan Foreign Minister Ahmed Balafrej, who later became Hassan's personal representative, did make one private trip to Peking. Otherwise the only prominent Moroccan visitors to China were men like Ben Barka, who by 1964 was Hassan's most determined political adversary, in exile and under double sentence of death in absentia, and Mahjoub ben Seddik, as well as a few other labor and student leaders. Hassan appointed Abderrahman Zniber, a friend of Ben Barka, ambassador to Peking, but he did not go until 1962, though recognition had taken place in 1958. Zniber was excluded from the Sino-Moroccan talks in Rabat when Chou En-lai visited Morocco in December 1963, though the Chinese ambassador in Rabat did take part. Evidently the government mistrusted Zniber because of his close contacts with some of the UNFP leaders.

Morocco, which kept a close relationship with France and the United States and depended in large measure on their financial aid (over $400 million from Washington between 1957 and 1965), rejected most offers of assistance from the East bloc. It appears that Ibrahim's interest in accepting an offer from Peking to send Chinese technicians to replace departing French ones was one of the reasons the King decided to turn his government out of office in May 1960.

The UNFP became an opposition party, often harassed by the police. At least two Chinese attachés kept permanent contact with it. They broke this off, however, just before the royal police arrested most of the leaders of the UNFP after the supposed discovery of a plot against the regime and the King's life in July 1963. Peking's propaganda media have never openly encouraged violent revolution against the monarchy, for reasons that will become apparent below. There was no evidence of any Chinese or other outside involvement in severe riots that shook Casablanca and other Moroccan cities in March 1965.

The Chinese Embassy also cultivated its contacts with the conservative, traditionalist Istiqlal party. Istiqlal's leadership had remained more or less grouped around the party's founder—scholar, writer and orator Allal el-Fassi. The merchants and traders of Casablanca and Fez were mainly Istiqlal supporters. They soon found it was profitable to do business with the Chinese: many fat import and export possibilities were offered, especially in the popular Chinese textiles and the green tea that is a dietary staple for most of Morocco's 13 million people.

Peking played upon Istiqlal's strongly Moslem flavor by inviting prominent Moslem educators and scholars from Morocco to China, and occasionally sending Chinese Moslems to Morocco on pilgrimages and "good-will tours." On several occasions this provoked some appreciative remarks by el-Fassi—who is probably as far from being Communist as anyone can be—about China's great "comprehension" of the Islamic world and its "enlightened policy toward Moslem nations from the Balkans to Pakistan."

Chou En-lai and other Chinese leaders have frequently declared that African and Asian countries have a right to alter, by force if negotiation fails, the frontiers left by colonial powers. This would logically have put Peking behind Morocco's frontier claims on Algeria. But Peking sided strongly with Algeria during the military hostilities in October and November 1963. Radio Peking gave a big play to Algerian claims of victory, which were untrue. It distorted a dispatch I sent to the *Christian Science Monitor* concerning a few transport flights made in Moroccan planes for Moroccans by U.S. personnel attached to the U.S. Air Force's pilot training mission in Rabat. The State Department itself denied my original story, and U.S. Ambassador John H. Ferguson ordered the flights halted almost before they had started. But the Peking broadcasts, supplemented by others from Cairo, Moscow and elsewhere, annoyed the Algerians, speaking as some did of "American planes" and "American troops . . . flying to the front."

During this period reports sent from Peking to Rabat by Ambassador Zniber were "damning," one Moroccan official told me. On several occasions the Chinese opened the diplomatic pouch and after tampering with the envelopes read the contents, the same official said.

Western experts who have watched Chinese Communist operations in North Africa for some time are convinced that a chief reason for Peking's failure openly to encourage subversion of Hassan's regime was Red China's need for Morocco's cobalt ore.

Morocco's cobalt beds lie in the rich mining region of Bou Azzer, south of the Atlas Mountains. They are controlled by a French firm, the Société Minière de Bou Azzer. In 1963 Morocco was the world's third largest producer. Most of the ore it sells is in cobalt arsenide compounds with a metallic content of 11 per cent, sometimes higher. China needs all the cobalt it can get for hardening steel in machine tools, but especially for its nuclear program. Cobalt above a certain concentration can absorb slow neutron particles in a nuclear reactor and so produce radioactive cobalt 60, a powerful source of gamma rays useful in nuclear weapons research. Under the old United States law of 1951, called the Battle Act, cobalt is on a list of strategic materials that the U.S. tries to prevent from reaching Communist countries. The State Department can cut off economic and military assistance to countries that sell such materials.

Moroccan sales of cobalt to Red China began under the Ibrahim regime when the sales contracts were signed. Two shipments were made in 1960, totaling 3,985 tons. The United States made quiet representations to Morocco. No more cobalt deals are known to have been negotiated after that until November 1963. The official Moroccan trade statistics for 1963 showed all the sales of cobalt for that year, totaling 13,707 tons, as going to France and Belgium. However, Western intelligence in Hong Kong discovered that a Greek freighter, the *Master George,* had in fact sailed from Casablanca in November with a cargo of 4,000 tons of cobalt listed as "phosphate," a very large shipment indeed for a single trip, bound for Hong Kong. The Greeks, as a NATO power, were so upset that the Greek consul in Hong Kong asked that the ship and the cargo be impounded. However, the cobalt was delivered to a consignee and is presumed to have certainly reached Red China.

Again the United States Embassy in Rabat made unpublicized representations. The Moroccan Foreign Ministry indicated in reply that the cargo had first been shipped to Europe, then resold. International trade being what it is, there was no absolute control over the final destination or use of the ore.

In February 1964 another problem arose over the fact that Moroccan ships were carrying cargoes to and from Cuba, which as a result of Moroccan sugar purchases is Cuba's third largest customer. Under the United States Foreign Aid Law aid might be cut off if this continued. Aid was, in fact, frozen at current levels until Morocco gave assurances that it would pull its vessels out of the Cuba trade.

On February 20, Foreign Minister Ahmed Guedira, one of the King's most intelligent and capable advisors, reacted with irritation against the pressure U.S. legislation was compelling the State Department to exercise on both the Cuba and China trade issues. "If we suspend our sales of cobalt to China we would risk profoundly perturbing our commercial relations with that country," Mr. Guedira said. He was letting the cat out of the bag, since up to then no one had publicly reported the new Moroccan cobalt shipment to China. "These relations," he went on, "are of essential importance to us. We cannot see where else Morocco would obtain the tea it now buys from [mainland] China [earlier, it had obtained much of it from Formosa]. On the other hand, we could not sell our cobalt anywhere else, since America, for instance, is not in the market."

In March the U.S. State Department, anxious to avoid the embarrassment of having to suspend aid again over this question, quietly announced that the cobalt had been found to be not of strategic value, though the criteria for establishing this were not made clear. The issue was dropped for the moment. However, a new Sino-Moroccan trade agreement signed in March 1964 for the coming year showed that China would take 5,000 tons of "non-ferrous metals." The strong probability was that this was cobalt again. Unless cobalt were taken off the so-called "A" list of strategic materials, or unless U.S. officials simply looked the other way, the whole matter was likely to arise again. In any case, experts who analyzed the Chinese nuclear test of October 1964 concluded the Chinese had ample stockpiles of cobalt.

Chou En-lai and his party stayed in Morocco on their African tour from December 27 to 31, 1963. Chou's reception in Rabat was courteous and on the state occasions even sumptuous, but the Moroccans who turned out at Rabat airport or lined the streets in Rabat and Casablanca to see him were more politely curious than enthusiastic. "China," one plump Moroccan woman remarked to me, "is so far away."

Chou's reception by King Hassan was the sort of moment when

direct human contacts are briefly more compelling than ideology. With its princes, pashas, halberdiers and medieval pomp, the royal court in Rabat might be considered the incarnation of everything that Chou and the Red Chinese revolution are dedicated to destroying. Yet the newsmen who had followed the Chinese party from its arrival on African soil in Cairo through its visit to "socialist" Egypt and Algeria said Chou never seemed so completely relaxed as in Morocco. Chou and his party, dressed in gray tunics and overcoats like Soviet commissars of the Stalinist era, had suddenly stepped into surroundings where tradition and trappings meant everything.

As the thirty-four-year-old King and his sixty-four-year-old guest, himself of aristocratic stock, relaxed at dinner in the luxurious surroundings of the palace, richly robed courtiers waited on them as the orchestra played Tchaikowsky's "Swan Lake" overture. They exchanged a few words in the excellent French they both command and both burst into laughter, obviously enjoying each other's company.

However interesting Hassan and Chou found one another personally, the brief fugue of Chou and his party in Morocco had a few more practical aspects. The Chinese group toured the Italian-built oil refinery in Mohammedia (formerly Fedala), 15 miles north of Casablanca. Chou and Chen Yi had some of their own top petroleum experts with them, including those who had been shopping for equipment in Europe. They listened to the Moroccan technical director explain that the refinery had treated 750,000 tons of crude oil from the U.S.S.R., Algeria, Libya and Saudi Arabia during 1963.

"Can you produce jet fuel and high-test aviation gasoline?" asked Chou. "We are not producing either now, but we easily could," was the reply. Chou's advisors took detailed, careful notes. They seemed eager to gather all the information they could on how European industrial techniques were being applied in North Africa. The same team toured Algerian oil installations a few weeks later.

The final communiqué approved Morocco's "non-alignment" and neutrality, supported peaceful coexistence between different social systems (as had the one on Algeria), and aimed for "a broad international cooperation based on equality and mutual advantage." Hassan received a polite if somewhat stilted "thank-you" for Morocco's consistent support for Red China's entry into the U.N., and congratulations for the evacuation of French and American military bases, which had recently been completed.

It looked for a while as if Chou's visit had been as much of a success for Morocco as for Red China. Now the Rabat regime had silenced its socialist critics in Cairo and Algiers who had called it "feudal" by receiving Chou in grander style than they, and in receiving his endorsement, or so it seemed, of the monarchist regime. The usual words in favor of the return of Palestine to its rightful Arab owners had been pronounced by the Chinese. Morocco had a chance to air its version of the Algero-Moroccan frontier dispute, and to hear the Chinese version of its own border difficulties with India.

All these impressions were shattered for the Rabat government when Chou En-lai gave his famous news conference in Mogadishu three weeks later, in which he was quoted as saying that Morocco, like Ethiopia, was still "under the control of foreign interests."

The reaction in Rabat approached cold fury. The newspaper *An Nidal* commented on February 8 that Chou "while he was on our soil, eating our food and negotiating with us the purchase of his green tea in exchange for our sardines, which he buys from us to resell to Europe, did not say that we are still subject to the domination of Western Europe . . . we would certainly not have refused our support to China, despite its idolatrous regime, if the words of those who speak in its name had been proper."

When all the Chinese embassies in the world, one full week later, finally issued a corrected text of the interview from which the derogatory remarks were omitted, it was, as one Moroccan official told me, "far too late." Apparently to make amends for the slip, Radio Peking and all the official Chinese agencies bombarded the royal palace and members of the cabinet with telegrams of congratulations and encouragement on every possible anniversary and other occasion for several weeks afterward.

There was another curious aftermath to Chou's visit, never reported before. Evidently it was decided by the nervous Chinese security men that the security for the small Embassy staff in Rabat—not more than about thirty in mid-1964—was far too lax. They were living in hotels, apartments or villas, and mixing with one of the largest cosmopolitan sets crowded together in any African city: there are about sixty-five diplomatic missions in Rabat, a town of perhaps 250,000, as well as a large United Nations group and economic assistance missions of various sorts.

The Chinese purchased for $900,000 a large villa in Souissi, an exclusive wooded district just outside Rabat where most of the royal family have villas. It was to be converted into a new embassy surrounded by a high-walled compound, where the entire staff would work and live. The last tenant received a call in May 1964, from a Chinese attaché who politely asked him when he planned on leaving. The Chinese then asked questions about the sewage pipes. Were they adequate and up to their task?

"They're not too good," was the reply. "Too narrow to provide good drainage."

"Fine," the Chinese replied. "We prefer narrow pipes, they are far less easy to plant bombs in!"

Quiescent though it seems, Red Chinese policy in Morocco might become more active if the massive Soviet aid to neighboring Algeria continues. Hassan might then choose to play Peking off against Moscow, the sort of thing he is capable of doing with superb skill. Certainly the Moroccans do not trust the Chinese: they use them. However, this sort of relationship can work both ways. China now has a good source of strategic materials, and contact with an important part of the Moslem world in Morocco. It is certain to exploit them to the utmost.

Like Moscow, the workaday little Moslem Republic of Tunisia (45,000 square miles, and about 4.5 million people in 1964) appeared to hold little ideological promise for Peking. President Habib Bourguiba, the self-educated son of a fisherman who led his country to independence in 1956, is one of the truly enlightened African statesmen. He also happens to be one of the more pro-Western, who has not hesitated to defy France, the former Protectorate power in Tunisia, when he felt that it suited Tunisian national interest to do so. This he proved in the crisis and battle over the Bizerte naval base in 1961, and again when he nationalized French farmland in 1964.

Since its independence Tunisia has also been especially close to the United States and has received nearly as much American economic aid as has Morocco, around $380 million from 1957 through 1963. During the Algerian war Bourguiba, like Morocco's leaders, staunchly supported the FLN at great risk and peril to himself and his country, and allowed the FLN to have its main military bases in his country. After the war, Bourguiba moved gradually closer to Gamal Abdel Nasser and the rest of the Arab world.

Though Tunisia has had diplomatic relations with the Soviets since soon after independence, East bloc activity in the country has been small. It was limited largely to a Soviet loan of $13 million to help finance a dam and a technical school advanced shortly after the Bizerte crisis. The Czechs, Poles and others have attempted some small-scale projects. Apart from some trade and visits by one or two Red Chinese agricultural experts, there had been almost no diplomatic contacts between Tunisia and the Peking regime. Then Bourguiba suddenly decided to recognize Red China.

Though Tunis had no previous ties with Nationalist China either, Bourguiba evidently had felt up to then that his good working relationships with Washington and his rather uneasy friendship with France might be jeopardized by early recognition of Peking. But when he discovered that De Gaulle was planning recognition in January 1964, the American objections that were probably passed on to him discreetly did not change his decision to beat De Gaulle to the punch if possible, even if only by a few days. There were some hurried consultations between one of Tunisia's top diplomats, Ahmed Mestiri, Ambassador to Algeria, and Tseng Tao, Red Chinese envoy in Algiers, in December. It was arranged that Chou and his party would stop off in Tunis after the brief sojourn in their European satellite of Albania, following their visit to Morocco.

The step had been heralded by Bachir ben Yahmed, editor of the Tunis weekly *Jeune Afrique,* who often spoke for Bourguiba. It was ridiculous, he wrote in an editorial on December 23, "to continue to feign ignorance of China . . . one of the greatest phenomena of the post-war world. . . . In recognizing China, the African states will contribute to its admission to the U.N. and in this way, make of it a member of international society . . ." This, he went on, would make it possible "not to play anyone's game in the Sino-Soviet conflict" since both Moscow and Peking would be given equal recognition.

Chou and his party stayed in Tunisia January 9-11. Before they left, Tunisian recognition was announced. Chou was given a tour of some Tunisian agricultural projects, including the Medjerdja Valley Development for which he expressed great admiration, not realizing, perhaps, that this was largely financed by American aid funds. But Bourguiba, with his usual force and frankness, caused Chou and Chen Yi some uncomfortable moments at a state banquet. During the usual toasts and speeches, he indicated that Tunisia could neither go along with China's rejection of the nuclear test ban treaty, nor with its hostility toward India in the Sino-Indian border dispute.

In a private exchange between President Bourguiba and Chou, Bourguiba confronted the Chinese Premier with the difference between statements on "peaceful coexistence" made in Tunis and the violent denunciations of the West, especially the United States, that

Chou had just finished making during a stopover in Albania. "What is your real face," Bourguiba asked him, "the face of Tirana, or the face of Tunis?"

In an interview he granted me on April 18, 1965, Bourguiba showed himself to be practically the only Afro-Asian statesman to support strongly the United States policy in Vietnam. "The real cause of American involvement in southeast Asia," he said, "is China's desire for hegemony in Asia. First they hit India. Now they are seeking to dominate Indo-China. China is trying hard to stir up all the trouble it can in Africa too, but I do not predict a brilliant future for them here."

On the final evening of his visit, when Chou had to make a speech to Bourguiba, it was phrased in highly prudent terms. One French journalist later remarked that "many of us thought Chinese diplomacy was about to line up with the principles of Bourguibism!" Chou thought it possible to arrive at a total ban on nuclear arms, he said. He was also far less acid in his references to the Formosa issue, proving once again that he is supple when the occasion demands.

Neither Peking nor Tunis seemed to be in any hurry to exploit their new relations. A Chinese chargé d'affaires, Chou Pui, took up his duties in Tunis on April 24. The first Ambassador, Hao Nien, arrived on May 4. For the time being Tunis appointed no envoy at all to Peking, offering as an excuse that there was a shortage of qualified diplomatic personnel for the post. Meanwhile Peking began to distribute its publications in Tunisia through a bookstore in the southern port city of Sfax. When Peking asked to send an Embassy staff of 250, the Tunisian Foreign Ministry cut them down to 40.

Bourguiba's move to recognize Peking, a purely formal one in many ways, was probably expected, however deplored, in Washington. It was one corollary of the general shift in power relationships caused by De Gaulle's own flirtation with China. Tunisia, a reasonably well-organized one-party state, was one of the soundest and most stable countries in all Africa. There was little organized opposition to the ruling Neo-Destour Party, though there was an illegal, and quite inactive, Tunisian Communist Party of Soviet orientation. Tunisia produces nothing of special interest to China, except possibly its phosphates and food products. Peking's role seemed likely to remain one of watchful waiting, and of using its new Tunis embassy as a listening post for possible revolutionary ferment in the Kingdom of Libya, just next door.

Libya, a huge (810,000 square miles, population 1.5 million) desert kingdom, independent since 1952 after centuries of Turkish and then two generations of Italian control, might seem at first glance to offer a fair "revolutionary situation," though certainly not an excellent one. The country is fabulously wealthy and getting wealthier all the time, as a result of oil discoveries in 1958, which were expected to net the government at least $100 million in revenue in 1965. The oil is being developed mainly by American, West German, Dutch, French and British firms. Libya has a progressive five-year development plan that is supposed to lift its largely nomadic population out of ignorance and poverty.

Libya's foreign policy is guided by seventy-four-year-old King Idriss and his son, Crown Prince Hassan Reda. They have been assisted by a succession of rather conservative governments. That of Premier Mahmoud Muntasser was formed January 24, 1964, after some vaguely pro-Nasserite agitation among students in Tripoli and Benghazi, the two main cities. The King aimed at a balance between Nasser in the east and the Maghreb in the west. Opposing this was the growing restlessness of the younger generation, which would like to have a secular, Nasser-type republic.

Libya in 1964 was the only North African state, from the Atlantic to the Red Sea, not to have recognized Red China, though it has had relations with the Soviets since 1955. It did, however, begin voting in 1961 for Peking's admission to the United Nations. There was a small but active Chinese Nationalist Embassy in Tripoli that regularly mailed out Arabic-language Nationalist propaganda to other Arab-speaking countries in North Africa and elsewhere. It warned against the dangers of Communist penetration in Africa.

Since no overt Communist Chinese propaganda agency exists, Peking mails material directly (as it also does in African states where it has embassies) to newspapers, government personnel, members of the Libyan parliament, and others. Sometimes Libyan newspapers pick up articles favorable to Peking from the Cairo press, especially *Al-Ahram,* and from Algerian newspapers and broadcasts. Libyan editors are inclined to be receptive to material favorable to Peking, since Red China supports the Arabs against Israel. Libya, which has some resident Palestinian refugees, marks the beginning of the Arab zone that is sensitive on this score.

A nationalist campaign in 1964, backed by President Nasser, to get rid of both the big United States Air Force base at Wheelus Field and the British military bases afforded Peking a good propaganda cause. Under a Peking dateline of March 4 the New China News Agency distributed an expression of support from the National Federation of Students of China for Libyan student demonstrations against the bases. It termed the American bases "part of the efforts of the American imperialists to subjugate Africa and all the world . . . The Chinese students are convinced that the students and the other sectors of the Libyan people will chase imperialism from their country, as long as they stay united and persist in their struggle."

One Libyan newspaper, *Al Balagh,* since closed by the government, published an appeal for Libyan recognition of Peking just before the January 1964 session of parliament opened, but the editor apologized to the Nationalist Chinese Embassy. Another paper, *Al Ra'id,* also advocated recognition of Peking during the parliamentary session. Direct Chinese Communist propaganda is an effective weapon in Libya as in other African countries, since it is much harder to filter it out by censorship, than it is to control local releases emanating from established diplomatic and information missions. Egyptian newspapers and Cairo radio, when they pick up pro-Peking themes, are probably the only really effective weapon Peking will have in Libya, until some Libyan government decides on recognition.

CHAPTER EIGHTEEN

Plots, Plans, Aid and Trade

THE COLORFUL MARKET TOWN OF NIAMEY, CAPITAL OF THE REPUBLIC of Niger, was the setting of an event on October 13, 1964, that was unprecedented in this sleepy place. Thousands of men, women and children, draped in the bright cotton prints worn everywhere along the southern edges of the Sahara, streamed into town to watch a public execution. In Niger, a relatively peaceful member of the former French African Community, political violence had been rare since the country won independence in August 1960. Capital punishment for it was even rarer; President Hamani Diori, a former schoolteacher, did not approve. But on this day, four men fell in the sunlight to the dust of the public square, riddled by the bullets of a firing squad. Forty-three other persons received prison sentences.

This was no ordinary, domestic African plot. Disclosure of its details in the Niamey courtroom had evoked echoes of the Cameroon and the Congo. Djibo Bakary, an exiled former vice-premier, had stubbornly opposed every aspect of Diori's policy, from his pro-French rule to his cooperation with a Nationalist Chinese aid mission. Bakary controlled an opposition party called Sawaba, based in Accra and Bamako, where the Chinese had been in constant touch with him and a few of his friends. Beginning in 1961, they began to train in China a small partisan force, intended to eliminate President Diori and throw the country into turmoil.

Bakary's partisans had been trained and ordered to destroy bridges and ferryboats, administrative posts, isolated customs sheds, electric and telephone wires, fuel depots and public savings institutions. They had been told to throw open the prisons, sabotage Niger's electric power stations and—following a technique learned at Stanleyville and elsewhere in the Congo—render useless the airstrips by blocking them. Communications were to be cut between Niamey and the interior of the country, so as to create "free zones" where independent military government and communes would be established as the Yenan and other "Red zones" of China were established during the Chinese civil war.

The guerilla chief, Abubakr Dandouna, disclosed after his arrest that his thirty-man force had been recruited in 1960 and 1961. They had spent 1961 and 1962 training at Nanking. The exact curriculum of the Nanking school was almost identical with that undergone by the UPC partisans from the Cameroon, who may indeed have been trained at the same school. It was reconstructed from individual "study books" taken from several of the partisans by French security officers specializing in the Chinese tactics.

On October 24, 1964, scarcely ten days after the public execution of Dandouna and his three fellow partisans, members of the youth movement of Niger's ruling *Parti Progressiste Nigerien,* intercepted a new group of Chinese-trained guerillas, this time fourteen. They had planned to operate in collusion with another small group crossing the frontier from neighboring Upper Volta: this group was commanded by a certain Tini Malélé, another Nanking alumnus. A third group of Niger exiles was trained at a camp near Mampong, Ghana. While the Niger security forces continued their investigation, President Diori observed strict silence. However, he kept Presidents Felix Houphouet-Boigny of the Ivory Coast and Maurice Yaméogo of Upper Volta, French-speaking neighbor states that with Dahomey formed the so-called Council of the Entente, fully informed.

Niamey Radio charged on May 6 that Ghana was training about 50 young Niger nationals in secret camps in Odumase and Konungu, where Cameroon nationals of the UPC were also trained. Twelve Chinese experts, said Niamey, were assigned to these camps. Nationals of Niger, Nigeria, the Ivory Coast, Togo and the Cameroon Republic, it claimed, were being indoctrinated by Ghana police officials at the African Affairs Center in Accra; others, from Nigeria, the Cameroon and Togo were said to be undergoing similar training at the Kwame Nkrumah Ideological Institute at Winneba.

There are strong indications that French agents, operating quietly in all these countries of continued heavy French influence, cooperated in smashing the plot: one of the first instances since the Indo-China war in which Frenchmen, whose government now recognizes and tries to entertain good relations with Peking, found themselves directly pitted against Peking's operations.

At a news conference at Abidjan, the Ivory Coast capital, on January 25, 1965, the three Presidents evoked the Chinese danger to Africa in the strongest terms yet used in public by African statesmen. "At Nanking, in China," said Houphouet-Boigny, "Africans are being taught to assassinate those whose eyes are open to the Chinese danger, in order to replace them with servile men who will open the gates of Africa to China." Vice-President Ahomadegbé of Dahomey, another French-speaking state of the former Community that had recently recognized China, felt the need to reassure his own nervous government. "For the moment," he said on February 9, "Dahomey has no cause to fear—like Niger—the Chinese Communist danger recently denounced by the other three heads of the Entente Council." The Entente Council states were so upset by the plots that they refused to attend any international conferences at which Ghana's delegates were present. Ghana, they said, was a "Chinese base" for subversion.

Dahomey, like Niger an independent republic since August 1960, has been one of the more unstable states of the former French Community. It is beset by ethnic and political quarrels, and in October 1963 was the scene of one of the many African *coups d'etat,* arising from a military plot that had nothing to do with the Chinese or, apparently, any other outside power. A "provisional" soldier-administrator, Colonel Christophe Soglo, Chief of Staff of the 1,000-man Dahomean Army, allied himself with the trade unions, overthrew the government of President Hubert Maga, and himself took over the five main portfolios of government. Colonel Soglo promulgated a new constitution, and a measure of stability returned in January 1964, when President Mignan Apithy was elected by universal suffrage for a term of five years.

But there were signs of major social unrest ahead. The economy was stagnant. A large group of French-educated Dahomean civil servants, many of whom had worked in the administrations of other states of the French Community, were unable to find jobs. The country had to support over 2 million people on only 44,290 square miles, the highest population density in Africa.

Nationalist China had established diplomatic relations with Dahomey, and in March 1963, Taipeh sent one of its agricultural aid teams to the country. Under the Soglo and Apithy regimes, however, the patient diplomacy of Huang Hua, the Chinese Communist Ambassador to Ghana, won over Dahomey for Peking. The Nationalist Chinese mission went home. On November 12, 1964, Huang Hua and Foreign Minister Gabriel Lozes signed an agreement for the establishment of relations at ambassadorial level. Five days later, a trade union in Niger—then in ferment over the smashing of the Chinese plot—claimed that Vice-President Justin Ahomadegbé of Dahomey had sent three emissaries to Brazzaville to ask for Chinese Communist aid from the Ambassador there, Chou Chiu-yeh, who had evidently assumed jurisdiction for this zone from Huang Hua. Li Fang-ping, one of the less-experienced Chinese diplomats, became first chargé d'affaires in Dahomey. The country received a Chinese loan that reportedly totaled $20 million.

Set in the very heart of Africa is another former French Community state where Peking has begun to make inroads: the Central African Republic, called Ubangi-Shari when it was part of French Equatorial Africa. Though its navigable rivers made it a trading center from early times, it lacks a railroad and is 900 miles from the nearest seaport. The country is poor, and since November 1962, when the cabinet of President David Dacko dissolved five opposition parties, has been ruled as a one-party state.

President Dacko maintained relations with Nationalist China and the two countries had reached agreement in May 1964 on Formosan aid to the Central African Republic's handicraft industries. Apart from some French aid, and a very small amount from the United States, the country had little other help. Ruefully, President Dacko observed that "foreign capital is little inclined to come and share the terrible handicap of our distance from the sea." From Brazzaville, Ambassador Chou Chiu-yeh sent word to Dacko that Peking might be interested in helping to alleviate the country's transport and communications problems.

In November 1964, simultaneously with the failure of the Niger plot and the recognition accord with Dahomey, President Dacko sent the Nationalist Chinese chargé d'affaires packing and recognized Peking. Chu Chun-yi arrived in Bangui, the capital, to be first chargé d'affaires for Peking. Then, after a meeting between President Dacko and Chou Chiu-yeh in Brazzaville on December 5, Peking announced that President Liu Shao-chi had appointed no less a diplomat than Meng Ying as Ambassador. Meng, as we noted earlier, had served as first Ambassador to Zanzibar after the revolution there, and had then worked as deputy director of a reorganized African Affairs Department of the Chinese Foreign Ministry during 1964. A series of trade and aid accords were signed in December 1964 and January 1965, under which the Central African Republic received a loan of $4 million. By accepting Meng Ying's overtures and this initial loan, President Dacko appeared to have immunized his regime, for a time at least, against the sort of troubles Niger had experienced.

As Red China unfolds its African offensive, it moves into contact with other areas. There were early signs of Peking's interest in Togo, and Peking was quick to recognize the independence of Gambia, Britain's last West African colony, in February 1965. Peking backs the Chad National Union, a violent revolutionary group opposed to the pro-French government of the Chad Republic.

The Sudan Republic was one of the first African regimes to recognize Peking, and sells cotton to it. Chou En-lai visited Khartoum on his tour of ten African states in early 1964. In the fall of that year, a popular revolution, exploited in part by the well-disciplined Moscow-line Sudanese Communist Party, overthrew the military regime of General Ibrahim Abboud. By early 1965 the Chinese had not drawn obvious profit from this situation, or from the clash of the Moslem northern Sudanese national authorities with the Christian, Negro south: one or two Peking Radio broadcasts and New China News Agency releases on this backed the official government position, in line with Peking's Islamophile policy.

CHAPTER NINETEEN

Nationalist China in Africa

THE COUNTER-EFFORTS OF NATIONALIST CHINA IN AFRICA, WHICH have been of some importance in undecided areas like Nigeria, are worth a closer and more serious look than they have had so far in the West.

Logically, Formosa should have some appeal for Africans. It is large by African standards (between 11 million and 12 million population). It has a semi-tropical climate, so that its agricultural techniques for growing rice and other crops can easily be transplanted to many regions of Africa. It doubled its farm output between 1954 and 1964. The Kuomintang philosophy includes many principles compatible with "African socialism." Like the African countries, it has a "developing" economy. In 1965, Formosa was able to announce it no longer needed United States economic aid.

Formosa seeks support among Africans in much the same way Peking does: by exchanging messages, greetings and delegations; by granting scholarships and even economic aid. In doing this, Formosa has sought to keep its United Nations seat by retaining the African votes it held and if possible winning more. It has worked against Peking's offensive in Africa, and wants both profitable markets for its produce and new worlds for its students and trained personnel to work in, since they often feel cramped and frustrated on their island.

In African eyes, Formosa is heavily identified with the United States and American policy. Only African states that are friendly to the United States, or earlier, France or Britain, have tended to open and to keep their relations with Nationalist China—though there are African states, such as Morocco, that are quite openly friendly to the United States, and yet have always recognized Peking, and only Peking. Nationalist China usually votes along anti-colonialist lines in the United Nations, even though it must keep up its good relations with European states that still recognize it, such as Spain.

The Sino-African Committee on Technical Cooperation is the government organism in Taipeh that administers Formosa's own African counter-offensive. It began this counter-offensive in 1960, and for a time it managed to step up the pace each year. Efforts are especially geared to African states that supported Taipeh in the U.N. In 1960 the Taipeh government sent good-will missions to eleven African countries, sometimes crossing the paths of the Chinese Communist emissaries. In 1961 a number of prominent Africans were invited to Formosa, and a Nationalist Chinese trade mission went to seven West African states.

Liberia requested and received the visit in March 1961 of a Nationalist Chinese technical mission that studied Liberia's agricultural needs and helped set up a development program. Taipeh also sent fourteen expert farmers to set up a successful model farm. Two months later a Formosan team visited Togo. Dahomey, before it switched from Taipeh to Peking, reached an agreement with Taipeh under which Nationalist China helped develop its water resources. One of Dahomey's ministers visited Formosa and sent trainees to Dahomey's fishing industry. There was an exchange of agricultural missions with the Congo (Leopoldville).

Libya asked for Chinese Nationalist agricultural aid in 1961. According to a Formosa newspaper, it was disappointed in United Nations efforts and hesitant as to whether it should take Western or Communist assistance for its irrigation and farming programs. The Tripoli and Taipeh governments signed an agreement on technical cooperation in February 1962. Nationalist China set up a model farm, and in March 1963, six Chinese farmers arrived from Formosa to train Libyan agriculturists. The mission in Libya, under the overall management of the Nationalist Chinese Ambassador, Chen Chih-ping, impressed Libyans with its ability to make rice grow in the middle of the desert.

In 1962, Formosa offered rice for flood relief victims in Kenya. Formosan experts studied rice cultivation in Gabon. Seminars on agriculture for chosen Africans were held in Formosa in 1962 and 1963.

Chad and the Ivory Coast also concluded agreements with Taipeh on technical cooperation. Formosan teams were sent to Gabon, the Ivory Coast and Ethiopia. In the Cameroon Republic, where the government rankled under the Peking-backed guerilla revolt, the Deputy Foreign Minister signed a cultural agreement with Formosa.

At the independence celebrations for Burundi, a Chinese Nationalist diplomat replaced Ho Ying, though Burundi soon recognized Peking instead of Taipeh, with the results we have seen. Uganda invited both Communists and Nationalists to its ceremonies: this time the Nationalists declined, and as we saw, Uganda opened full diplomatic relations with Peking.

In March 1964, Formosan agricultural teams of ten experts apiece were sent out to Nigeria and Senegal. Under an agreement signed the same month, another team specializing in truck gardening and mountain crops arrived in Sierra Leone to work in that still British-supervised territory. By this time more than 100 African specialists had been trained in three separate courses organized in Formosa since 1962. These Africans return home generally satisfied with their experiences and equipped to contribute some new skills to their national economies. Israel has a training and technical aid program for Africans that is similar in some respects.

Formosa cannot, of course, compete in the scope or financial amount of its aid with that of Communist China, and certainly not with the Soviet Union. All that it has been able to do, and all that it can hope to do, is to select certain targets that are important to its own well-being. If it loses its United Nations seat to Communist China, its efforts are likely to be forgotten.

CHAPTER TWENTY

Sino-Soviet Competition in Aid and Trade

IN BOTH THE COMMUNIST CHINESE AND THE SOVIET CONCEPTS, trade and aid are integrated components of the same policy toward the underdeveloped countries. Unlike many Western countries, the U.S.S.R. and Red China are able to exercise absolute control over the initial patterns, if not all the end uses, both of assistance and of trade.

In Africa, Peking and Moscow both often present their trade agreements and medium-term credits in a single, businesslike package, wrapped in the friendly tissue paper of "peaceful coexistence" and "non-interference in internal affairs." The impact of such offers can be strong in a new country that is short of capital, and is generally getting unfavorable terms for its export sales in the West.

But what about the competition between Red China and the Soviets in aid and trade?

Bilateral agreements, as we have seen, are attractive because they establish a fictitious equality of status, as in the case of China's green tea, a consumer item, against Morocco's cobalt ore. Generally, East bloc purchasing missions operate in Africa without giving assurance that trade will reach the projected level: the glare of publicity surrounding the signing is the main thing. Since the starting level is so low, almost any increase can be made to look huge. Of all the Communist bloc states, only the Czechs seem to act at least as much, if not more, from purely commercial motives as from political and ideological ones in their aid-trade policies. The same is more true for the Red Chinese in certain areas, such as Morocco, where they see genuine chances of expanding the market for some of their foods, textiles and manufactured goods.

Nearly all African states, including those with white-supremacy governments, now have trade agreements with one or more members of the Communist bloc. Generally East bloc trade before 1965 accounted for 5 to 6 per cent of the total: African trade is still overwhelmingly directed toward Western groupings such as the European Common Market and the British Commonwealth's sterling area. Guinea, with 25 per cent of its trade going to the Communist bloc, and the Republic of Sudan, which sells it a great deal of its cotton, are the big exceptions.

As we have seen, the Red Chinese are more selective in their commercial dealings than the Soviets, just as they are forced to be far more sparing in their aid. Red China is tightly limited by its own internal economic difficulties in the aid it is able to offer, and doubtless in its trade as well. In recent years, visitors to the Export Exhibition Hall, over the Pearl River in Canton, where China displays all the goods it is offering, have been struck by the fact that where Red China used to import far more raw consumer goods—the kind the African states can offer—the emphasis has shifted to industrial goods since 1960. At the same time, China's own exports are shifting from raw to manufactured goods, which are what African countries still need most. In most African markets, as in most Asian, Chinese manufactured goods cannot compete with those from Japan. The Japanese, with their astounding energy and astuteness, might drive the Red Chinese right out of their African markets in years to come, just as they seek to do in Asia.

Japan, unlike any other major industrial and commercial power, has so far been able to remain entirely nonpartisan in African politics. Tokyo's largest trading partner on the continent has been the Republic of South Africa, but it has also signed preferential agreements with several West African states. In May 1965, Japanese industrialists were negotiating their largest achievement in Africa yet: construction in Zambia of a fertilizer plant and a copper factory—the latter important as a source of supply to Japan's burgeoning shipbuilding industry. Despite its own astoundingly fast industrial development, China was far from being in a position to offer the Africans any such industrial riches as these.

Peking seeks to convince Africans that the best way to build truly independent national economies, free of links with former colonial powers, is through the "mutual" aid offered by China, rather than the "tied" or "one-sided" aid of the Soviets and the West. Repeatedly the Chinese propaganda media charge that the white nations seek to impose "neo-colonialism" through their aid programs. This argument is effective in countries where programs of aid to imports are made contingent on "buying American."

Geographically, up to 1965, at least, West Africa, especially Ghana, Guinea and Mali, had been more of a Soviet than a Red Chinese preserve. China had shown a stronger interest in aid and trade along the East African coast. In Tanzania, Kenya and the Somali Republic, as well as in Algeria, Sino-Soviet competition was especially keen.

Quantitatively, Red China's aid has lagged far behind Russia's. Studies show that only in Algeria, Guinea, Mali and the Somali Republic did Chinese aid before 1964 amount to 20 per cent or more of the Soviet-bloc commitment. Kenya and Tanzania were added to this list in 1964, when the Chinese redoubled their offensive in East Africa.

Before Chou En-lai's visit to Africa in the winter of 1963-64, China's total commitment in Africa since 1954 had been scarcely $400 million and had been limited to Algeria, Ghana, Guinea, Mali and the Somali Republic—if we set aside clandestine military aid to revolutionary movements in areas like the Cameroon Republic, the Congo and Portuguese Africa, and some military aid to several independent governments such as Algeria. The Soviet commitment, however, was about $1.5 billion, and this went well over the $2 billion mark in 1964 with massive new promises to the United Arab Republic and Algeria. The net total commitment of the Western nations probably ran close to $6 billion during the same period.

How does the character of Chinese Communist aid compare with that of its Soviet and Western adversaries?

The assistance of the Soviets and their satellites is generally in the form of credits granted at low-interest rates (usually 2.5 per cent). These are tied to execution, under Communist supervision, of projects agreed upon with the interested government. In one typical year, 1960-61, Western aid in the form of grants represented 38.5 per cent of governmental disbursements to Africa and the Middle East. Many long-term loans are also included in the Western programs: in 1961, nearly 8 per cent of United Kingdom and 35 per cent of United States loans were for twenty years or more.

By contrast, the Chinese loans are usually interest-free, and repayment often is to start only ten years after the loan is accorded, and then in goods, not cash. Simplicity is the keynote in administering the loans. This is attractive to the African countries, which lack trained civil servants. Chinese aid is supposed to be granted in accordance with eight more or less inflexible principles. Peking is constantly repeating these for Afro-Asian consumption (see Appendix B).

Half or more of Soviet and Chinese aid taken together has been industrial schemes. In these, emphasis is placed on plants that produce capital or engineering goods, and that employ local raw materials, which African governments of course prefer. Transportation and communications receive a sizable share. So do geological surveys and the generation of electricity. Just as in the Communist homelands, especially Red China, encouragement to local production of consumer goods comes last. This has been the reason for the sharp drop in popularity of Communist aid programs in such countries as Guinea, where a modest but rather effective United States aid program concentrated on getting more consumer goods into the country and getting them sold cheaply.

Whereas the Soviets have favored heavy industry and major projects such as the great Aswan High Dam and the eastern Algerian steel complex, China concentrates more on commercial ventures, such as a special program of imports at the time of the 1964 Casablanca Trade Fair, which appears to have netted a handsome profit for Peking.

Generally, the rate of progress on Communist-bloc development programs in Africa has been slow, with the Aswan High Dam a notable exception. The Chinese agricultural programs—both Communist and Nationalist—seem to have produced a more favorable impression so far than the Soviet industrial projects, always with Aswan as the great exception. In 1963, according to British sources, the Soviets and their satellites had about 2,000 technicians in Africa, with very few Red Chinese (my own estimate would be less than 500, though this undoubtedly rose in 1964). Salaries and living expenses of Soviet-bloc technicians are usually charged at full rates to the credit financing the project. This created a bad impression in Guinea and Mali. The Chinese profited by this through their famous program of obliging their technicians to live at the level of their hosts.

African states with long experience of Communist-bloc aid, such as Egypt, Guinea and Ghana, have become rather wary of it. Only the Congo (Leopoldville) has rejected it outright, although Morocco made it clear that Communist aid offered up to 1964—with the exception of Polish aid for a beet sugar refinery—had far too many strings attached.

There has been no perceptible private investment from the Communist bloc in Africa to my knowledge, with the possible exception of very small amounts from Czechoslovakia. Africans often complain that Communist offers do not correspond to real needs: the Red Chinese, of all the East bloc states, have been the most attentive about correcting this. There are also complaints of sharp Communist trading practices, and the on-trading of exports, such as Moroccan sardines, which are sold cheaply to Red China and then sold by the Chinese to East European countries at a handsome profit.

Countries depending on one or two major crops for their foreign exchange earnings (such as the cloves of Zanzibar or the cocoa of Ghana) are especially vulnerable if agreements with Communist countries tie up a major part of their exports, yet do not produce the needed industrial imports and raw materials. This has been the case with both Soviet and Red Chinese purchases of Egyptian cotton. If Communist exports lag, the recipient African country may be pressed to lower specifications and discriminate against non-bloc imports. This can harm both its home economy and its foreign trade. Probably the most chronic examples were in Guinea between 1959 and 1961.

Another big drawback of the barter accords the Communist countries prefer is that the recipient African country is committed to a certain price level over a period of months or even years. This means that it cannot take advantage of world market price fluctuations in its favor. This happened to Morocco with Cuban sugar purchases in 1964. Mali mortgaged a large part of its peanut crop to Communist states against machinery and services, while France, which would have been willing to pay preferential rates, was denounced as "neo-colonialist."

In sum, the Communist Chinese offers of "mutual" aid and trade, microscopic as they are by comparison with the total of Western, Nationalist Chinese and Soviet aid programs, have a strong appeal, especially in countries that have been disillusioned with Western "neo-colonialist" programs or grandiose Soviet-bloc ones. The spectacle of Chinese technicians and even Chinese laborers modestly working side by side with Africans has already captured many African imaginations in places like Guinea and Mali. However, the Chinese with their strained domestic economy, very limited resources and relatively large expenditures on propaganda and military subversion against Western and pro-Western African governments, cannot soon begin to approach the productive value of the programs offered by their rivals. This puts their emotional and sentimental appeal, strong as it is, under heavy strain. It also makes it difficult to predict the degree of their long-term success, since this will depend as much on the mistakes of the West and the Soviets as on the powerful subjective factors that, in seeming defiance of practical economics, often seem to govern African destinies.

CHAPTER TWENTY-ONE

Peking's Propaganda Push

SOMEWHERE IN THE AFRICAN BUSH A TRIBESMAN SMEARED WITH RED camwood paint, wearing animal skins, bends over a transistor radio. A Radio Peking speaker exhorts him in his own language to throw out the white colonialists who are robbing his country. In a nearby town an African schoolteacher listens to a Peking broadcast in French, English, Swahili or Lingala on political economy, telling him how Africans must shake loose the domination of the monopolists and imperialists, "with the United States at their head." In his classroom, because no other materials are available, he uses books and magazines from Peking for teaching English. One of his students has just received an airplane ticket for Peking from the Chinese Embassy: he is going on a grant for a year's study in China. In another farming community a village policeman is startled to find a manual on guerilla warfare tactics sandwiched between innocent-looking textbooks on how to repair tractors.

All over Africa, from Casablanca to Capetown, such scenes take place daily. Peking is engaged in a propaganda effort on the African continent that is probably unprecedented anywhere, unless perhaps by the Soviet propaganda in Eastern Europe after the Second World War.

This propaganda drive has two main objectives. The first is the obvious one of influencing Africans to embrace Chinese Communist theory and especially the Chinese doctrine of violent revolution against white rule and Western influence in all its forms. This is represented as part of a world-wide struggle against "U.S. imperialism and racism," a struggle taking place from Santiago, Chile, all the way through Jackson, Mississippi, to Harlem, Johannesburg and Singapore.

Its second objective, though generally sought through far more sophisticated channels and methods, is equally ambitious and daring. It is to force the Soviets and their satellites out of their positions of control in international Communist fronts and organizations for African workers, youth, students, journalists, women, lawyers, doctors and "peace workers" and to set up Chinese-dominated organizations in their place. This, in turn, is one part of the larger Chinese design for control of the entire world Communist movement, and if possible, the support of the whole "non-aligned" world as well.

The central control mechanisms from which Red China works toward these objectives are nearly all in Peking itself, though some have been transplanted to Jakarta, Indonesia, especially since the Indonesian dispute with Malaysia became acute in 1964. In some cases operational centers have been set up in Africa, though a guiding hand is always exercised from China itself.

Most of these control organs were formed in 1960 and 1961. One is the Committee for the Support of Afro-Asian Liberation Movements. This has had the least publicity of any, and is rarely mentioned by Chinese Communist information media. Western intelligence agencies are convinced that one of its most important functions is to distribute military aid to armed forces, such as the Algerian army, and to the liberation movements wherever an interesting "revolutionary situation" may arise.

The Chinese Institute of African Affairs, though more publicized than the Committee for Support, is also an organization about which Peking is rather reticent. This is because it trains African Communist Party cadres. Its role is bound to increase as Peking seeks to swing the allegiance of more and more of the handful of African Communist leaders away from Moscow and toward itself.

Well publicized, in contrast, is the Chinese-African Peoples' Friendship Society. This arranges cultural and economic exchanges. A Vice-President, Chang Tieh-shang, has been especially active in organizing occasions like "African Freedom Day" each April 15, at which the usual speeches are made by Chinese and Africans in Peking.

Another organization with the innocent-sounding name of the

Committee for Cultural Relations with African People apparently has the mission of controlling all Chinese Communist agents in various fields who have been sent to Africa. These control operations are of course ultra-secret. Some have been disclosed by Chinese defectors, such as Tung Chi-ping.

Parallel with these, and probably closely coordinated with them, are the overt diplomatic activities of the Ministry of Foreign Affairs under Marshal Chen Yi, and the operations of the New China News Agency. In 1964 and 1965 New China transmitted by radio to a number of regional bureaus in London, Berne, Algiers, Cairo, Conakry, Brazzaville and Dar es-Salaam a long daily news file in high-speed Morse code. Adapted to each region, this was transcribed, mimeographed in French or English, and either mailed free or sold for nominal fees to newspapers, periodicals and radio and television stations all over Africa.

New China has concluded a series of exchange agreements with the news agencies of those African countries Red China is most interested in. A typical example is Algeria. In July 1964 Chu Mu-chih, one of New China's senior staffers, signed an exchange accord with the director of Algérie Presse Service for cooperation between their respective agencies. Chu signed such agreements with Ghana, Pakistan, Burma and numerous other Afro-Asian countries. Chu also appears to act as a sort of inspector-general of the New China News Agency, making certain that New China correspondents fulfill their appointed role. This was defined for them by a party journal in China in 1957 as "acting as the ears and mouth of the Party, the government and the people." We have already seen how in Africa this involves performing quasi-diplomatic or intelligence functions.

Radio Peking is the best-known and most effective propaganda channel of Red China in Africa. It began its African service in November 1956, fully two years ahead of the Soviets. The early broadcasts had only a very limited reception, because they were in Morse code at dictation speed, and very few Africans read Morse. In November 1958 Peking began a daily program in Cantonese for the Chinese communities in southeastern Africa and the Malagasy Republic. This had little propaganda content. It was probably intended as a technical experiment to measure reception possibilities and test listener reaction among the resident Chinese.

By September 1959 Peking had begun its first two-hour program in English beamed to Africa. Two years later it was already well ahead of Moscow in air time: African listening posts were logging thirty-five hours weekly in English, seven in Cantonese, seven in Portuguese, seven in Swahili, four in French, and three also in English that were not beamed exclusively to Africa. This probably gives a fair idea of what Peking's propaganda priorities were at the time. In addition, there were other broadcasts in Arabic, beamed primarily to the Middle East, but also picked up in Arab North Africa (when not jammed by the French).

The programs were generally of good technical and editorial quality, and were obviously intended to be entertaining. Since Red China did not sign the international convention on radio frequencies, it completely ignored other stations and used any frequency it chose, changing frequently and often crowding up against broadcasts from Moscow, the BBC, the Voice of America, or Radio Brazzaville.

I have monitored Peking broadcasts in both American-accented English and British-accented English beamed to Africa. In the latter case, frequencies are often right next to the BBC frequency, and chimes that sound startlingly like BBC chimes are sometimes used.

By September 1963, Peking was giving daily commentaries in Hausa, one of the principal languages of sub-Saharan Africa from Guinea to Chad. At that time, its total broadcast time had risen to 68.5 hours weekly, including seven each in Hausa, Swahili and Portuguese—as compared with Moscow, which had by then forged well ahead in air time with 115.5 hours.

As the Sino-Soviet split widened, Peking broadcasts included more and more anti-Soviet polemics. They carried the full texts of the main Chinese doctrinal statements, and many Soviet ones as well. They also used militant declarations by African political and labor leaders visiting China and, of course, reports of successful "armed struggles" in various parts of Africa. Radio Peking marked the independence of Zanzibar on December 10, 1963, with a special broadcast, and in 1964 began to use more and more "on-the-spot" accounts by its own correspondents—as well as those of New China—of African political, economic and cultural developments. There were also some straight travelogues, feature material and many detailed programs on various aspects of life inside Red China—always stressing the similarities with conditions in Africa. According to a BBC report from Cairo in May 1964, the ranking in foreign broadcast radio time in Africa was Red China, Russia, the United States, Britain and the United Arab Republic in that order.

Red China has a well-coordinated publication program aimed at

Africa. Its political backbone is the weekly review *Peking Review,* published in French as *Pékin Informations,* and mailed around the world by Chifa, the China Publications Center, directed by Guozi Shudian, a Chinese Moslem. It is interesting to note in passing that many copies were found in Stanleyville amid litter the rebels left behind. Special consideration is shown toward stamp collectors by putting a different group of colorful Chinese stamps on magazines mailed in successive weeks to the same subscriber. *Peking Review* reaches individual subscribers and distribution centers in Africa in English, French, Spanish and Portuguese by air mail, direct from Peking. Giving each week's Chinese and world events through Peking's eyes, *Peking Review* is given away in some areas, and sold at subscription rates ranging from about fifty cents to $1.25 a year in others. Local Chinese emissaries regularly compile address lists of key persons, who then receive free introductory copies. An African subscriber who buys an additional subscription for himself or someone else receives a color calendar. A second extra subscription brings a Chinese scroll, and a third, a desk diary.

The monthly magazines *China Reconstructs* and *China Pictorial,* often beautifully printed and always well-illustrated, present Chinese art, life, landscape, letters and of course Chinese Communist society in gay and vivid colors. Other specialized magazines on foreign trade, Chinese cinema and Chinese literature reach key Africans in these fields at nominal or no cost. Chinese Embassies in Africa distribute many press releases (as distinct from the dispatches of the New China News Agency) with special studies on such subjects as light industry, agriculture and petroleum in China. From Switzerland there came the slick-paper *Révolution,* edited by French Communist Jacques Vergés and American Richard Gibson, pushing the Chinese line, though this was suspended in 1965. Through Guozi Shudian, Peking sends around the world a large variety of brochures, pamphlets and books in the major European and African languages. Mao's works, of course, are available in abundance, especially his military writings. There are Chinese folk tales for children and adults; books on Chinese art, art reproductions of Chinese painting, drawing and artisan products, treatises on the new Chinese theater. There are many purely political pamphlets with such titles as *Statement Calling on the People of the World to Unite to Oppose Racial Discrimination by U. S. Imperialism and Support the American Negroes in Their Struggle against Racial Discrimination.*

Literature is also pressed into the service of African, Asian and

American Negro "revolutions." For example, the home service of
Radio Peking reported on April 9, 1964, that poetry recitals had
been gaining popularity in the theaters, factories, communes, schools
and army units of China. To coordinate this activity with political
goals, the cities of Shanghai, Peking, Canton and Harbin held poetry
recitals in support of Cuba, the American Negroes and Panama in
their "just struggle against American imperialism." African students
in China are sometimes invited to these recitals, at least when they
are held in Peking (since African students are not allowed to leave
the capital).

The theme of race in the United States is an increasingly persistent
and extremely effective leitmotif of all Red Chinese propaganda in
Africa. In 1965 a campaign was launched to convince the world that
the Black Nationalist leader, Malcolm X, shot in Harlem, was really
killed by "white racists." The first issue of the French-language magazine *Littérature Chinoise,* which Peking distributed widely in Africa
in 1964, gave some details about a giant poetry recital in which "over
1,000 poets, including many foreign ones, took part," sponsored by
Tsang Keh-kia, chief editor of the Chinese magazine *Poetry.* This
recital concerned mainly the American Negroes. Kwang Wei-jan recited his poem called "I Sing of the Combat of Liberty," which
"saluted the heroic epoch when the flames of anger spread around the
world" and "the slaves rise up to become the masters."

When the Ghanaian poet George Awooner-Williams recited "The
Awakening of the Black Eagle," he "marked the rhythm by beating a
drum with his hands, in the traditional manner of Ghana, and ended
with the cry *'Uhuru'* (Liberty)." The program also included recital of
a poem called "To My Black Brothers of Alabama" by the exiled
Sudanese poet Ahmed Kheir; "Black Friends, We Are With You," by
the Vietnamese poet Pham Nag Hong; and "Those In Search of
Liberty," by the Indonesian poet Lisakotta.

Tasteful and interesting displays of Chinese traditional painting
have been shown in many African capitals. One I saw in Rabat
featured eighty reproductions of celebrated Chinese paintings from
the Tang Dynasty (A.D. 618-907) to the present. The exhibition drew
much favorable comment from the students, artists and intellectuals
in Morocco. A brochure explained that "under the direction of the
People's government, this excellent traditional art was continued,
renovated and developed, since the very founding of New China,
according to the directives 'may a hundred flowers blossom' and 'let

the new detach itself from the old.' " In Bamako the same show was accompanied with a lecture by Chen Yin, a visiting Chinese painter.

Chinese specialists in everything from art to entomology are sent to any African country that will receive them. One such scientific mission, which visited Ghana, Mali, Guinea, Algeria and Morocco in the spring of 1964, included Chen Ki-yi, assistant rector of the Higher Institute of Agriculture of Peking, Chang Mao-kiun, assistant rector of the Peking Mines and Metallurgy Institute, and Chang Yiu-cheng, assistant chief engineer of the Kwantung Geological Bureau.

Even philately is pressed into the service of Peking's propaganda efforts in Africa. In 1964 the Chinese Postal Ministry issued a new series of stamps to mark "African Freedom Day," on April 15. One of the stamps, reported the New China News Agency, shows a Chinese and an African with linked arms, "symbolizing Sino-African friendship"; the other, an African "beating a war drum."

The cinema is gaining importance as a Chinese Communist weapon in Africa. This involves both an offensive against the influence of Hollywood and American films, and the promotion of films about Africa from China and Chinese-dominated areas. Both objectives have been pursued at a series of three Afro-Asian Film Festivals, the last of which was held at Jakarta, Indonesia, in April 1964. The fourth was scheduled to be held in Pyongyang, North Korea, sometime in 1966.

At Jakarta delegates from twenty-three African and Asian countries, under Peking's benevolent eye and with active Red Chinese participation, passed a resolution vowing to end "imperialist domination of the film world in Africa and Asia." They proposed to "develop national cinema industries as well as the Afro-Asian cinema in general, inspired by a democratic spirit that cherishes liberty and peace."

Indonesian President Achmed Sukarno welcomed the delegates with a rousing anti-imperialist speech, and told film workers they should work together on the basis of the principles of the first Bandung Conference. The delegates resolved that the "imperialist domination of the United States" was a threat "to our culture and national identity." The resolution went on to say that "imperialist films, especially Hollywood films" spread various "attitudes, philosophies and ways of life" that are harmful. Some of the qualifying adjectives used for Hollywood influence were "pessimistic, defeatist, fatalistic, anarchist, nihilist, adventurist, racist, non-patriotic, warlike, against peace and the independence of nations."

"If we do not take guard, if we do not oppose them sufficiently," it said, "all this will act as a poison that will finally destroy our peoples, physically and mentally." The motion picture was "the weapon we hold" for "support of all the liberation movements of the peoples of Africa, Asia and Latin America." The New China News Agency reported that more than eighty films from Asian and African countries had been shown in mainland China since 1950.

Some of the documentaries made on African subjects by Chinese cameramen in Africa, processed in Chinese studios, and shipped back to Africa are the color film "Resolute Algeria" and black-and-white films called "Cities of Morocco," "An Ode to the Nile," "Independent Mali," "The Horn of Africa," "Chinese People Condemn the Murder of Patrice Lumumba," and others on Ghana, Guinea and Tanganyika. Two Chinese films, "The White-haired Girl" and "The Daughters of the Party," were dubbed in Bambara with the cooperation of Malian film artists in May 1964. This was the first time Chinese films had been dubbed in an African language.

"Chinese film weeks" are frequently organized in African capitals. During one in Algiers in April 1964 some of the titles offered were "Hurricane," "Intrepid Algeria," "The Flowers Open" and "The Cuban People in Battle." Chinese lecturers explained to the Algerians how the Communists in China made clandestine films under Kuomintang rule, and claimed that Red China has exported 5,000 films. I watched Red Chinese film stars, quite glamorous in their Hong Kong split skirts, flouncing up the carpeted steps of the Aletti Hotel, pursued by solemn-faced Chinese security police in gray suits and crepe-soled shoes. (The Aletti, which during World War II, was the Allied headquarters in Algiers, in 1962 sheltered French Secret Army terrorists who murdered Arabs indiscriminately in the desperate hope that this would keep Algeria French forever.) Though the Algerian newspapers printed glowing reports of the film week, and the Chinese Education Minister, Yang Hsiu-feng, was told after leaving money for the rebuilding of Algiers University, burned by the Secret Army Organization in June 1962, that "Algeria will not forget the aid of China," many Algerians showed irritation that Yang had chosen the week of the FLN's first party congress, a crucial test for Ben Bella's power, in which to hold the "Chinese Film Week."

One interesting Chinese cultural propaganda venture in Africa has been a troupe of dancers and musicians about 400 strong. They present not only dances of China and the "national minorities" (such as the Uighurs and Mongolians, many of whom live in the zones disputed with the Soviet Union), but also of most of the African and Asian countries. In each country they visit they study local dances and music and, somewhat in the manner of Isadora Duncan, make arrangements of them.

I attended their presentation in Casablanca in July 1964. Their idea of a "Berber mountain song" was embarrassingly far from the mark. It drew only a smattering of polite and somewhat pained applause from the Moroccans. But their version of a Berber dance, put on by Chinese lads and lasses clad in authentic Moroccan costumes who obviously enjoyed the dance immensely, was an instant hit. Africans, like anyone else, are tremendously flattered by a conscious and serious foreign attempt to portray their own folkways, however clumsy the attempt may be. Of all the various American, French, British, Belgian, Spanish, Soviet, Czech, Polish and miscellaneous other cultural groups sent to entertain Africans or win their approval, only the Chinese had the imagination to try this.

On "African Liberty Day," in April 1964, all of the African diplomats, students and visitors in China were invited to Peking for a super-production of the troupe, which included songs and dances of fourteen African countries. The climax of the evening, according to a Radio Peking report, was a rendition by China's Central Philharmonic Orchestra of a "Hymn to Chinese-African Friendship," composed especially for the evening by Chairman Mao himself.

Few Chinese activities in Africa are as important in their possible future impact as the training of African students in China. Precise data on their numbers are lacking, but one Western estimate in 1964 was that there were several hundred, mainly at the University of Peking, but probably fewer than the total number in Russia. World attention was attracted to the failure of much of this program, and the hypocrisy it has revealed in China's racist propaganda, by the publication in 1964 of the account of Emmanuel John Hevi of Ghana, general secretary of the Union of African Students in China, describing his own disillusions and disgust (*An African Student in China;* London: the Pall Mall Press).

Hevi did not go to China until 1961. Peking's African student program seems to have begun in 1958, when the Prague-based International Union of Students (IUS) began to operate a sanatorium especially for African students near Peking. From this year on Peking issued blanket invitations for students from countries just gaining independence, in particular the Congo (Leopoldville), the Somali Republic in 1960, and Algeria in 1962.

By 1961 there were about 500 students from Morocco, Algeria, the United Arab Republic, the Sudan, the Somali Republic, Kenya, Zanzibar, Cameroon, Chad, Ghana and Uganda. They were sent first to a course at the Institute of Foreign Languages in Peking to learn enough Chinese to be able to tackle their other courses. The Union of African Students in China was formed in April, with Elias Okidi of Uganda as President and Hevi as general secretary. Its aim was given as "promoting cooperation and unity among African students struggling for the total liberation of Africa from colonialism and neo-colonialism and ousting imperialism from Africa and the whole world."

Life for the students seems scarcely ever to have been easy. Chinese racial discrimination against them was flagrant and generalized, according to many accounts. Western intelligence sources, for example, learned of a riot in March 1962 that began with a brawl between a Zanzibari student and a Chinese outside a Peking hotel. Several people were hospitalized and the Chinese authorities eventually sent an apology to the student concerned.

The main complaints of students coming out of China were against "racial discrimination," prohibitions against African students shopping at stores open to other foreigners, and even the "ban on friendship between Africans and Chinese." A crisis between the Africans and the Peking authorities was resolved only after the intervention of the Guinean Ambassador and the Ghanaian chargé d'affaires, who also secured the release of the Africans arrested on various charges during the protest meetings that followed the riot.

In 1961 four Sudanese students refused to stay in China for the full seven-year course they had begun. They returned home at the end of the first year, complaining that segregation made life impossible for them. A Chilean student, Manuel Migone, complained bitterly over the difference between conditions in China portrayed in *China Pictorial* and the real ones as they existed in 1961. He said that dissatisfaction was such that in addition to the four Sudanese, four Indians, fifteen Iraqis and twenty Somalis had "gone home in disgust."

Foreign students at Peking University were forbidden to travel more than nineteen miles from the center of the city, were only allowed out of the precincts of the university on group outings, and, perhaps most serious of all for China's anti-white propaganda abroad, were not permitted to mix with Chinese students or attend regular students' meetings. Chinese students were forbidden to frequent foreigners or give them information.

In his book Hevi discloses other aspects of the African students' ordeal. He says that they were given scarcely any peace by organizers of demonstrations and by Communist Party officials who wished to make sure Peking got its money's worth out of their presence. Even their Chinese-language instruction was inadequate. Hevi had six months of this, during which he learned sentences about how Mao Tse-tung, like the new-risen sun, brought joy to the toilers of the East. On the other hand, he was lacking the vocabulary for "a glass of water," and so did not know how to ask for one.

"Out of a total of 118 African students who studied in China in my time," reports Hevi, "96 had actually left and a further 10 had signified their intention to leave by the time I had packed my bags. . . ." Their reasons included boredom, poor quality of instruction, and—by far the most important—racism.

Peking keeps trying to impress its stamp on every facet of youth activity. In sports it has sponsored, with Indonesian collaboration, what amounts to its own Afro-Asian Olympic games. They are called the "Games of the Newly Emerging Forces," or GANEFO. One series of these was held at Jakarta in November 1963. The New China News Agency reported on November 23 that, after the games, sports delegations from Algeria, Morocco, Tunisia and Nigeria met "leaders of art troupes" from the U.S.S.R., China, North Korea and Cuba. The Chinese sportsmen in Jakarta had entertained with special solicitude some thirty Algerian delegates to the games, led by the Algerian athlete Ali Buwadi. To combat the Moscow-line World Federation of Democratic Youth (WFDY) in Africa, Peking helped to sponsor a Pan-African Youth Movement, headed in 1964 by a Guinean, Bangara Kanfoury.

This organization and similar ones in Asia, as well as many less-aligned youth leaders in Africa, received regularly from Peking copies of an English-language Red Chinese magazine called *Evergreen*. The issue for April 24, 1963, carried a map entitled "Development of the African Peoples' Struggle Against Colonialism." The map's key shows "Countries still under the rule of white colonialism" and repeats stock anti-American slogans.

One of the many Afro-Asian Communist front groups that the

Chinese have tried to split is the Women's International Democratic Federation (WIDF), founded in 1945 by women of the French Communist Party and very active in Africa. It has a subsidiary International Committee for the Defense of the Rights of Children, to ease the plight of children exposed to "imperialist" aggression. African women from Nigeria, Mali, Senegal, Ghana, Guinea and other countries have held office in it. Many have been given training in bloc countries so that they can implant organizations in their home countries. It was gaining much ground in areas where women were kept in the most tribalistic or backward countries, but less in others, like Kenya and Egypt, where they have been more emancipated. The Chinese and Chinese satellite (North Vietnamese, North Korean and Albanian) branches worked to complete the split of the WIDF, and so win many of its adherents to a new pro-Chinese Afro-Asian women's organization set up in Algiers.

The Chinese succeeded in excluding the Soviets from the executive committee of the International Journalists' Organization (IOJ) at Jakarta in April 1963, exploiting the propaganda theme that the Soviets are not an Asian power. But Soviet-bloc members remained dominant in the IOJ, which is based in Prague. At its next executive meeting in Algiers in April 1964, Chou Yu, the chief Chinese delegate, made what a Czech journalist attending the meeting told me was a "scorching attack" on the IOJ leadership. But his resolution was defeated 18 votes to 4. At this meeting Algeria, Cameroon, Ghana, Uganda, South-West Africa and a group representing the staff of the outlawed South African daily *New Age* were admitted to IOJ.

The IOJ's pro-Chinese rival, headed by Mamadou Gologo of Mali, is the Afro-Asian Journalists' Association (AAJA). An editorial carried in the second issue of its organ, *The Afro-Asian Journalist,* published in Jakarta on April 22, 1964, said AAJA will seek to make itself an effective instrument "serving the Afro-Asian revolution," Radio Peking reported on April 24. Its affiliate, the Afro-Asian Writers' Conference, sent a delegation from Jakarta to Ghana and the Congo (Brazzaville) in the same month. Subsequently it threw active support to the Congo rebellion.

Also subjected to the Chinese splitting tactics was the Soviet-line International Association of Democratic Lawyers. In 1964 the Chinese won some of its members over to a new pro-Chinese group called the Afro-Asian Lawyers' Association, whose secretary-general in 1964 was a Guinean, Keita Faiala. One of its principal organizers was neither African nor Asian, but an Albanian named Hirano. New China News Agency dispatches attribute to him the usual quotes about "fighting" and "struggling" against U.S. imperialism, and attacks on the Soviets as well.

Chinese attacks on the Soviet Union at the Communist Fourth International Teachers' Conference at Algiers in April 1965 were so violent that at one point the Algerian president of the session resigned from the presidium. Fang Ming, the Chinese delegate, managed to combine anti-American and anti-Soviet diatribes with attacks against "West German militarism" and Israeli Zionism. Fang Ming made especially scornful comments about Soviet reluctance to support North Vietnam against U.S. air attacks. Chinese behavior was similar at an Afro-Asian Economic Seminar in Algiers in February 1965.

Even the venerable World Peace Council, perhaps the most solidly established of all the Communist front groups, which has often attracted support from non-Communists, was a target for the Chinese. On October 17, 1963, the Soviet Committee for the Defense of Peace warned against Chinese plans to split the peace movement and set up a rival body. At the World Peace Council meeting in Warsaw (November 28-December 3, 1963) the majority of the delegates at the opening session stood in silence for a minute to express sympathy for Mrs. Kennedy and her children upon the assassination of President Kennedy. Radio Peking claimed that a Chinese delegate's protest at this tribute was approved by delegates from "Mozambique, Uganda and many other African countries." (The unfavorable impression this made on Africans, who deeply respected President Kennedy, seems to have been too much for Premier Chou En-lai. When he arrived in Egypt on his African tour two weeks later, he told a news conference in Cairo that President Kennedy's assassination was an "odious act.")

China's future image on the African continent is more likely to be determined by Chinese deeds than by words. Yet, in the course of one decade since the Bandung Conference, China has emerged from obscurity to being one of the countries Africans most often talk about, as a result of one of the most vigorous propaganda efforts ever seen.

CHAPTER TWENTY-TWO

Peking and African Labor

A SHORT, SPARE MAN WITH THINNING HAIR AND FLASHING EYES FACED me across a wide desk in his Casablanca office, lined with curios he had collected from all over Africa. He smiled at me, revealing some gold teeth. He looked out over the busy port of Casablanca, Africa's largest artificial harbor, and the center of some of its largest industries and one of its most active labor movements. He was Mahjoub ben Seddik, the shrewd and capable head of Morocco's Labor Federation. More, he was the newly elected President of the neutralist All-African Trade Union Federation, with headquarters in Accra.

I had asked Mahjoub about the possible aims and impact of the Chinese. Did African workers regard them, like the Russians and Americans, as foreigners? If anyone was in a position to know, he was. *"Voyez-vous,"* he told me, shifting in his chair, "the Chinese are quiet and discreet. Certainly they are foreigners, but for Africans, workers or otherwise, they are brother underdeveloped people.

"They do not come to Africa wanting something, or at least Africans do not think they do. What their long-term goals may be, we don't know. The racial angle is not so important. After all, they are not black men either. But they adapt themselves to the countries they serve. They know how to find out discreetly what they want to know and how to stay out of trouble, which is more than most others can say. If they do have definite political goals in Africa, we shall not know in our lifetime."

Any Soviet and most Western labor leaders would have taken issue with Mahjoub on the last point. For, since 1961, the Chinese have been very obviously trying to do the same thing in African labor that they have in the world-wide "front" organizations: split its ranks, exclude the Soviets altogether and set up, as a final goal, an "Afro-Asian" labor federation under Chinese leadership.

In this battle Indonesia has provided Red China with the base and the facade of "neutralism" that it needs to approach African workers. The task is not easy, for many African labor organizations are not affiliated with the Moscow-line World Federation of Trade Unions based in Prague, but with the pro-Western International Confedera-tion of Free Trade Unions (ICFTU) in Brussels. The ICFTU is, in turn, heavily supported by the AFL-CIO in the United States, as well as by most European labor movements. The ICFTU has money and influence, and a good record because it has used both fearlessly to champion many of the same anti-colonialist causes—the Portuguese territories, apartheid in South Africa, discrimination in Southern Rhodesia, and Algerian independence—that the Communists other-wise claim to monopolize.

Red China's labor offensive in Africa set itself two medium-term objectives: to win the minority of African unions (eight in 1964) away from ties with the WFTU, which might not prove too difficult, and then to win the majority (twenty-eight in 1964) from the ICFTU, which would be much harder. The neutralist AATUF is necessarily a target because it includes unions from each.

Peking began its efforts by sending Lin Chang-sheng, a member of the central committee of the Chinese Communist Party and Vice-President of the All-China Trade Union Federation, on a four-month tour of a number of African countries in the spring of 1961. Lin sought out extremists or pro-Communist labor organizers, such as Assi Camille Adam of the Ivory Coast, and invited them to Peking for the beginning of an indoctrination process that the Red Chinese probably realized would take a long, long time.

Peking suffered its first defeat at Casablanca in May 1962. It was largely engineered by Mahjoub ben Seddik and the Yugoslavs. After the neutralist labor conference organized by the AATUF in May 1962, Mahjoub helped sponsor a second meeting of "non-aligned" unions in Casablanca. This gave rise to a third conference in Casa-blanca in January 1963. Here it was decided to exclude Communist China and its allies but to include that other socialist country with a large interest in Africa, Yugoslavia, as one of the sponsors. Others were labor groups in Japan, Singapore, Egypt, Algeria, Morocco, Ghana, Ceylon, Chile and Brazil. Some of these were Moscow-oriented; others independent or pro-Western.

Peking's counter-move was launched in 1963 through the convenient intermediary group from Jakarta called the Indonesian Joint Secretariat of Labor. It was led by Ahem Erningpradja, the Indonesian Minister of Labor. This Indonesian delegation visited numerous Asian and African countries, including Algeria, Egypt, Ghana, Guinea and Morocco. It was not successful. The AATUF remained independent. At the same time China completely failed to get an "Afro-Asian Workers Conference" off the ground at the preparatory meeting in Jakarta in October 1963.

At the same time Peking acted directly by sending a Chinese labor delegation in the summer of 1963 to tour Africa and to invite, with all expenses paid, union leaders from Tanganyika, Zanzibar, Angola, Congo (Leopoldville), Burundi and Northern Rhodesia to Jakarta to discuss a proposed "Afro-Asian Labor Conference." Most of these Africans were from opposition or splinter unions. They represented almost no one but themselves.

It became clear to Westerners and Africans alike that this portended a major Peking attempt to create a gigantic non-white world labor federation, beholden neither to Moscow, Washington nor any other capital outside the Chinese Communist sphere of influence.

Moscow did all it could to nip this in the bud. It was jealous of what WFTU ties it still controlled in Africa, mainly in the two Congos, the Cameroon Republic and Zanzibar. Despite Moscow's efforts, a preparatory meeting for the prospective Afro-Asian Workers' Conference, as it was henceforth called, was held in Jakarta, October 28-November 3, 1963. Tawfik Bendahou, who represented the Moroccan unions at the meeting, said afterward that it had been hastily convened and badly prepared. African countries, he added, were inadequately represented. They should have been consulted before an executive committee was set up, or a final date for the conference finally established.

Undaunted, Peking went ahead with its plans. With the Labor Federations of Zanzibar and Pemba, and later with that of Tanganyika, the All-China Trade Union Federation put out joint appeals for convocation of the Afro-Asian Workers' Conference "as early as possible" in 1964.

Moscow was determined to establish Soviet status as an Asian power and to take part as such, if possible, in the "Second Bandung" Afro-Asian conference at Algiers in June 1965. So the Russians, through their own intermediary, veteran French Communist labor organizer Louis Saillant, the general secretary of the WFTU, announced that the WFTU favored the Chinese idea. Saillant said that the WFTU's participation in an Afro-Asian Workers' Conference would "help to ensure that this Workers' Conference does not complicate the problem of world trade union unity." In other words, a Soviet and pro-Soviet presence would ensure that Peking would not be successful in taking the perhaps irreparable step of splitting the Communist-led portion of the world labor movement, something very close to splitting irreparably the very world Communist parties themselves. The Somali trade unions seconded the Soviet motion and said that the Afro-Asian Workers' conference ought to be prepared by as many committeemen as possible, "to avoid any unilateral approach." To rationalize its compromise, the WFTU in late 1964 and early 1965 urged the holding of a Moscow-backed "Afro-European Workers' Conference."

It seemed likely that some sort of Afro-Asian Workers' Conference would take place in 1965 or 1966, and that it would see a major clash between the Soviet and the Chinese camps. The Africans themselves, meanwhile, were quickly losing interest. Mahjoub and Algerian labor leaders told me: "We are sick and tired of the Chinese and the Russians fighting their battles among us. The only answer is a free, strong and *completely independent* African labor movement. Eventually, this is what we will have."

CHAPTER TWENTY-THREE

Mao's Master Plan

WHAT CAN CHINA HOPE TO GAIN FROM ITS MULTIPLE ACTIVITIES IN Africa, and what may it lose? To state that Peking seeks total political control or domination in Africa, even of countries it has chosen for its greatest efforts, would be to overstate and vastly oversimplify the case. But outside domination, as history has shown, has sometimes come about, at least for brief periods, on entire continents, as in the Americas. Therefore, even though complete domination in Africa may not be a fixed objective in Chinese policy, some African leaders have already said that they worry about this as a long-term possibility.

The immediate goals of China in Africa may be sought in some of the motivations of Chinese policy everywhere. Three principal sources of these motivations, as identified by Professor Donald Zagoria in lectures at Columbia University, are tradition, nationalism and ideology. The first is expressed in China's age-old view of itself as the center of the civilized world. The second is the new nationalism that is the heritage of both the Kuomintang and the Communist revolutions. The third is the revolutionary ideology of Marxism-Leninism as interpreted by its Eastern prophet, Mao Tse-tung.

In its diplomatic, commercial and propaganda drive to capture African sympathies and influence in Africa, China today continues a tradition of Sinocentrism apparent from the dawn of Chinese history. In Confucian and pre-Confucian times, Chinese rulers looked nostalgically backward to the sage-kings of a legendary Golden Age, when China was the center, as they saw it, of the civilized world. The Chinese explorers and seafarers who crossed the Indian Ocean and Southwest Asia to the Hellenic world, or visited the Arab and African lands between the birth of Christ and the fifteenth century, sought, like the Chinese of today, information, raw materials, markets and prestige. But they also sought to spread to barbarian shores what they considered a superior civilization. The same idea is inherent in today's Chinese arguments about a new, superior, Afro-Asian civilization that will rise from the ashes of the old one that they see as having been destroyed by Western imperialism.

In terms of the new nationalism that swept over China after the revolt against the Manchu dynasty in 1911, China seeks aggrandizement and prestige as an independent world power, beholden to no other nation of East or West. Africa is a continent that, like China, has been throwing off the shackles of white, European colonial control in the last few generations. By aiding Africans to eliminate Western influence, as did the Chinese, while seeking their friendship and alignment with China's new brand of supranational, Afro-Asian diplomacy, Peking pursues essentially nationalistic goals and a foreign policy of expansion. Strategically, by securing lookout posts and spheres of influence along the East African coast, it seeks to secure its extended Indian Ocean flank, while setting up listening stations in other parts of Africa, from the Mediterranean coast at Algiers to the Atlantic shores in Dakar.

In terms of Communist ideology, the third fundamental aspect of Chinese foreign policy, Peking's rulers seek to spread their own brand of world revolution to the exclusion of others. They believe that their model, in which the purging flame of armed revolt is to be accompanied and followed by a total social revolution that will transfer land, power and the means of production to armed peasants and workers, is exclusively correct. They appear to believe that the triumph of their model in the "intermediate zone" or "storm centers" of Africa, Asia and Latin America is inevitable. They hope that the Soviet, Yugoslav and other brands of socialism will prove inept and fail in these "storm centers." They are willing to do whatever they can to discredit the other models, as well as to eliminate the "neo-colonialist" influence of the West to make way for the inevitable victory of the Leninist-Maoist faith.

How has Mao's thinking evolved on the means to bring this about, and where does Africa fit into his plan?

The answer, I believe, can be clearly read in Mao's own statements for public record since 1946.

Since that date the Red Chinese have advocated isolating the United States by setting up geographical belts or "zones" in the world. These would be either under direct Chinese Communist control or influence—like Southeast Asia—or at least independent of United States policy, as in the French concept of a Western Europe standing alone and refusing to take orders or guidance from Washington.

Mao first proposed a "Pacific Ocean zone of peace," which by 1955 included the United States. Chou En-lai suggested that his "Five Principles of Peaceful Coexistence" be extended to the entire Pacific area, with the then peaceful relations between China, India and Burma as the model. The "Five Principles," which Chou enunciated once again during his African tour of 1963-64 and subsequently are: (1) mutual respect for sovereignty and territorial integrity; (2) non-aggression; (3) non-interference in internal affairs; (4) relations based on equality and mutual benefit; and (5) peaceful coexistence between regimes with different social, political and economic systems.

Both Nehru and Mao successively proposed a number of "peace" or "atom-free" zones. These included the Pacific, the Middle East and the Baltic and Balkans area. The Chinese by 1959 had correctly concluded that Khrushchev's inclusion of China in Russia's own proposals for "nuclear-free" zones was designed to preclude China's receiving Soviet nuclear weapons and to cover this decision. Since August 15, 1963, Peking has frequently and bitterly attacked Moscow for unilaterally tearing up, on June 20, 1959, the Sino-Soviet agreement of 1957 on new technology for national defense, and especially for refusing to provide China with a sample of an atom bomb and the technical data for its manufacture.

Peking was thus anxious to prevent anyone else, especially Western-influenced regimes like those of Japan, Laos or the Philippines, from getting the weapon that the Chinese themselves were denied by the Russians. At this point China sought to fashion buffer zones between itself and both Soviet- and Western-dominated areas. This led to talk of peaceful coexistence and "secure frontiers" with such neighbors as Burma and India.

Africa first appears as part of the "zone" concept in a *People's Daily* editorial of August 28, 1960. Africa was included among regions where Red China desired relations based on the "Five Points."

This, as we have seen, was also the time when Peking's activity in East and West Africa began to expand in earnest. When Peking made new peace proposals in July and August 1963 it omitted the old references to a nuclear-free zone for the Asian and Pacific areas, and instead recommended that they be created immediately—in Africa and Latin America.

The "intermediate zone" got world attention in February 1964, just after President de Gaulle took up his new relations with Peking. According to the French Communist newspaper *Humanité* of February 21, 1964, Mao told François Bernard, leader of a French parliamentary delegation visiting China: "France, Germany, Italy, Britain—if she can cease to be America's agent—Japan and ourselves: that is the third force."

Anna Louise Strong, an American expatriate writer who lives in Red China and who has followed the entire Chinese revolution, suggested how the "intermediate zone" might include Africa. It is recorded in "Talk with the American Correspondent Anna Louise Strong," in Volume IV of Mao's *Selected Works*.

During a talk with Miss Strong in Yenan in 1946, Mao moved tea cups and wine cups on a table to show how the "American people" and all the other capitalist countries were being "manipulated" by the United States government. They would revolt before Washington could make war on the socialist camp. This is a prime source of the Peking dogma, constantly repeated in Africa, that "American reactionaries will one day be opposed by the peoples of the entire world."

In January 1964 the *People's Daily* said events had proved the thesis of the 1946 Strong interview to be correct. The growing resentment of U. S. policies in the West, *together with the growing resistance of the developing areas,* constitutes the new intermediate zone. If U. S. policies are to be defeated, and the wrong ideas of the Soviet Communist Party corrected, then a vast intermediate zone must be created between the United States and the U.S.S.R. Its first part would be independent countries and those fighting for independence in Asia, Africa and Latin America. Its second part would be all of Western Europe, Australia, Canada and other capitalistic states. Countries in this second part, or "second intermediate zone," though they "exploit" their own people, are themselves bullied by the United States. Therefore they want to shed United States influence, which is something they have in common with both the socialist camp and the peoples of Africa, Asia and Latin America.

"Scorn the enemy strategically, but have respect for him tactically," says Mao. While on the one hand the Chinese tell Africans and others that the Soviets are guilty of "treason" toward the developing peoples in seeking better relations with the United States—especially since intensification of the war in Vietnam in 1965—on the other hand the Chinese took up relations with France, a country they have accused of the worst "colonialist" and "imperialist" sins in the past.

But in Chinese eyes can a truly neutral "third world" really exist? In his essay "On the People's Democratic Dictatorship," published in 1949, the year the Chinese revolution triumphed, Mao said: "We oppose illusions about a third road. Not only in China but throughout the world, without exception, one inclines toward imperialism or toward socialism. Neutrality is merely a camouflage: a third road does not exist."

For Red Chinese thinking on African revolution—not the words of its propaganda releases—one of the best sources is probably the *Work Bulletin* of the General Political Department of the Chinese People's Liberation Army. This is a publication prepared for study by selected Chinese Communist cadres. The issue of April 25, 1961, reached the outside world. It contains a remarkable comparison between the stages of development in various parts of Africa and the situation in China itself, from the period of the anti-Western Boxer revolt of the last century to the overthrow of the Manchu Emperors in 1911 and the student revolt of 1919.

The *Bulletin*'s conclusion was that no part of the African continent had yet reached a stage comparable to that of Chiang Kai-shek's offensive of 1926 in China, or even to the period after 1936, when Communists and Nationalists temporarily joined forces against the foreign invader, the Japanese. It found that African countries "are far from the 1949 era" of total Communist control.

In Africa [the *Bulletin* continues] there are many rightists, not many leftists in power. . . . We must explain the Chinese revolution from the time of the Taiping revolt [in the last century] through the Boxer Rebellion and Sun Yat-sen to the present Communist revolution. They [the Africans] must act for themselves, foreign assistance being secondary only . . . [but] if there were one or two among the independent countries that would effect a real nationalist revolution their influence would be great and a revolutionary wave would roll up the African continent.

Just as Lenin made a temporary alliance with the bourgeoisie when he needed its help to overthrow the Czarist regime, between March 1917 and April 1918, Mao at first supported the "bourgeois and nationalist" Kuomintang of Chiang Kai-shek. He constantly urged formation of what he called "a single national front" with Chiang against the Japanese. Once a Red exile government had been securely established in the remote mountains of northwest China, Mao reassured the Chinese middle classes that they had nothing to fear for the moment. "The transformation of our revolution," he wrote, "into a socialist revolution is a task for the future." After the withdrawal of the Japanese the tune quickly changed, and the real socialist offensive began in earnest.

The major new tactic that China has introduced in its African offensive is, as we have seen, race. The solidarity of all the non-white races, against the whites, from Jakarta to Jacksonville, is now stressed strongly.

Even if the West was slow or reluctant to see the theme of race growing ever stronger in Peking's program, the Soviets were not. We saw that as far back as August 10, 1963, Moscow issued a statement assailing Peking's propaganda aimed at separating the Asian, African and Latin American continents from European Communist states on the basis of "color of skin."

On November 27, 1963, Radio Peking carried remarks supposed to have been made by Robert Williams, an American Negro, fugitive from Monroe, North Carolina, living in Cuba, during his visit to Peking for celebrations on October 1. When answering questions about the "Negro struggle in the United States" Williams said:

We know that racism inside the U. S. is a threat to the security and the peace of the world. Also to be considered is that the only people ever bombed with an atom bomb were what they call in the United States colored people. So in looking at the world situation, Negroes are seeing that the same people who oppress them also oppress other colored peoples throughout the world, and some people have said this is racial discrimination.

However, there is nothing racist about this. We did not create our enemies. If they happen to be white, it is not our responsibility, it is not our fault. We did not make them white and we did not make them oppress us, and we see—our people now can see—that this racism and imperialism runs hand in hand and it runs around the world. The struggle of the colonial people for independence has been an inspiration to our people. . . .

Williams visited China at least twice in 1964 and 1965 and continued such broadcasts for Peking. Similar ideas were voiced in the

United States, especially after the Harlem riots of the summer of 1964 in New York, by the pro-Chinese splinter group, the Progressive Labor Movement, and by such Negro revolutionary groups as the "Black Liberation Front," convicted of plotting to blow up the Statue of Liberty and other U. S. monuments. Such pronouncements drew a great deal of attention in Africa.

The Soviet response is that the liberation struggles in Africa, Asia and Latin America should be based on class solidarity, not color; and that the Soviet bloc's propaganda for peaceful coexistence does nothing to hinder these struggles. G. Mirsky, a commentator on Radio Moscow, criticized the idea that the world was divided into white people "who have brought with them coercion and suppression" and colored people "who personify the virtues." This, Mirsky said in August 1963, "is racialism turned inside out" and a degeneration of "healthy anti-imperialist nationalism of the oppressed peoples." Communists, he went on, rejected any "opposition of peoples to each other because of the color of skin," and it was "monstrous and inexcusable" for the Chinese to try to set colored people off against white peoples. The reasons for Soviet anxiety about this were probably never better demonstrated than when less than a year later the Chinese distributed throughout many parts of Africa issue No. 9 of their Paris-published magazine *Révolution* with a cover photo of Khrushchev, pink and perspiring as though at a country fair, bearing the caption: "We, the Whites . . ."

The Chinese Communists are far from invulnerable on the race issue. They risk, in some situations, falling prisoner to their own inconsistencies and hypocrisies. As President Bourguiba of Tunisia told me in an interview in April 1965, "The Chinese should remember that in Africa 'colored' means black, not yellow." It is all very well for the Chinese to call for the solidarity of the non-whites. They are, however, treading on dangerous ground when they suggest colored solidarity in regions like East and South Africa, where African resentment of Asians (including Indians, Indonesians and Chinese, among others) is often as great as or greater than of whites. China's persistent and increasing trade with the white-supremacy government of South Africa, which Africans have attempted to boycott—often at considerable sacrifice—is another example that has already been exposed and criticized by Africans.

Another weak point in Peking's argument in Africa is its opposition to the Moscow-Washington-London nuclear test ban treaty, especially since China began its own tests in 1964. During his African tour, Chou En-lai had to perform feats of verbal dexterity to explain this. Most of the African countries had signed the treaty. Several African leaders, notably President Bourguiba, said that they could not approve Peking's uncompromising stand. Well-informed Africans understood quite well that Chinese opposition, like that of France, was based on China's own desire to win parity as a major power by achieving nuclear status, and resentment that Moscow had refused to give Peking nuclear data. The Africans, moreover did not enjoy hearing Radio Peking broadcasts that described a document they had signed as a "dirty fraud" or "nuclear blackmail."

Chou En-lai wrote personal letters to all the heads of state on August 2, 1963, appealing for support for China's alternative to the treaty, a world disarmament conference. Tanganyika's reply was typical of many other African reactions: President Nyerere welcomed hopes for total world disarmament, and said that major responsibility for this lay with the nuclear powers. Progress toward total disarmament was possible only by "taking every possible step," so Tanganyika had signed. Ethiopia said that Peking's ideal of world disarmament was a good one, but that they signed the treaty because it was an important first step toward this ideal.

Peking frequently criticized, for African consumption, the Soviet leaders' denial of atomic weapons to Red China and claimed that Soviet publications were distorting Chinese views about nuclear war. The Soviet riposte was to tell the world that Mao had said in a secret speech in Moscow in November 1957, officially disclosed in Peking on September 1, 1963: "If the worst comes to the worst and half of mankind died, the other half would remain while imperialism would be razed to the ground and the whole world would become socialist."

Another source of trouble for the Chinese in Africa is the basic contradiction between the special tasks Peking demands of its diplomats in Africa and their traditional diplomatic role. This contradiction makes their mission difficult. While their instructions require them to win the confidence of the new governments and establish friendly and mutually profitable relations, these same diplomats must often aid local subversives to undermine the established order, so that pro-Chinese elements can eventually seize power.

What Peking ultimately demands from Africans, as from Asians, is choice: choice between Peking and Taiwan, between Peking and Moscow, and certainly between East and West. By pressing these demands for options too insistently, the Chinese risk committing the same blunders that others, especially the United States, and the Soviets have committed in Africa. Impatience may be another quality that vitiates the Chinese effort: impatience for quick results, and occasional crudeness in seeking them, caused Peking's setback in Burundi in late 1964, and it may cause others.

African leaders themselves, though fascinated by the size of China and the revolutionary innovations of its society and its policies, generally seek their own road to their own socialism. Statesmen like Kwame Nkrumah, Sékou Touré and Julius Nyerere, as we have seen, prefer to extract what they can use from both Western and Eastern models, and from this synthesize a purely "African" socialism. In varying degrees they tend to mistrust the slavish imitation of Chinese models, Chinese intrigue or Chinese revolutionary dogma as much as they mistrust the same things when propagated by other foreigners. This has already led to collisions between African and Chinese interests in some fields and in some countries.

The Chinese are a patient people. If their long-range scheme is actually as grandiose as the remaking of all Africa in an image favorable to themselves, they are bound to collide increasingly with the wish of the Africans to be themselves, just as the West and the Soviets have already done. These collisions are likely to bring about tactical and perhaps strategic Chinese retreats.

One of the prime *short-term* objectives Peking pursues in Africa is the training of indoctrinated revolutionary groups capable of aligning their states with Chinese policy. Many of Africa's rulers are becoming aware of this. It led them anxiously to ask the real meaning of Chou En-lai's ambiguous phrase as he concluded his African journey in 1964: "The revolutionary situation in Africa is excellent." Against whom, ask the Africans, will the new revolution be waged?

The answer appears clear enough. China feels that Africa needs a second revolution. The first was the conquest of political independence. China now tells those Africans who are out of power that independence has benefited only the "haves" and that the "have-nots" must seize power, which brings with it the good things of life. The new revolutionary troops must be those used in China: the poor peasants in the countryside, the unemployed workers and intellectuals in the towns. In other words, the black proletariat, having helped the black bourgeoisie to expel the white rulers, must now seize power from the black bourgeoisie, originally put in power by the Western colonialists.

It is barely possible that the entire Chinese offensive in Africa, spread over several decades or generations, may prove to be a total failure. Chinese methods of diplomacy, agriculture, statecraft and organization of society may prove totally inapplicable to many African situations. They could turn out to be signal failures in Africa as a whole. Such a breakdown, particularly if the Chinese overextended themselves, might take on great proportions indeed. But for Westerners or others confidently to predict such an outcome would be merely another example of the smug and narrow wishful thinking that has dogged Western diplomacy and hampered its ability to think about the world dynamically.

There is another snare in judging the Chinese effort in Africa. The Chinese, as Marshal Chen Yi has observed, should be judged by their deeds, not their words. The overblown, verbose propaganda world of "paper tigers" and "armed struggle" is colorful and often effective. But neither Africans nor anyone else should allow it to obscure the often cautious and prudent nature of what the Chinese actually do in a given situation, as opposed to what they say about it. Chinese words in Africa have spoken louder than Chinese actions, and it has often been evident that the Chinese welcome Western exaggeration of their "revolutionary" efforts: this helps make it appear that they are outdoing their Russian rivals, and adds to the overall impact of their propaganda in Africa and Asia.

By the end of our own generation, or perhaps of our century, the final nature and magnitude of Red China's African offensive—still complex, multiform and perhaps still inchoate even in Chinese minds —will doubtless be more apparent. Like most of the movements of history, it is likely to be drawn out in time and not immediately conclusive in its effects.

What, then, should be the responsibilities of the West and most of all, of the Africans themselves? Ultimately, the Africans themselves will decide the outcome of China's offensive in Africa. They are seeking their own pathways out of a tragic past and toward what they hope is a happier future. Perhaps all the West can do is play a relatively marginal role: that of judiciously offering Western models and Western assistance, where these seem appropriate or needed.

Whatever the stake of the West and the stake of other parties, that of the Africans themselves is infinitely greater: their own destinies and their own salvation. Political and subversive warfare, military force and cold war tactics, while obtaining successes in spatially and temporally limited situations such as the Cuban crisis of 1962, have a habit of backfiring. This is more apt to be true when the adversary operates in the realm of ideas, as do the Chinese, than when he is threatening with rockets. On a continent such as Africa, where the hearts and minds of people, rather than the calculations of politicians, are still vital in directing the course of nations, the uses of naked power are dubious indeed.

Winds of revolution, winds of social change are blowing over Africa. Perhaps the best that sane men everywhere can hope for is that the wind which finally prevails shall be neither an East wind nor a West wind, but an African wind.

Postscript to Afro-Asian Solidarity

The most ambitious diplomatic project Red China had ever undertaken collapsed at the last moment before it could be realized. This was the "second Bandung" Conference of African and Asian nations, scheduled to be held in Algiers starting June 29, 1965. The background of its collapse, the accompanying circumstances and the consequences reveal some lessons about the realities of China's role in Africa and the world.

Peking had envisaged and represented the meeting, which was supposed to include sixty-four heads of state, as a grand sequel to the first Bandung Conference a decade earlier. Its postponement until November 5, 1965, was at best a doubtful formula. It was conceived chiefly to save face for the Algerian hosts, as well as for China, Indonesia and China's Asian satellites, North Vietnam and North Korea, which pressed for holding the meeting right up to the instant of its collapse. Theoretically it may prove possible to hold the Conference in the autumn of 1965 or later, though Algeria as a setting seems unlikely in view of the endemic instability there following Colonel Houari Boumedienne's overthrow of President Ahmed ben Bella on June 19, 1965. But the crucial United Nations session opening in the autumn of 1965 will take much of the time and energy of the world's diplomats, particularly those from Africa and Asia.

The postponement or cancellation of the conference, whichever it finally turns out to be, is one of the gravest setbacks Communist China's diplomacy has ever suffered, even if temporary. Since Chou En-lai's African tour of 1963–64, and even before, Peking's diplomats and more recently Indonesia's had tirelessly trekked across Africa and Asia, and made overtures to Latin America, to arouse support for the meeting. A fifteen-nation preparatory committee, on which such firm friends of China as Indonesia and Cambodia were most active, had labored over the arrangements. Algeria's impoverished treasury had managed, with Chinese

help and encouragement, to find nearly $50 million to spend on the
lavish arrangements, which were still far from complete at the moment
the conference was supposed to open.

China made its prime objectives amply clear. First, it wished to convert
the "intermediate zone" countries of Africa, Asia and Latin America into
a vast anti-American front, with emphasis on United States involvement
in Vietnam. Second, the Soviets, who clung to hopes of an invitation,
supported principally by India and the United Arab Republic and despite
Chinese efforts to exclude them, were to be attacked on a scale and with
a vehemence hitherto unseen. A preliminary foreign ministers' meeting,
twice postponed and finally abandoned after a bomb mysteriously exploded
in the still uncompleted conference hall, was to have decided whether or
not to honor the Chinese insistence that the Russians be barred, along with
Malaysia, as Indonesia and China demanded.

The immediate cause of the meeting's collapse was Colonel Houari
Boumedienne's coup d'état against President ben Bella. The coup was
followed by small but noisy demonstrations against Boumedienne and his
"Revolutionary Council," which was soon to take on a distinct anti-
Communist (especially anti-Soviet) cast, by supporters of Ben Bella,
mainly young people. Chinese, Korean and Burmese diplomats, strolling
on Algiers' central Rue Didouche Mourad on the evening of June 23,
were caught in a pro-Ben Bella student demonstration. Red-tinted water
from the high-pressure hose of a police pump truck drenched them.
Chinese students were jeered and chased from a university restaurant by
pro-Ben Bella Algerian students, because Peking had quickly and ostentatiously recognized the Boumedienne regime—a recognition given in the
mistaken hope that this would help the regime go through with its plans
for the conference. A Chinese flag was burned in the streets of Algiers.
Three evenings later came the bomb explosion, the work of unidentified
saboteurs.

Obviously Algiers was no place for more than sixty presidents and
kings to gather. Added to these circumstances was the embarrassment
caused many of them by the fall and imprisonment of Ben Bella, hailed
only the day before as one of the world's foremost anti-imperialists and
a close friend of some of the participating heads of state.

Even before Colonel Boumedienne's coup, however, it was clear that
the enthusiasm of the African and Asian governments and their Latin
American friends had waned considerably. Premier Chou En-lai's new
call for universal revolution during his visit to Tanzania in early June had
awakened unfavorable echoes in much of Africa. India, the leader of the
"moderate" bloc that opposed Chinese hegemony in Asia and feared it
even in Africa, and basically pro-Western regimes like those of Morocco
and Tunisia in Africa, and Thailand and the Philippines in Asia, had
agreed to come only with reluctance. Nations of the French-speaking
African community turned down their invitations, mainly because Ghana,
which they said was a base for Chinese subversion against them, was
planning to attend. After the coup, thirteen Asian and African nations
and Cyprus, attending the Commonwealth meeting in London, asked for

a postponement. The Chinese chargé d'affaires in London and two Algerian envoys sent by Colonel Boumedienne tried to dissuade them, but in vain. Delegates of Kenya, Tanzania, Nigeria and Uganda, despite previous acceptances, simply avoided showing up at Algiers, as did those of Afghanistan, Laos, Cyprus and Burma. On the day perhaps most crucial for the fate of the conference, June 23, six members of the preparatory committee—Malawi, Guinea, Tanzania, Zambia, Ethiopia and Cambodia—boycotted the meeting. Working against it behind the scenes were the Soviet Union and even the United Arab Republic. The Egyptians did this even while President Nasser and Premier Chou En-lai were conferring in Cairo, and both expressing in public the fervent hope that the conference would take place.

The failure of Red China's major effort at Algiers, and the unlikelihood of any similar conference succeeding in the near future, caused widespread relief throughout Africa. From broadcast and newspaper comment it was plain that Africans, like Asians and others, had dreaded an aggravated repetition of the Sino-Soviet squabbling they had already witnessed on innumerable occasions on their soil since 1960. Diplomats were gratified, too, that the continent was spared the new airing of feuds between Presidents Nasser and Bourguiba; Ethiopia and Somalia; and Ghana and her neighbors; and even more fruitless philippics of the black Africans against the white rulers of South Africa, Rhodesia and the Portuguese territories. In a sense, the temporary defeat of Chinese extremism at Algiers had given the entire non-aligned world a breathing spell, however brief. Statesmen such as Presidents Nasser and Tito, the Soviet leaders and others whom the Chinese had been attacking in terms nearly as violent as those reserved for President Johnson, now had hopes of making their voices heard again above the din of Chinese propaganda. More than that, the leaders of Africa were strengthened in their growing conviction that their future lay, not in Peking, Moscow, Washington or elsewhere, but on their own continent.

The Eight Principles
Governing Red Chinese Foreign Aid

(As announced by Premier Chou En-lai during his tour of ten African countries, December 1963–February 1964)

1. In the assistance it furnishes to other countries, the Chinese government constantly observes the principle of equality and mutual benefit. It never considers this assistance as a type of unilateral charity but rather as mutual aid. Thanks to this assistance, friendly and newly independent countries can progressively develop their national economies, free themselves from colonial control, and consolidate world anti-imperialist forces.

2. In furnishing aid to other countries, the Chinese government strictly respects the sovereignty of the recipient states. It never asks for any privilege and never poses conditions.

3. The Chinese government furnishes its economic assistance in the form of loans exempt from interest or at a minimum rate of interest and provides long periods for their repayment, so as to reduce to a minimum the burden carried by the recipient countries.

4. In furnishing economic aid to foreign countries, the Chinese government does not seek to place the recipients in a state of dependency on China but rather to aid them to move forward, step by step, on the pathway of self-sufficiency.

5. Projects that the Chinese government helps the recipient countries

to realize are, as much as possible, those capable of yielding rapid results for a minimum investment. This makes it possible for the recipient governments to increase their revenue and accumulate capital.

6. The Chinese government furnishes the best material manufactured by its own plants at prices prevalent on the international markets. If the material proves not to be in conformance with the norms and the quality desired, it promises to replace it.

7. To be sure that personnel of the recipient country has fully assimilated the necessary knowledge to use its technical aid, the Chinese government offers it the appropriate professional training.

8. The experts that the Chinese government sends to recipient countries to aid them in their tasks of construction have the same standard of living as the experts of these countries. Chinese experts are forbidden to formulate any special demands or to benefit from special advantages.

Approximate Foreign Aid
Commitments to African Countries, 1954–65 *

	U. S.	U. K.	France	West Ger-many	Israel	U. S. S. R.	Eastern Europe	Red China
(in millions of dollars)								
Algeria	125.0	10.0	3,000.0	17.0	—	229.0	10.0	50.0
Egypt	1,250.0	700.0	—	500.0	—	875.0	10.0	80.0
Ethiopia	175.0	60.0	15.0	10.0	3.0	105.0	15.0	—
Ghana	200.0	600.0	—	15.0	25.0	115.0	95.0	40.0
Guinea	8.0	—	250.0	12.5	7.0	70.0	25.2	45.2
Kenya	40.0	230.0	—	10.0	3.0	28.0	25.0	44.8
Mali	12.0	3.0	175.0	10.0	8.0	56.0	16.0	26.0
Morocco	500.0	12.0	1,500.0	35.0	—	—	15.0	—
Nigeria	400.0	300.0	—	20.0	3.0	—	10.0	—
Somali Republic	32.0	40.0	—	12.0	—	56.0	16.0	26.0
Sudan	65.0	190.0	—	15.0	—	22.4	—	—
Total	2,807.0	2,145.0	4,940.0	656.5	49.0	1,556.4	237.2	312.0

* Includes government grants and loans, in cash or goods, for development, promised and committed directly; budgetary support; "emergency" assistance following disaster; bilateral technical assistance; government-guaranteed private loans. Not included are other private loans, military assistance and aid through international bodies or Peace Corps-type assistance. Sources include United Nations publications, announcements by countries concerned, U. S. Agency for International Development, and U. K., French and West German official statistics. Israeli aid is almost entirely in training courses.

African Countries Recognizing
Communist and Nationalist China, June 1965

Diplomatic Relations with the Republic of China

Cameroon	Liberia	Rwanda
Chad	Libya	Sierra Leone
Congo (Leopoldville)	Malagasy	South Africa
Gabon	Mauritania	Togo
Ivory Coast	Niger	Upper Volta

Diplomatic Relations with the People's Republic of China

Algeria	Guinea	Somali Republic
Burundi	Kenya	Tanzania
Central African Republic	Mali	Tunisia
Congo (Brazzaville)	Mauritania	Uganda
Dahomey	Morocco	United Arab Republic
Ghana	Senegal	Zambia

Recognizing Neither

Malawi

Recognizing the People's Republic of China but Having No Diplomatic Relations

Ethiopia
Mauritania
Nigeria

Red Chinese Diplomats in Africa

In March 1965, Peking had fifteen ambassadors directing its embassies on the African continent. The three most experienced, and undoubtedly the most important from the viewpoint of their responsibilities, both geographically and geopolitically, were Chen Chia-kang in the U.A.R., Huang Hua in Ghana, and Ho Ying in Tanzania. Six of the others deserve special mention.

CHEN CHIA-KANG

United Arab Republic

Shortly after the victory of the revolution in 1949, Chen was assigned to the Asian Affairs Department of the Ministry of Foreign Affairs. He remained until 1954. As department chief he accompanied Chou En-lai to Moscow in 1952 to negotiate the return to China by the Soviets of the Changchun Railway. In 1954 he aided Chou again at the Geneva Conference that led to the partition of Indochina. In the same year, Chen worked with the small Chinese team that negotiated the Sino-Indian treaty of April 1954 on the status of Tibet.

In 1955, Chen was again an advisor to Chou En-lai, this time at the Bandung Afro-Asian Conference. A year later, when Egypt agreed to the establishment of an embassy in Cairo, Chen was chosen as the logical man to staff this first Red Chinese diplomatic mission in Africa. He arrived in Cairo in mid-1956 and from there negotiated the establishment of diplomatic ties with the Somali Republic and the Kingdom of Yemen.

In 1958 Chen visited Khartoum and arranged for the establishment of an embassy in the Sudan in 1959. Chen was named concurrently Minister to the Yemen, and in February 1959 he visited the Yemen to inspect

Chinese highway construction. By late August 1960 he had appeared at Leopoldville as an "observer" at the Conference of African Foreign Ministers.

Chen kept in close touch with the Algerian leaders in Cairo and other African and Arab capitals from 1955 on. In 1963 he took an active part in the visit of Chou En-lai and Chen Yi to the U.A.R. He was sent to Addis Ababa to arrange for their visit to Ethiopia in January 1964, and participated in their talks with officials of Emperor Haile Selassie's government after they arrived.

Cairo is probably the controlling Red Chinese mission for all of North Africa and the Middle East. Very many of the thousands of delegations and individual visitors between Africa and Peking pass through Cairo and have contacts with the embassy there. Peking has chosen to keep Chen in Cairo longer than it has kept any other Chinese ambassador at an overseas post. Many Western diplomats and journalists know Chen personally. They credit him with high intelligence and a sense of humor.

HUANG HUA

Ghana

Huang, who speaks fluent English, has a long background of contact with Westerners. In the 1930s he acted as interpreter for some of the interviews that Edgar Snow later incorporated into his classic work *Red Star Over China* (republished by Gollancz in London, 1963). Huang, like Chen Chia-kang, served as a liaison officer with the United States Military Group in Yenan during World War II. Afterward he was stationed on the Communist side during the attempt of a mission headed by General George C. Marshall in 1946–47 to reach a truce between the Communists and the Kuomintang.

From 1949 to 1953, Huang was senior Foreign Ministry official in Nanking, where there was still a U. S. Embassy even after the city's capture by the Communists in April 1949. He was supposed to have sounded out U. S. Ambassador J. Leighton Stuart on recognition of the Communist government.

In 1953 Huang took part in the Korean truce talks. The American negotiators came to know him as a tough bargainer. Like Chen, Huang went with Chou En-lai to the Indochina talks in Geneva in 1954 and to Bandung in 1955. Between the two events he ran the European and African Affairs desk in the Ministry of Foreign Affairs. African matters were assigned to a single new desk created in 1956, leaving Huang in charge of European affairs only.

Huang was posted to Accra as soon as diplomatic relations were established with Ghana in 1960. The post was active, and Huang made arrangements for a steady stream of Chinese visitors to Ghana, as well as managing liaison work with guerilla movements in the Cameroon Republic and other areas receiving Red Chinese aid.

In December 1961 Huang attended the Tanganyika independence ceremonies at Dar es-Salaam. While there he negotiated the establishment of diplomatic relations between China and Tanganyika. In January 1964, Huang participated in talks between Ghanaian officials and Chou En-lai's delegation during the latter's visit. A month later Huang negotiated the opening of relations with the Congo (Brazzaville), after France had recognized Red China. Although a hard-boiled negotiator and doctrinaire Communist, Huang is said to be well informed, affable and charming.

HO YING

Tanganyika and
The United Republic of Tanganyika and Zanzibar

Ho once lived in Malaya and was subsequently a deputy political commissar in the Red Army. In 1951–52 he was consul-general and minister-counselor in Indonesia. Between 1952 and 1954 he served under Chen Chia-kang, subsequently ambassador to the U.A.R., in the Asian Affairs Department of the Foreign Ministry. He also worked with Chen as a negotiator of the Sino-Indian treaty of April 1954 on Tibet.

In 1954, Ho became Ambassador to Outer Mongolia, where he stayed until 1958. During this time Sino-Mongolian relations were at their best. Some ten thousand Chinese laborers worked in Mongolia under the direct control of the Chinese Embassy in Ulan Bator, just as laborers from Red China were to do later in Guinea, Mali and the Somali Republic. Peking gave Mongolia financial aid, and a rail line was opened between the two countries.

After returning to Peking, Ho became deputy director of the first Asian Affairs Department (dealing with non-Communist nations) in 1958–59; then chief of the West Asian and African Affairs Department in 1960–62. He was posted to Dar es-Salaam after relations were established with Tanganyika in early 1962. He used Dar es-Salaam as a base for operations in many neighboring countries. In September 1962, for instance, he went to Bujumbura to attend ceremonies marking the independence of Burundi. A Chinese Nationalist emissary was also present, and Ho left after denouncing the "two Chinas" plot of "U. S. imperialism and the Chiang Kai-shek clique," depicting the Burundi government as the innocent dupe of both, but being careful not to blame Burundi.

In October 1962, Ho negotiated the establishment of diplomatic relations with Uganda. He was accredited there from April 1963 until April 1964, when Chen Chi-fang was appointed to the Kampala post. In November 1963, Ho returned to Burundi. This time he negotiated the establishment of diplomatic relations. He represented Peking at the Zanzibar independence ceremonies in December 1963 and also opened relations there. By the summer of 1964 he was attempting to effect diplomatic relations with the newly independent state of Malawi (formerly Nyasaland).

Ho's vantage point in Tanzania is a strategic one for Peking's operations throughout East Africa. Tanzania touches Northern Rhodesia (the new nation of Zambia), Malawi and Mozambique. Alastair Matheson, of the Observer Foreign News Service, described Ho as "China's most valuable agent" in East Africa, where his American limousine is probably "the largest and flashiest car" in the area.

WANG YU-TIEN

Sudan–Kenya

Before turning to African affairs, Wang served as counselor in East Germany for six years and was first Ambassador to the Sudan from 1959 to 1962. He also had a total of five years' experience with the Foreign Ministry in Peking, the last two as head of the African desk. Wang was accredited to Nairobi immediately after the opening of diplomatic relations in December 1963.

LAI YA-LI

Mali

Lai's posting to Bamako when Mali opened relations with Red China in October 1960 was especially interesting, since Mali was the scene of Sino-Soviet competition, and Lai had experience in dealing with the Soviets. He had taken part in the original Sino-Soviet negotiations leading to the Russo-Chinese Treaty of Alliance of February 1950.

Before going to Mali, Lai had six years' experience in the Foreign Ministry in Peking. For five years he met regularly with American diplomats as deputy to Wang Ping-nan during the Sino-U. S. talks held in Geneva and Warsaw, the only formal diplomatic contacts between Washington and Peking after 1955.

CHANG YUEH

Somali Republic

Chang served for about four years in the Foreign Ministry before being sent to Cairo as trade representative in 1955, before the establishment of China-U.A.R. diplomatic relations.

After the establishment of an embassy in 1956, he became counselor and then, under the supervision of Chen Chia-kang, senior Communist Chinese envoy in the Yemen. He arrived in Mogadishu soon after the Somali Republic and Red China opened relations in December 1960.

MENG YING

Central African Republic

The Red Chinese diplomat on the spot who was evidently in charge of directing Peking's contribution to the Zanzibar revolt, Meng brought to Africa long experience in dealing with sensitive Asian areas on the periphery of Red China's expanding empire. He served for five years in Burma, spent another five in Outer Mongolia, and also spent three years in the Foreign Ministry in Peking.

When Zanzibar and Tanganyika formed a united republic in May 1964, the Red Chinese Embassy was moved to Dar es-Salaam. Meng was sent to his new post in Bangui, Central African Republic, in late 1964.

LIU YU-FENG

Burundi

Liu, who like his counterpart in the Congo (Brazzaville), Chou Chih-yeh, probably has had considerable responsibility for the Red Chinese backing of guerilla operations in the Congo (Leopoldville), is another diplomat well versed in Asian affairs before he began to exercise his talents in Africa. He was consul-general in Calcutta for four years and embassy counselor in Jakarta for two years.

Liu spent several years in the Foreign Ministry in Peking. He was never personally involved in any of the opening phases of the Congo crisis from 1960 to 1963. This enhanced his value in the strategic Bujumbura post, where he arrived in June 1964. However, he was recalled when Burundi suspended diplomatic relations in January 1965, and was temporarily assigned back to the Foreign Ministry.

TSENG TAO

Algeria

Before 1960, Tseng served in the Red Chinese civil service in Shanghai. He spent 1960–61 in Cuba, ostensibly as director of the New China News Agency. In 1961, Tseng served as an advisor to Foreign Minister Chen Yi at the Geneva Conference on Laos. He was posted to Algeria in 1962 and has probably held some sort of controlling authority for Red Chinese activity west of Cairo since then. He took part in Sino-Algerian talks during the visit of Chou En-lai and Chen Yi in December 1963, and also helped make last-minute arrangements for Chou's unforeseen visit to Tunis in January 1964, when Tunisia recognized Red China. In 1964 and 1965 he was active in organized work for the scheduled Afro-Asian Conference and in promising support in June 1965 to the new Boumedienne government in Algeria.

Yao Nien became Ambassador to Tunisia in May 1964. He had spent several years in India, an interesting fact in the light of President Bourguiba's criticism of Peking for its attitude during the Sino-Indian conflict.

The Congo in Arms: An
Order of the Day of Pierre Mulele

(This document was captured by Congolese security forces from guerillas under the political direction of Pierre Mulele in Kwilu province in early 1964. It was released in Leopoldville in March 1964. The resemblance of its provisions to those of Mao Tse-tung's instructions for guerilla warfare are too strong to be coincidence. The "Eight Orders" to partisans and the "Three Tasks" they are supposed to execute in territory they occupy are virtually transplanted from Mao's military writings and from standard Red Chinese handbooks used during the civil war in China and subsequently. The translation from the rather awkward and childish French of the original is the author's.)

Purpose of Their [The Partisans'] Work

1. To watch over the region where they are staying and to know everything that is going on in the villages. You should know everything that the enemy possesses with it:

a) Their number, each group that is traveling.

b) Know what the purpose of their travel is: whether they are searching for us, the partisans. If they are searching in the forest or in the brush or in the village or on the road.

c) What objects they are carrying in their hands; what their names are.

d) Give no false information if you have truly seen nothing.

2. You should know whether peace reigns among them, the villagers; whether the villagers are satisfied with the reactionary soldiers or not; whether the villagers talk with them often or not. Are the reactionary

soldiers in contact with the chiefs of the villages and of the sectors too, and the territorial administrators?

3. You should know at what time of the day they travel; what they have in their hands; do they have two or three [objects] in their hands? The places they travel to most often; are they accompanied by many women or not? Do they go out often to drink palm wine and where (in a bar or at someone's house)?

4. You should know the name of their chief who is with them. What is his village? His faults and those of all his soldiers. Try to learn the name of the battalion or the company or their platoon.

5. To have all this news, it is preferable that you get along perfectly with all the villagers of their region and that you tell them all the bad doings of the reactionaries. Before talking with a man or with men, you should know their character ahead of time. Do not talk with everyone. All your conversations with the villagers should always concern the political affairs of the country.

6. You should trick the enemy by every possible means. First, send to the enemy sentinels pretty girls to tempt them in places where there are reactionary soldiers. Before doing this, you should know the character of their officers, from the eldest to the youngest, because their characters are not the same. Destroy all their objects or vehicles; trick them by writing them false letters; point out to them the places where you are not.

7. To draw up charts on the enemy positions is the work of the group chief. To reveal everything about the enemy is the work of every partisan.

8. Partisans should not ask the villagers for a great deal of food, because once all the food is gone, we will be lacking during the days to come.

9. Partisans should live a communal life in all things (work and all other affairs).

10. All of the power of the partisans is in the hands of the villagers.

11. Partisans should make their camp far from the negotiable roads or from all major roads.

12. Partisans should not perform any work that they have not been asked to perform.

13. Partisans should *try to confiscate all the weapons their opponents possess.*

14. Partisans should be men who travel rapidly, men who are brave during the day, under the rain, in cold weather, when they are sick, at night, when they are hungry or whenever they are suffering bodily. Each move should be made secretly by footpath and not through villages. While they are underway they should make no noise, and they should not smoke en route if they are traveling at night.

15. During a patrol, partisans cannot march together. If they should split up, they should appoint a meeting place; underway they should send a scout ahead. If there are enemies, they should make a detour to avoid them if possible, and they should keep watch behind to make sure no enemies are following. They should notify their chiefs if they see enemies coming.

16. Partisans should not wait for the enemy. They should look for him wherever he may be found *so as to confiscate all his weapons, or also to kill him or arrest him.*

17. If the enemy regroups to disperse the partisans, the partisans should disperse. If their opponents are divided or dispersed, the partisans should regroup, so as to fight the weaker ones.

18. Partisans should harass the enemy in order to wear him out and fight him afterward without difficulty.

19. Partisans should fight the enemy if they are very sure of beating him. Any fight with the enemy should be an improvised one. After such combat, they should leave that location to make their base elsewhere (far away).

20. Partisans should make propaganda for the Party and show in all of the villages the reasons why they are entering the Party (or affiliating with the Party). They should do this work even among the Party's opponents.

21. Partisans should help the villagers in solving all their grievances.

22. Every partisan should do everything possible to confiscate rifles from any isolated enemy, among enemy guards who may be drunk and from those who often have a good time with girls.

23. Partisans should obey every order of their chief.

24. Do not confiscate any object belonging to the villagers; not even a needle or a thread.

25. *Turn over to your leaders* everything confiscated from the enemy during fighting.

26. Partisans should not leave their brother in enemy hands if he is wounded in fighting or if they are being pursued.

27. If partisans take an enemy prisoner, they should observe the most absolute secrecy.

Eight Orders That The Partisans Should Follow:

1. Show respect to all men, even bad ones.
2. Buy the objects of the villagers honestly and without theft.
3. Return borrowed objects promptly and without difficulties.
4. Pay for objects you destroy, and do it cheerfully.
5. Do not strike and do not injure anyone.
6. Do not destroy and do not walk on the fields belonging to the villagers.
7. Respect women and do not amuse yourselves with them at will.
8. Do not torment those whom you make prisoner during fighting. Do not confiscate and do not take their personal property, such as rings, money and all other objects.

Three Tasks That Partisans Should Accomplish:

1. Do not quarrel [among themselves].
2. Voluntarily perform all manual labor.
3. Teach and advise the villagers.

Selected Bibliography

Books Related to Chinese Foreign Policy

Adler, Solomon. *The Chinese Economy*. New York: Modern Review Press, 1957.

Boyd, R. G. *Communist China's Foreign Policy*. New York: Praeger, 1962. (Paperback.)

Brzezinski, Zbigniew K. (ed.). *Africa and the Communist World*. Stanford: Stanford University Press, 1963.

Clubb, O. Edmund. *Twentieth Century China*. New York: Columbia University Press, 1964.

Crankshaw, Edward. *The New Cold War: Moscow vs. Peking*. Baltimore: Penguin Books, 1963. (Paperback.)

Dallin, Alexander (ed.). *Diversity in International Communism: A Documentary Record, 1961–1963*. New York: Columbia University Press, 1963. (Paperback.)

Garvey, James E. *Marxist-Leninist China: Military and Social Doctrine*. New York: Exposition Press, 1960.

Griffith, Samuel B. (tr.). *Mao Tse-tung on Guerrilla Warfare*. New York: Praeger, 1961.

Halperin, Morton. *Communist China and the Bomb*. New York: Praeger, 1965.

Hsieh, Alice Langley. *Communist China's Strategy in the Nuclear Era*. Englewood Cliffs, N. J.: Prentice-Hall, 1962. (Paperback.)

Hudson, Geoffrey F., Lowenthal, Richard, and MacFarquar, Roderick. *The Sino-Soviet Dispute*. New York: Praeger, 1961. (Paperback.)

Kirby, E. S. "Foreign Policy of Communist China," *International Journal*, XV, No. 1.

Levenson, Joseph R. *Confucian China and Its Modern Fate*. 2 vols. Vol. I: *The Problem of Intellectual Continuity*. Berkeley: University of California Press, 1958.

Li, Dun J. *The Ageless Chinese.* New York: Scribner, 1965. (Paperback.)

London, Kurt L. (ed.). *Unity and Contradiction: Major Aspects of Sino-Soviet Relations.* New York: Praeger, 1962.

Lowenthal, Richard. *World Communism: The Disintegration of a Secular Faith.* New York: Oxford University Press, 1965.

Mao Tse-tung. *Selected Military Writings, 1928–1949.* San Francisco: China Books and Periodicals, 1963; Peking: Foreign Language Press, 1963. (Paperback.)

————. *Selected Works,* IV, V. New York: International Publishers, 1962; Peking: Foreign Languages Press, 1964.

————. *Strategic Problems of China's Revolutionary War.* San Francisco: China Books and Periodicals, 1954.

Mehnert, Klaus. *Peking and Moscow,* tr. Leila Vennewitz. 1st American ed. New York: Putnam, 1963.

Pentony, DeVere E. (ed.). *China, the Emerging Red Giant: Communist Foreign Policies.* San Francisco: Chandler Publishing Co., 1962. (Paperback.)

Schatten, Fritz. *Afrika Schwartz Oder Rot?* Munich: R. Piper, 1961.

Schram, Stuart R. (tr. and ed.). *The Political Thought of Mao Tse-tung.* New York: Praeger, 1963. (Paperback.)

Smets, Paul F. *De Bandoeng à Moscou: Contribution à l'Etude des Conférences Afro-Asiatiques.* Brussels: Université Libre de Bruxelles, Institut de Sociologie, 1964.

Snow, Edgar. *The Other Side of the River.* New York: Random House, 1962.

Steiner, H. Arthur. *The International Position of Communist China.* New York: Institute of Pacific Relations, 1958.

Thornton, T. P. "Peking, Moscow and the Underdeveloped Areas," *World Politics,* XIII, No. 3.

Whiting, Allen S. In Roy C. Macridis (ed.), *Foreign Policy in World Politics.* 2d ed. Englewood Cliffs, N. J.: Prentice-Hall, 1962. (Paperback.)

Zagoria, Donald S. *The Sino-Soviet Conflict, 1956–1961.* New York: Atheneum, 1964. (Paperback.)

General Reference Books on Africa

Adam, Thomas R. *Government and Politics in Africa South of the Sahara.* Rev. ed. New York: Random House, 1962. (Paperback.)

Almond, Gabriel A., and Coleman, James S. (eds.). *The Politics of the Developing Areas.* Princeton: Princeton University Press, 1960.

Ashford, D. E. *Political Change in Morocco.* Princeton: Princeton University Press, 1961.

Duffy, James. *Portugal in Africa.* Baltimore: Penguin Books, 1963. (Paperback.)

Hoskyns, Catherine. *The Congo Since Independence*. New York: Oxford University Press, 1965.

Legum, Colin (ed.). *Africa: A Handbook to the Continent*. London: Anthony Blond, 1961.

McCord, William. *The Springtime of Freedom: The Evolution of Developing Societies*. New York: Oxford University Press, 1965.

Middleton, John, and Campbell, Jane. *Zanzibar: Its Society and Its Politics*. New York: Oxford University Press, 1965.

Moraes, Frank. *The Importance of Being Black*. New York: Macmillan, 1964.

Morgenthau, Ruth Schachter. *Political Parties in French-Speaking West Africa*. New York: Oxford University Press, 1964.

Munger, Edwin S. *Bechuanaland: Pan-African Outpost or Bantu Homeland?* New York: Oxford University Press, 1965.

Murdock, George P. *Africa—Its Peoples and Their Cultural History*. New York: McGraw-Hill, 1959.

Nasser, Gamal Abdel. *Egypt's Liberation*. Washington, D. C.: Public Affairs Press, 1955.

Okuma, Thomas M. *Angola in Ferment*. Boston: Beacon Press, 1962.

Oliver, Roland, and Fage, J. D. *A Short History of Africa*. Baltimore: Penguin Books, 1962. (Paperback.)

Post, Ken. *The New States of West Africa*. Baltimore: Penguin Books, 1964. (Paperback.)

Robinson, Ronald (ed.). *African Development Planning*. Cambridge: Cambridge University Overseas Studies Committee, 1964.

Segal, Ronald. *Political Africa: A Who's Who of Personalities and Parties*. New York: Praeger.

Wallerstein, Emanuel. *Africa, The Politics of Independence*. New York: Random House (Vintage Books), 1961. (Paperback.)

Wiedner, Donald L. *A History of Africa: South of the Sahara*. New York: Random House, 1962. (Paperback.)

Articles in Periodicals or Anthologies

Adie, W.A.C. "The Middle East: Sino-Soviet Discords," *Survey*, No. 42 (June 1962).

Brook-Shepherd, Gordon. "Red Rivalry in the Black Continent," *The Reporter*, January 10, 1962.

Cooley, John K. "China's Push in Africa," *The Commonweal*, January 10, 1964.

Counts, Robert. "Chinese Footprints in Somalia," *The Reporter*, February 2, 1961.

Der Ostblock und die Entwicklungslander: Vierteljahresbericht der Friedrich-Ebert-Stifung (Hanover), No. 4/5.

Draper, Theodore. "Castro, Khrushchev and Mao," *The Reporter*, August 15, 1963; also in *Quest*, No. 39 (Oct./Dec. 1963).

Fitzgerald, C. P. "The Chinese View of Foreign Relations," *World Today*, January 19, 1962.

Garthoff, Raymond L. "Unconventional Warfare in Communist Strategy," *Foreign Affairs* (July 1962).

Griffith, William E. "Communist Polycentrism and the Under-developed Areas." In Kurt London (ed.), *New Nations in a Divided World*. New York: Praeger, 1963.

Halpern, A. M. "The Chinese Communist Line on Neutralism," *China Quarterly*, January–May 1961.

————. "Communist China and Peaceful Coexistence," *China Quarterly*, July–September 1960.

————. "Communist China's Foreign Policy: The Recent Phase," *China Quarterly*, July–September 1962.

————. "The Foreign Policy Uses of the Chinese Revolutionary Model," *China Quarterly*, July–September 1961.

Hinton, Harold C. "China: A Dragon Rampant," *Commonweal*, February 15, 1963.

————. "Political Aspects of Military Power and Policy in Communist China." In Harry L. Coles (ed.), *Total War and Cold War*. Columbus, Ohio: Ohio State University Press, 1962.

Hornbeck, Stanley K. "Background of American Policy Regarding China," *Chinese Culture*, Vol. 5, No. 1 (June 1963).

Katzenbach, E. L., and Hanrahan, G. Z. "The Revolutionary Strategy of Mao Tse-tung," *Political Science Quarterly*, September 1955.

Kirby, E. S. "Foreign Policy of Communist China," *International Journal*, XV, No. 1.

Numade, N. "Marxism and African Liberation," *The African Communist* (London), April 1960.

Scalapino, Robert A. "Foreign Policies in a World of Change," *Foreign Affairs*, Vol. 42, No. 4 (July 1964).

Schneyder, Philippe. "Pékin à l'assaut du tiers monde," *Revue militaire d'information* (Paris), April 1960.

Seton-Watson, Hugh. "The Communist Powers and Afro-Asian Nationalism." In Kurt London (ed.), *Unity and Contradiction*. New York: Praeger, 1962.

Silberman, Leo. "Change and Conflict in the Horn of Africa," *Foreign Affairs*, July 1959.

Thornton, T. P. "Peking, Moscow and the Underdeveloped Areas," *World Politics*, XIII, No. 3.

Zagoria, Donald S. "The Sino-Soviet Conflict and the West," *Foreign Affairs*, Vol. 41 (October 1962).

Newspapers and Periodicals of General Background Value

Africa Digest (London).
Africa Report. African-American Institute (New York).
Al-Alam (Rabat).
Alger-Républicain (Algiers).
Al-Shaab (Algiers).
Central African Mail (Lusaka).
China News Analysis.
China Quarterly (London).
Communist China Problems Research Series. Union Research Institute.
Le Courier d'Afrique (Leopoldville).
Dipanda (Brazzaville).
The Ethiopian Herald (Addis Ababa).
Le Figaro (Paris).
Foreign Affairs. Council on Foreign Relations (New York).
Horaya (Conakry).
Maroc-Information (Casablanca).
Le Monde (Paris).
Pékin Informations (Peking).
Peking Review (Peking).
Problems of Communism (Washington, D. C.).
The Spark (Accra).
West Africa (Lagos).
The West African Pilot (Lagos).

Index